JANET'S STORY

THE STORY OF A MOTHER AND A SON
STRUGGLING TO COPE WITH ALZHEIMER'S
DISEASE

BIOGRAPHY
THE LAST YEARS OF THE LIFE OF A GREAT
WOMAN
AS SHE BATTLES ALZHEIMER'S WITH THE HELP OF
HER
LOVING SON

THIS BOOK DEDICATED TO THE LOVING MEMORY
OF
JANET OWENS LEFLORE
THE KINDEST AND MOST GENEROUS PERSON I
HAVE EVER KNOWN
DECEMBER 26, 1926 – OCTOBER 18, 2015

WRITTEN BY:
BURTON R. LEFLORE

Copyright: © 2018 Burton LeFlore

All rights reserved. No part of this book may be reproduced, stored, or transmitted by and means ----- whether auditory, graphic, mechanical, or electronic ----- without written permission of the author, except in the case of brief excerpts used in critical articles and reviews. Unauthorized reproduction of any part of this work is illegal and is punishable by law.

This book is a work of non-fiction. Unless otherwise noted, the author and the publisher make no explicit guarantees as to the accuracy of the information contained in this book and, in some cases, names of people and places have been altered to protect their privacy.

ISBN:

9798804416028

LIBRARY OF CONGRESS CONTROL NUMBER:

Because of the dynamic nature of the Internet, unlawful use or republication of this work without the express written consent of the author is prohibited. The views expressed in this work are solely those of the author and do not necessarily reflect the views of the publisher, and the publisher hereby disclaims any responsibility for them.

PREFACE

JANET'S STORY is a true account of the last years of the life of Janet O. LeFlore. Janet was my mother. As her son, I witnessed how Alzheimer's and Dementia slowly stripped her of her memory; her recollections; her orientation to time and space; her independence, and her ability to perform daily routine tasks she had taken for granted the majority of her life.

Alzheimer's and Dementia also deeply affected my life in a multiplicity of ways. First it was difficult and sometimes horrifying to watch a woman who I had always admired, respected and looked up to, regressing. She had always been an amazing beacon of intelligence, light, ray of hope and love. She slowly and consistently became someone other than the woman I had known as all my life. I had to sacrifice aspects of my daily routine to care for her and make sure all was well with her. It tested my patience as many days, I found myself being asked the same questions over and over about the simplest and most trivial things. There were days when she would exhibit behavior that was completely irrational and beyond comprehension, other than perhaps she no longer had the capacity to understand.

In many ways it is like taking care of a young child. However, instead of you seeing the child's growth and maturity with each passing day and finding joy in the process, you are watching an adult as their condition deteriorates with each passing day. Very often observing the onset of Alzheimer's brings feelings of desolation and helplessness. There were many difficult days trying to deal with a person who had been independent all of their life now vehemently resisting the idea or thought of people being remotely in control of their life. There are many days when you have to deal with the frustration, anger, depression, sadness, mood swings and confusion the person faces as Alzheimer's progresses and they struggle to coexist autonomously.

I decided to write this book because seeing my mother Janet LeFlore suffer from this devastating condition had such a profound effect on me. Some days it hurt me so deeply to see the things she was going through. Challenges she faced in her day-to-day life trying to remember and recall simple things. Challenges she underwent as she endured being misunderstood and rejected by some of her closest family members who she loved so much. Sadly, and helplessly watching as she became increasingly withdrawn from the real world and isolated from society. Helpless in not being able to do anything to prevent the onset of neurological changes that occur in a person with Alzheimer's.

Similarly, there was the feeling of isolation I felt because there were not many people who I could depend on or talk to about what was going on with my mother. I found that most people find it hard to comprehend and relate to what a caretaker may be experiencing from day to day, unless they have experienced it themselves with someone in their own life. Very few people understand, so many caretakers feel alone with regard to emotional or spiritual support in their quest to care for a loved one.

By sharing and relating this story about Janet Owens LeFlore, I want to try and help more people to understand the condition called Alzheimer's. I want to give to so many of the people out there who are suffering in silence or who have suffered in the past with their loves one; feeling hopeless; unfairly criticized; unappreciated; overworked; stressed and alone. I want to let you know you are not alone. I pray for you and your loved one. I pray you will find strength and joy in being there for them, and contentment in knowing you are blessed with the understanding that you are performing one of the noblest tasks known to man, caring for someone who cared for you.

INTRODUCTION

The Preface of this book is intended to provide the reader with the "why," giving the many reasons I decided to and needed to write this book and tell the story about the last chapters of my mother's life. The Introduction is intended to provide the reader with the "how."

The book is laid out chronologically. In deciding where to start, I had to pick a place in time. Certainly, I had to let the readers know a little about who she was and who she had been for the majority of her earthly existence. I also wanted to pick a starting point where she may have been showing very mild signs of having Alzheimer's and Dementia. A happier time, so to speak, but in many ways, it was a sad time because her husband was suffering from cancer.

JANET'S STORY is written in a narrative style. All of the subject matter and material in the book is based on my knowledge, experiences, accounts, perception, recollections, observations, perceptions and thoughts. In addition, there is a significant amount of material transcribed and copied from actual trial transcripts. There is nothing fabricated or sensationalized with regard to the content designed to make it more appealing, interesting or awe inspiring. Nothing more than the simple truth about the last chapter in my mother Janet LeFlore's life.

There were many names changed in this Biography to protect the privacy of those individuals. There was no attempt to disparage, misrepresent or to demean anyone. However, any and all statements in this book are absolutely and without a doubt true and accurate despite any disclaimers. So, if anyone feels the need to come for me, please understand I will meet you with the absolute truth. Libel is only actionable in court of law if the statements were false. However, in this case any and all statements made it this book are true beyond any shadow of a doubt and to the best of my belief.

The names of some of my deceased family members are also included in this book. I am glad those names did not have to be changed because that helps to maintain the authenticity of the work. My most sincere desire during the writing of this book was to be as authentic as possible with the story I was telling. Names of some of my living relatives have remained the same also, similarly for me it helps to maintain and preserve the originality and genuineness of the work.

Most importantly, even though I have modified some names within the lines of this narrative. I have not changed, altered, nor modified anything related to my mother's character or her life. The book is all in part a tribute to her legacy and life. Herein I have also attempted to provide a window and greater understanding of how Alzheimer's affects people and the people living with a loved one suffering from this malady. In order to tell this story, I had to discuss some things about her that were somewhat private; however, for the sake of authenticity those things had to be revealed.

There are many scenes in the book that I find to be humorous as I look back on it, even though at the time when it occurred it was alarming, disturbing or unsettling. Certainly, I want the reader to take this book seriously, but do not be afraid to laugh every once in a while. Janet is a sympathetic character because she is an elderly woman and she has Alzheimer's. Although, there are times when Janet comes hard toward people around her. She would not hesitate to tell you exactly how she felt and it was not always in the most kind and courteous manner. Another common trait of elderly people with Alzheimer's.

There are instances when I may break off into descriptions of my perceptions and intellectual or emotional impressions regarding her idiosyncrasies and sometimes misunderstood mode of behavior or way of thought peculiar to her. However, I tried to keep it focused within the confines of what might have been happening at that point with Janet and how I may have perceived it at that point in time.

CHAPTER ONE

"I have a class. I got to go and teach," Janet said. "Dr. Bishop called, he said he had given me some classes to teach this semester. I need to hurry up or I'll be late," as she searched through her drawers trying to find something to wear.

"You retired back in 93," Burton said. "You haven't taught chemistry in over twenty years."

"No. I'm trying to tell you," Janet said. "I have a class. I'm going back to work. I got to work. I don't have any money. I need money. We need money."

"You're an RSA, Retirement Systems of Alabama employee, having worked for many years in the Alabama College System."

"I got a class to teach," Janet said. I got to be there at 9 o'clock. I can't be late."

"There are no classes," Burton said. "You have taught hundreds of classes over the years," Burton replied. "Hardly a day goes by when someone doesn't come up to me and says, do you know Mrs. LeFlore was my chemistry teacher."

"I'm a chemistry teacher?" Janet said. "Can you take me there? I need to teach my class. I want to try and be on time if I can."

"You have money, Mom," Burton said. "You get a check from the retirement systems every month and you also get social security. Now you could probably benefit a lot of folks if you would go back to work, but you don't have to go back to work today."

"I need to get dressed," Janet said. "My class will be waiting for me."

"Mom, did you hear what I just said?" asked Burton.

"I heard you, but I don't think you're listening to me," said Janet.

"First of all, Dr. Bishop couldn't have called you because he's been dead for quite a while and you have been retired for quite a while," said Burton.

"But I don't have any money," Janet said. "I have no money."

"Yes, you do," Burton said. "You have money, Mom. You have plenty of money. You have worked practically all of your life and you do not have to worry about money."

"What money?" Janet asked. "Are you sure I've got some money, Baby?"

"Yes, I'm sure," Burton said. "I work. As a matter of fact, I'm on my way to work right now."

"What kind of work do you do?" asked Janet.

"I'm in the real estate business," said Burton.

"Could you give me a job? Janet asked. "Can I go to work with you? I'm tired of sitting here at the house all the time doing nothing."

"You want to get your real estate license and start selling real estate?" asked Burton.

"What do I have to do to get a real estate license?" asked Janet.

"You'll have to take a real estate licensing class," Burton said. "I teach real estate classes."

"Can I get in your class?" asked Janet.

"You can," Burton said. "I'll let you know when the next class is coming up."

"I want to work though," Janet said. "I'll take the class if I have to."

"You'd probably do pretty well in the real estate business," Burton said. "But now you know you have been a scientist and a chemistry teacher for most of your life."

"I was a chemistry teacher?" asked Janet.

"Yes, Mam. You were a chemistry teacher for twenty seven or thirty years." Burton said. "I thought teaching was your love. But now there's a possibility that you could get a real estate license and do pretty well in real estate now that you're retired."

"I just need to make some money," said Janet.

As time passed, Janet became increasingly isolated. By now, she rarely had any contact with her brothers and sisters. She also had little interaction with her grandchildren. Janet spent the majority of her days around the house. Occasionally, she would have a visitor, but they were few and far between. Since Janet did not get out as much, she had little contact with the world. As she became more and increasingly involved in her day-to-day struggle to remember. Janet was a highly educated and intelligent woman. She had grown up in a large family and had a wide circle of friends, associates, coworkers, students and the like all of her life. She loved people and she loved being around people. Now it seemed she spent most of her time feeling lonely and confused.

Mavis came to work every day, Monday through Friday and often Janet said that Mavis got on her nerves. Although most days they got along, and Janet would be nice and noncombative toward her. By now her son Burton had totally assumed the role of caretaker and power of attorney for Janet. Janet was becoming increasingly dependent upon Burton to handle all of her affairs and pay all of her bills. She was also the go-to for any and all information that she needed. She asked a lot of questions. Janet still had an inquisitive mind and she could still formulate effective responses. However, she was becoming increasingly forgetful about everything. In addition, she was becoming more disoriented. She seemed to rarely know where she was, even though she was home most of the time. She did not seem to recognize her surroundings at home even though she had lived in her home for over thirty years.

There was no doubt that Janet was suffering from Alzheimer's and dementia. This devastating disease affects different people differently. However, for the most part, there is a common thread to the symptoms and how they manifest themselves. She became more withdrawn from society and less concerned. She would spend hours outside or in the house with her broom sweeping. She would literally sweep with a given broom until all of the straw had worn down the stick. If she could not find a broom, she would find a mop. Sweeping became like a reflex action for her and somehow it seemed to calm her and soothe her. Janet was a very focused woman over the years. She found it difficult to keep her thoughts focused now since she might be thinking about something and the next moment, she would forget what it was she had been thinking about. However, when she was sweeping, she was able to stay focused, at least as far as the physical aspect of the repetitive motion. The back-and-forth strokes of the broom.

During the early part of December, Burton decided that he would get Janet a little dog. He thought a small dog would be a good companion for Janet. He went to the Mobile Dog Pound and found the cutest little Dachshund named Misty. Burton knew immediately that this was the dog he wanted to get for Janet. He decided to adopt Misty that day. He filled out the paperwork for Misty and paid her fees and took her home. Janet liked Misty very much and Misty made herself right at home. Somehow Misty seemed to understand that part of her job there in the house was to watch Janet and keep her company and that Misty did from the day she arrived.

As the year 2010 was nearing an end, and the Christmas Holidays arrived, Burton was at home with Janet one night two days before Christmas. He was in his room on his computer when he got a phone call from his cousin Patsy. Patsy indicated that Janet's brother Warren had passed away. Burton was flabbergasted. He knew his uncle's health was waning, but he never expected that he would pass so soon. Burton offered his cousin his condolences. Patsy explained that since it was so close to Christmas, they were just going to wait until after the new year to have his funeral. Now he realized why his uncle had been so heavy on his mind last summer when they traveled to North Carolina and why for some reason the main objective he had during that trip was to make sure his mom saw her brother. Now it all made sense to him. He was saddened to hear the news and knew he had to tell Janet.

"Mom," Burton said. "Patsy just called."

"How is Patsy doing?" asked Janet.

"She said Uncle Warren passed away this evening," said Burton.

"What," Janet said. "My brother Warren is dead?"

"Patsy said he died a few hours ago," replied Burton.

"Oh my, Warren is dead," Janet said. "Will you take me to his funeral?"

"Of course, Mom," Burton said. "You know we're going to going and pay our last respects to Uncle Warren."

"I still remember that day I sat there in the window and watched my brother leave our house as a teenager and go to that farm. He helped Papa run that farm. He got put out of school for getting into a fight. He told Papa he didn't want to go back to school. He said he wanted to go to the farm and work on the farm, and Papa let him. He could have gone back to school, but he just wanted to be out there on that farm."

"Uncle Warren was quite a character," Burton said. "He was quite a man. I had a lot of respect and admiration for him. I'm glad we got a chance to go and see him last summer. Who would have thought just a few months later he would be gone? Do you remember when we went to see him last summer?"

"Yes, I remember," said Janet.

"I'm glad we went to see him," said Burton.

"Did you call Papa and tell him?" asked Janet.

"I'm sure Papa already knows," Burton replied. "He's probably in heaven with Mama and Papa right now, Mom."

"Mama and Papa are dead too?" asked Janet.

"Yes, Mom. You already know that," said Burton.

"Will you take me to his funeral?" asked Janet.

"Yes, Patsy said the funeral won't be until after the New Year," Burton said. "And yes, we will go to Virginia for his funeral."

"Okay," Janet said. "You promise?"

"Yes, I promise," Burton said. "Why don't you lay down and get some rest mom."

Janet was somber and melancholy about the news regarding her brother Warren. She and Warren had been extremely close over the course of their lives. Even though she struggled to remember practically everything, she had no problem remembering when they were children growing up at 1013 S. 12th Street in Wilmington. She was saddened to hear of his demise. Burton helped her to bed and tucked her in for the night. She lay there for a while thinking about Warren. Janet was having a moment of clarity. She fully remembered and recalled what Burton had just told her. Her brother Warren had passed away. She said a prayer for him before she fell asleep.

Following the news about Warren, the remainder of the Christmas Holiday and New Year's was like a blur. The first week of 2011 Burton made preparations to travel to Hampton, Virginia with Janet for Warren's funeral. Burton booked a flight for them out of Pensacola. They would fly from Pensacola to Atlanta and then from Atlanta to Hampton. Their flight left early that morning, so they had to leave the house before dawn to get to the airport in Pensacola on time.

Burton had called his cousin Rita and asked if he and Janet could stay there with her and she agreed. Burton was appreciative of Rita because he needed help with his mom getting her ready for the funeral; however, he did not want to put too much on Rita since her father had just passed. He did not know how Rita was handling his death and ultimately, he wanted to make sure his mom got a chance to go to his funeral but did not want to add too much to her plate given all the other circumstances she was facing. They arrived in Hampton where Rita picked them up from the airport and took them to her condominium.

They arrived at Rita's house and started to get prepared for Warren's funeral in the morning. Rita said the family was all going to meet at Warren's house in the morning and they would all ride to the Church from Warren's. Rita had just lost her father, and this was obviously a tough time for her. Burton and Janet appreciated Rita allowing them to stay with her while they were in Hampton to attend the funeral; however, they wanted to be mindful of her and as unobtrusive as they could possibly be. They settled into one of her downstairs bedrooms. Burton gave Janet her medicine for the night and helped her to get into her nightclothes. It had been a long trip and they were tired. Janet soon drifted off the sleep. Rita's son Brandon was there. Burton spent a little time with his little cousin Brandon in his home recording studio, before going to bed.

The next morning, they were up early, got dressed and the drove over to Warren's house. By the time they arrived at Warren's house, practically the entire family was there. Bethany and her husband, Julia and her spouse, as well as Warren's wife. Practically all of Janet's nieces and nephews were also there. Burton escorted his mom inside and she sat down in the living room on the sofa. The house was packed with family members. A lot of Janet's family lived in Hampton, Virginia.

Her brother Peter lived there as well as Warren. In addition, her sister Carol and her oldest brother A.B., all lived in Hampton. A host of Janet's nieces and nephews also lived in Hampton. It was not long after Janet sat down on the couch that her sister rushed over and sat down beside her. In her hand, she had a small bowl of grits and a spoon. Anna said hello to Janet and literally before Janet even had a chance to reply, had scooped a spoonful of grits and started spoon feeding Janet. Janet opened her mouth and started to spoon-feed her some grits.

"Excuse me," Burton said. "She can feed herself."

"Oh okay," Anna said as she sat the bowl down. "How are you?"

"Hey, Burton," said Janet's brother Peter.

"Hey, Peter. How are you?" replied Burton glad Peter had interrupted.

"Hi, Janet," Peter said. "How's my sister doing?"

"I'm fine. How are you, Peter?" said Janet.

"Warren's gone Janet," Peter said. "We got to go and do our last farewell to him and put him in the ground. Well actually we're not putting him in the ground, his plot is above ground. But we got to pay our last respects to our brother."

"Yes, we do," said Anna.

"Hey, Janet," said Julia who walked over and hugged Janet.

"Julia," replied Janet.

"It's Jeannie," said Bethany as she ran into the living room.

"It's Bethany," said Janet with a smile.

"Burton, come here. How are you?" said his cousin Patsy.

"Patsy," Burton said as he walked into the kitchen. "Give me a hug. I want to tell you I'm sorry for your loss. Uncle Warren, your father was an incredible man, and I know I will certainly miss him."

"Yea we all will," said Patsy.

"Well, hello Burton," Ann said. "How are you? Burton looked at her and did not reply. "I'm going to give you a hug no matter if you like it or not." She said as she approached Burton giving him a hug. "How are you?"

"I'm great," said Burton looking at Anna as if to say this conversation is over.

"The cars are ready for the family if everyone will come outside, we can proceed to the church," said the funeral attendant.

"Mom, let's go," Burton said. "You come with me."

They proceeded to the church for Warren's funeral. As they drove along the streets of Hampton. Burton started to think about how his Uncle Warren had sat there at his father's wake mistakenly thinking for a moment that he was looking at himself. Burton had witnessed his uncle go from the vibrant, energetic, kind-hearted, leader in his family and community to an aged man becoming increasingly forgetful and dependent, slowly drifting into an increased vegetative state of existence slowly relinquishing his independence, autonomy, and self-awareness to this creeping neurological disorder called dementia and Alzheimer's. One of the pillars of the family had taken his last breath and said his last goodbye.

Alzheimer's is such a devastating disease. Here Burton was experiencing the magnitude of this diagnosis and how it was affecting Janet, and now Warren had basically died from the same disease. Janet was intensely sorrowful about the death of her closest brother. Ironically Janet and Warren both suffered from Alzheimer's disease. They were born within two years of one another to Angle and Mable T. Owens in a small town called Wilmington, North Carolina and had been very close and dedicated to one another and their family for all these years. Now Janet would say her final goodbye to her brother Warren.

Janet was very quiet during the funeral as the preacher eulogized him and numerous friends and family members commented about Warren and the noble life he led. Janet did not go before the church and make any comments or statements. She did not cry but she was noticeably saddened by the loss of her brother Warren. Janet did not appear to be confused at all about who's funeral it was or who had died. She just sat there quietly and listened as the service proceeded. Burton was seated there next to her and put his arm around his mother on several occasions in an effort to comfort her. When the service was over, they got into several cars waiting outside and drove to the cemetery where Warren was placed in a tomb which would be his final resting place. They all proceeded back to Warren's house.

Janet and Burton went back to Warren's house with Warren's family. Most of the other family members went to Peter's house. After spending some time with Warren's family, Burton and Janet decided not to go around to Peter's house. Instead, they decided to go back to Rita's house. They spent the remainder of the evening at Rita's house. Janet remained relatively somber and mournful. Burton helped to take off her clothes and change into her nightgown. She was not asking a lot of questions like she usually did, and she did not inquire about where they were.

She seemed to be caught up in her own thoughts and did not really express what might have been going through her mind. Janet loved all of her brothers and sisters immensely; however, she was perhaps closest to Warren over their lifetime since they were born less than two years apart. It was a difficult day for Janet. On top of losing Warren, she felt alienated from her sisters who she had not had much contact with for the last few years.

The following day their flight was scheduled to leave about noon. They awoke that morning and organized their luggage. Rita prepared a wonderful breakfast for them of Waffles, Turkey Bacon, Hash Browns, Orange Juice and Coffee. Janet, Burton, Rita and her son Brandon had an enjoyable breakfast together that morning. Afterward, Janet and Burton got ready to fly back to Mobile. Rita drove them by Peter's house on the way to the airport.

Her sisters came outside and said hello to Janet and Rita. Burton sat stoically there in the passenger seat without replying or saying a word to her sisters. After a brief interaction with Julia and Bethany outside of Peter's house, Janet said goodbye and Rita drove them out to Hampton Roads Executive Airport. Burton and Janet hugged Rita goodbye when she dropped them off.

They had arrived about an hour and a half before their flight so they would check their baggage, go through security and wait there at the airport until their flight was ready to depart. They would fly through Atlanta and then back to

Pensacola, Florida where they would make the short drive back to Mobile from Pensacola.

"Are you okay?" asked Burton.

"I'm fine," said Janet.

"Uncle Warren was quite a character," Burton said. "I'm going to miss Uncle Warren."

"What happened to Warren?" Janet asked. "You mean my brother Warren?"

"Yes, your brother Warren," Burton said. "He's dead, Mom. You do know he's dead. We just went to his funeral yesterday."

"Warren is dead?" asked Janet.

"Yes," Burton said. "You know he's dead, we just buried him yesterday."

"Warren was a pillar of strength in our family for so many years. I still remember when I was in grade school this little girl hit the girl in front of us. When she saw the teacher coming over to where we were, she told me if I told on her she was going to beat me up. I was scared of the girl, but the teacher asked me who did it and I told her. I didn't want to get in trouble."

Janet continued, "So when the teacher left, the girl said she was going to fight me after school for telling on her. When school got out, I ran and tried to get off the schoolyard and to the house as quickly as possible. There was a little overgrown field that we used to have to walk through to get back and forth from school. When I got to the field, I decided I would hide there for a while. A few minutes later Warren came walking through the field, and he asked me what I was doing. I told him that a girl at school said she was going to beat me up. Warren said he was going to teach me how to fight. We went home and he taught me how to fight. The next day I went back to school and beat that girl's behind, and she never messed with me again. Shoot after that, I wasn't scared anymore. I knew how to fight. I'd just whoop somebody's ass just for the hell of it."

"Seemed like you and Uncle Warren were definitely the go-getters and the fighters in the family," said Burton.

"You sure he's dead?" Janet said. "I don't remember him being dead."

"Mom, we went to his funeral yesterday," Burton said. "We saw his lifeless body lying in a casket. We went to the burial site where they laid him to rest."

"And I was there?" asked Janet.

"Yes. You were there, Mom," replied Burton.

"Where are we going now?" asked Janet.

"We're flying back to Mobile," Burton said. "We fly into Pensacola and then we'll drive the rest of the way back to Mobile."

"Where do we live?" asked Janet.

"We live in Mobile," said Burton.

"So is that where we're going now," said Janet.

"Yes, we're going back to Mobile," Burton replied. "We just left Hampton."

"What's in Hampton?" asked Janet.

"I told you," Burton said. "We went to Uncle Warren's funeral."

"I remember when Papa decided to give Warren half of the farm," Janet said. "Papa said Janet I'm going to give Warren half the farm and I'm going to give you the other half. I said papa if you choose to give Warren half the farm then that's your decision. He told me he thought that Warren deserved it and I agreed with him, but I told papa that I didn't want the other half of the farm because there were so many of us. We had all worked on that farm. Perhaps Warren had done more than the others," she said.

"Perhaps he had sacrificed his education to work that farm for papa. Warren loved the land so much. He loved the country. He loved to hunt and fish. But I told papa that I thought we all should share in the farm and I did not want to accept half of the farm. I told him I would prefer to share it with all of them, and he said that was fine with him. Boy, they were not happy about papa having given Warren half the farm. Eventually, they talked him into taking a third of the farm. Warren agreed to take a third even though papa gave it to him in his will. That's the type of man he was. He's loving and tried to be fair."

"Yea, Uncle Warren was a pretty good guy," said Burton.

"Where did you say we were going?" asked Janet.

"For the tenth time, Mom," Burton said. "We're going to Mobile."

"The tenth time," Janet said. "You never told me we were going to Mobile. Why are we going to Mobile?"

"Because we live in Mobile," Burton said. "I got to get back to work."

"I thought we were in Wilmington," said Janet.

"No, we haven't been to Wilmington," Burton replied. "We went to Wilmington last summer, and we went to see Uncle Warren. You know when we went to Wilmington it was so seriously in my heart and mind that we see Uncle Warren. Who would've thought he would be dead four months later? I'm so glad I took you to see him when we did. Didn't realize it would be our last time seeing him alive."

"Are we going to Wilmington?" asked Janet.

"No, Mom. We're going to Mobile," Burton said. "One more time, we just left Hampton, Virginia and we are flying to Pensacola. We have to make a stop in Atlanta to change flights and then we're catching another flight to P'cola and then back home to Mobile. Now, why don't you sit back, relax and enjoy the ride. Don't make me keep repeating myself about where we're going, okay."

"I love you, Baby," said Janet.

"I love you too, Mom," said Burton.

"Please don't be mad at me," Janet said. "I'm sorry if I get on your nerves."

"Mom, I'm not mad at you and you don't get on my nerves," Burton said. "It's just that let's enjoy the rest of this flight without me having to explain again where we're going. We're going to Mobile. That's where we're going."

"Okay," replied Janet.

They arrived in Atlanta where Janet requested a wheelchair. She said the jet was causing her equilibrium to be off. Janet said she was dizzy and felt like she might fall if she tried to stand up. Burton assisted his mother into the wheelchair. They deplaned in Atlanta and went to the gate where their connecting flight was waiting.

Since Janet was in a wheelchair, they allowed her to board the plane to Pensacola before the other passengers. Before long she and Burton were on the final leg of their flight from Atlanta to Pensacola. Burton tried to catch a nap for the remainder of the flight to Pensacola. In less than an hour, they were in Pensacola.

They found their car and left the airport. Burton was hungry so they stopped at a Bonefish Grille in Pensacola and had dinner before getting on the road for the short trip back to Mobile. Before long they were back in Mobile and pulling up at the house. Janet was still a little off-balance following the flight, so Burton helped her into the house. He took their luggage out of the trunk. Burton put her bag in her room and carried his bag to his room. Afterward, he sat Janet down at the kitchen table and gave her medicine. Administering Janet's medicine was starting to become like a little daily ritual for them.

Burton was learning about his mother's condition and was of the understanding now with Janet that when his mom got a good night's sleep her cognitive functioning was better. At this point, her cognitive ability was diminished. It became important to try and create circumstances where she would function at her best, whatever that might be on any given day. She was also less irritable and combative when she had rested well the previous night. The better Burton was able to manage his mother's symptom's by trying to keep her on a schedule, by staying consistent and by trying to make sure she got a good night's sleep. The easier things were on him as her caregiver, not to mention Mavis who was there at the house with Janet most of the day, except on weekends.

The next morning Mae arrived at work about 8 o'clock. She rang the doorbell as she usually did. Janet got up and let her into the house with her key. Since Janet was not able to keep up with any keys on a key chain, he had purchased a key ring that she could hang around her neck. He had done this several years ago so that Janet could let Mae in the house when she arrived at work in the morning. For the most part, he did not try to restrict Janet from coming in and out of the house as she pleased, as long as it was not dark. He would make her come inside after dark. Rarely did she ever try to go outside after dark if she was in the house; however, she would sometimes stay outside until a little after nightfall and not want to come inside. Although Burton still wanted his mom to have at least the autonomy of having a key to the door.

However, this morning Janet got up and went to the door. She stood there gazing through the glass at Mae who was eager to get in out of the cold. Janet tried the doorknob, but the door would not open because it was locked. Mavis stood outside trying to communicate with Janet. She pointed at the key around her neck, but Janet looked puzzled as if she did not know what Mae was talking about. Janet again tried to open the door again without unlocking it.

Janet stood there and started to rub the wall. She stood there by the door and started to lightly run her fingers across the surface of the finished wood on the wall next to the door. Mae desperately tried to direct Janet's attention to the key around her neck. She rang the doorbell again to see if Burton might hear it ringing and come open the door. Cold and exasperated from having been outside waiting for Janet to open the door, she sat down on a chair which they kept on the porch by the doorway.

"Janet, the key is on your neck," Mae said. "It's hangin' right there around your neck. Will you please open the door, it's cold out here?" She pointed at the key around Janet's neck. Finally, Janet looked down at the key.

"Oh this," Janet said. "This is the key." She took the key and opened the door.

"Good morning," Mae said. "It's chilly out there this morning."

"I feel it," said Janet.

"How was your trip?" Mae asked. "Glad you made it back safe. You hungry?"

"Yes," Janet said. "I would like a cup of coffee."

"Did Burton buy any?" Mae asked. "He hadn't been buying any coffee lately."

"I would like a cup of coffee if you can find some, thank you," said Janet.

"I'll look and see," Mae said. "I don't think there's none in there. We can ask him if he'll get some…"

"By the way," Janet said as she sat down at the kitchen table. "Burton wanted me to tell you something."

"What's that?" asked Mae.

"He wanted me to tell you that he will no longer be needing your services," said Janet.

"What you telling me?" Mae said. "I'm fired now."

"That's what Burton told me to tell you," Janet said. "I guess you could finish out the day,"

"Well, I'll have a talk with Burton about that if you don't mind," replied Mae.

"I think you should ask him," Janet replied. "I think he wants to tell you himself."

"Ms. Janet if you want him to let me go then so be it," Mae said. "But Burton was the one who hired me to work here. I work for him and if I'm fired, I want to hear it from his mouth." She said as she started to prepare breakfast.

"That's fine," replied Janet.

"That sounds like Burton coming downstairs right now," Mae said. "Good morning, Burton."

"Morning, Mae," replied Burton. "Hey, Mom."

"Burton, your mom told me you said you no longer need my services," said Mae.

"When did I say that?" Burton said. "Mom, you're at it again. I got to go to work. Well, talk later."

Later that day, Mae left about 4 o'clock. She made sure Janet was inside the house before leaving work because she knew it was cold outside and this was not a good day for Janet to be outside sweeping. Mae let herself out and not long after Mae left Janet went outside with her broom. She walked all the way around the driveway barefoot out into the cul de sac directly in front of the house. She had been outside sweeping the street for over an hour when Burton arrived at the house. Burton was disturbed to see his mother outside sweeping in the middle of the street. Janet was in a cotton gown and barefoot sweeping the street and seemed to barely notice him when he drove by. He pulled into the driveway and got out to go and talk with Janet.

"What are you doing, Mom?" asked Burton.

"What does it look like," Janet said. "I'm sweeping."

"But you," Burton said. "Mom, you can't be out here in the middle of the street sweeping like this and you don't have any shoes on. You're going to catch a cold."

"Have you ever known me to have a cold ever in your life," Janet said. "I've never had a cold."

"Mom, never say never," Burton replied. "Your first cold could be your last."

"I've never had a cold," said Janet.

"But you can't be out here sweeping in the middle of the street like this," said Burton.

"It's my street dammit!" Janet said. "We built this street, and I will sweep it whenever I get good and got damn ready."

"Mom," said Burton.

"Do you see all this pine straw out here on the street," Janet said. "I just wanted to sweep it up and make it look nice."

"I understand that," Burton replied. "But this scenario right here is not a good look."

"I don't care how it looks," said Janet.

"Do you want the neighbors calling DHR? Please, Mom. You've got to come inside now," said Burton.

"I'm sweeping my street and I don't care about any of that you're talking about," Janet replied. "I need to get all this pine straw up."

"I understand that you just want to sweep the pine straw up, but you promised me you would work in the back yard. You can't be out here in the street sweeping. Sometimes people sweep their carport or walkway, but people don't try and sweep the street. That's why they have street sweepers to do that. Sweeping an entire street is a little more of an undertaking that a single person would want to do without machinery."

"I don't want to stop right now," Janet said. "I don't care anything about what anybody has to say, much less you."

"Let me ask you a question," Burton said. "What if I was to pull my pants down and walk around in public with my pants pulled down to my ankles. People might think there's something wrong with this picture and why is this guy walking around in public with his pants down. Just like people might say why is this old lady outside in the cold sweeping the street in a gown with no coat wearing no shoes. Mom, you need to come inside right now."

"I'm not coming inside now," Janet said angrily. "There's still light outside and I need to finish my work."

"No," Burton said. "No, Mom. You, you're not going to finish this right now. I need you to come inside before you catch a cold. It's not safe for you to be out here for a multiplicity of reasons. I need you to come in the house right now, please."

"I said I'm not quite ready to come in there yet," said Janet.

"Mom, I'm going to have to insist that you come inside," Burton said. "I tell you what, maybe you can come out here and finish up tomorrow but right now I need you to take a break and come inside."

About a month had passed when Bethany called Janet and Burton indicating that she would like to come to Mobile and visit Janet. At first, Burton was skeptical. Bethany's timing was severely suspect considering the fact they had just seen her at Warren's funeral not long ago. Burton wondered if Janet's sisters were up to some of their old tricks. However, he and Janet had talked with Bethany on several occasions, and she had clearly expressed her opinion that the actions they took where wrong.

Bethany had at least been willing to admit she thought their course of action was inappropriate and not guided in real empathy and compassion for their sister Janet. Bethany had legitimately tried to apologize and make peace with Burton and Janet over the court action they took. After giving it some thought, Burton called Bethany back and told her it would be okay for her to come as long as she did not show up with Ann and Julia. Bethany indicated to Burton that she was going to make a reservation to travel there and would get back with him regarding her travel arrangements.

One Sunday evening, Burton was at home cooking some catfish strips and french-fries. Janet was outside working in the yard. Janet was sweeping the carport and she heard a dog barking. The dog bark sounded like it was coming from the other end of the yard. Janet thought it was her dog Misty, so she decided to follow the sound of the dog bark to see where the dog was. The barking came from the other end of the yard somewhere behind the bushes.

Janet's back yard was rather large and there was a fence around the perimeter of the yard. Surrounding that fence is heavy foliage and brush. Janet wandered off behind the bushes in search of the noise she heard coming from that end of the yard. Once she walked behind the bushes at the very far end of her yard, she had no idea where she was. Burton finally went outside to get her to come in. As dusk and nightfall were quickly approaching, Burton did not find his mother on the carport in the back yard where she was supposed to be.

First, he thought Janet might have gone around to the front of the yard, so he walked around front, but did not see her anywhere. By now he was becoming a little alarmed since it appeared that Janet may have wandered off somewhere. He walked all the way to the edge of the driveway but did not see Janet anywhere. He started to call her, but she did not answer. Burton walked around to the back yard to take a look to see if she was back there somewhere. He called her again and got no answer. Janet could hear Burton calling her and she replied to him in hope that he would be able to find her.

Finally, when he got further toward the other end of the back yard, Burton heard her reply. He called her again and she yelled out that she was right here. He could not see her anywhere and could not tell where she was. He looked and looked and did not see here anywhere; although, she answered him and did sound as if she was alright. Besides the fact, she was lost somewhere in the back yard. Now it was dark. Burton went inside to look for a flashlight, but he could not find a flashlight anywhere. The closest flashlight he knew he had was at the office.

Burton ran back out into the yard and told Janet that he was going to get a flashlight. He told her to stay put and he would be right back. He jumped in his truck and hauled ass down the street to get to his office. At the corner he did not see any cars coming so he ran the red light at the corner. As soon as he ran the red light, he saw some blue lights behind him. Burton did not get far from the intersection outside of his street before he was pulled over.

At first, Burton could not believe that he was being pulled over by the police. In his haste and disbelief, he realized the officer might be able to help him find Janet. When the officer approached the vehicle as his blue lights could be seen vividly from Burton's rearview mirror. Burton rolled down his window and held his driver's license out of the window. He did not say anything or engage the officer who had pulled him over. The policeman took the driver's license from Burton who was now parked on the side of Pleasant Avenue. Burton remained and sat quietly in his vehicle.

"May I see your license and registration please?" asked the Officer. "You know you ran that red light back there."

"Sir my mother suffers from Alzheimer's and she has wandered into the yard and I can't find her, I was trying to get to my office so that I could get my flashlight to try and find her. You have a flashlight, perhaps you could help me. I live right down the street, less than a block from here. I just stay right down there. Please sir, if there is any way you can help me, I would appreciate it."

"Wait right here," said the cop. "I'll be right back."

"Did you hear what I said," Burton said. "I have a serious emergency here. My mom is lost in the back yard and I need some assistance, do you think you could help me, sir?"

The officer took Burton's license and went back to his police cruiser. The officer kept Burton waiting for a considerable amount of time, approximately fifteen minutes. Burton anxiously sat there waiting in his truck as the blue lights from the officer's police cruiser continued to blast behind him. Finally, he saw the officer emerge from his patrol car and walk back toward his vehicle. Burton watched him through his rearview mirror. He did not reflect any sense of urgency in his demeanor as he came back up to Burton's truck and handed him a ticket. Burton, who is usually very noncommunicative with police officers during a traffic stop, became angered as the police officer handed him the ticket. He did not take it. The officer threw it up on his dashboard.

"You wrote me a ticket," Burton said. "You actually wrote me a ticket. You kept me here waiting all this time when I told you my Eighty-year-old mother is lost somewhere in our back yard. I'm sure you probably hear a lot of stories out her on your beat, but I know you don't think I made that up," said Burton.

"Here," he said as he threw the ticket at Burton.

"Are you serious," Burton said. "So, you can't help me find my mom."

"No sir," the officer replied. "If you have a problem, you can call the non-emergency number."

"Appreciate you," said Burton as he drove off headed toward his office to get his flashlight.

Burton retrieved the flashlight and hurried back to the house. He still did not see Janet. He flashed his flashlight but could not find her anywhere. He called her and she continued to answer; however, she was still not visible as she was hidden somewhere deep within the brush. When he still could not find her, he decided he would call the police for assistance since the asshole who stopped him would not help him.

He called the police non-emergency number and continued to look for his mother. Finally, he spotted her in the brush. Burton reluctantly waded his way into the bushes to where Janet was trapped between a fence and the high shrubbery that lined her back yard. Janet was relieved to finally see Burton come to get her out of this place. He took her by the arm and led her out of the bushes into the main part of the back yard.

Janet had been scared and now felt relieved that Burton had found her. He took his mother inside. Burton sat Janet down at the table and he gave her something to eat. He called the police department and told them not to worry about coming to the house to help him find his mom. He was relieved that Janet was safe and had not hurt or injured herself. However, he resolved to go and fight the traffic ticket that he had gotten earlier for running the red light.

Janet sat there and ate her dinner as Burton prepared her medicine. He gave her a glass of juice and she drank it emptying the glass in a matter of seconds. He had to pour her another glass of juice before he could give her the meds. Janet ate all of her dinner. Burton was quite relieved that he was able to find Janet in the yard and that she had not been hurt or wandered off from the house. So far Burton had continued to allow her to go out into the yard and work outside, and she had not wandered away. Besides occasionally wanting to go out and sweep the street, she had not left the house and wandered off to God knows where.

About a month later Janet's sister Bethany arrived in Mobile to visit with her. Burton picked her up from the airport and took her to the house. Janet seemed happy to see Bethany and Burton stayed home that evening and cooked fajitas. He cut up some chicken and steak. He chopped some lettuce, tomatoes, cilantro, and onion for the fajitas. Janet and Bethany sat there at the table and talked with Burton while he prepared the food. He finished cooking and they ate dinner and spent about another hour talking before Janet went to bed. Bethany was tired and went to bed not long after Janet.

Although Burton had decided to allow her sister Bethany to come and stay with them and visit with Janet, he was still skeptical. He still did not feel totally comfortable leaving his mom alone for too long with Bethany. Not so much that he was concerned that Bethany would try anything underhanded where Janet was concerned, he had learned by now that he could no longer let his guard down around her family. As far as he was concerned, there were some family members that were not welcome at all, because he did not feel like they could trust them. He had to be totally realistic about the fact that Janet had Alzheimer's.

Someone could come to her and ask her to sign documents or do any number of things, and his mom could not remember what had happened. At this point, he was not about to give them another chance to exploit his mother or take advantage of her kindness, trusting nature, or a condition that affected her memory. He had learned his lesson and was not going down that road with her family ever again. Burton vowed that he would never allow them to hurt his mother like that ever.

Instead of leaving his mom at home alone with Bethany and going to work the next day, Burton decided to take the day off. It was a Friday and he had not taken a day off in a while. He decided to drive to Orange Beach and take his mom and her sister Bethany out on his boat. The next morning after they had breakfast, they got dressed and drove over to Orange Beach in Baldwin County. Burton had his boat stored over there at Zeke's Marina. So, they went and picked up his boat from the marina and went for a ride.

It was an incredibly beautiful day on Cotton Bayou. The sun was glistening on the incredibly calm water. It was warm and hardly a cloud in the sky. A perfect day to be out on the boat. They rode along the intracoastal waterway down to Perdido Pass into the state of Florida. This was a boat ride that Burton enjoyed. Janet who was not as fond of water as her son was having a good time herself. The three of them had a nice afternoon, eating lunch at Pelican Bay Restaurant not far from Perdido Pass. They skirted around Ono Island where Burton stopped and told his mom and his aunt that he wanted to own a house one day. He commented on how he could not believe the wealth these people must have to be able to afford houses on Ono Island. Burton went on to tell them about how it was a gated community pointing out to them that most of the boat docks had not one, but two boats moored there.

    They sailed into Florida and then back to Alabama. Later in the excursion, they cruised around the lagoons of Cotton Bayou where many more fabulous homes along the waterway are located. Fish were jumping out of the water in the calm and windless afternoon as the sun set on Orange Beach, Alabama. There is nothing Janet and her sister Bethany took the entire ride and they enjoyed being out there on the water with Burton. There is nothing more that Burton loved and adored than being on a beach by the sandy shore. He was a water person and a swimmer.

    Burton is an incredible swimmer having swum on the City of Mobile's swim team in high school and spending his summers working as a lifeguard. Burton almost died in the water when he and his family were visiting Madrid, Spain. He would have drowned, but his brother Champ saved him. He was also pushed into the deep end of a pool by a little girl when they were visiting Greece and his brother saved him again. He did not know how to swim, but he resolved to learn and became an incredible swimmer. So now, this being known, it was time to take the boat back in to the dock. Nightfall had arrived and they had to slowly navigate their way to the marina.

    Burton arrived at Zeke's Marina. He pulled up to the dock and tied his boat. He helped his mom and his aunt out of the boat, and they returned to his truck. They drove back through Baldwin County through Foley, Robertsdale, Summerdale, Loxley and onto I-10 which would take them to Mobile. They crossed the Bayway back into the city and proceeded to return to Janet's house.

For a day and a half Burton had tried to be there to facilitate this visit between Janet and her sister Bethany, but he needed to get to his office attend to some business. For the most part, Bethany seemed genuine. However, Burton experienced something that caregivers frequently experience, in that he was doing everything he could do to try and make sure Janet was taken care of; however, people still want to come into the scene and talk about what you're not doing or to be critical when they have no clue exactly what's going on or how much you are actually doing.

As was previously indicated, Janet also had issues with nerve pain in her jaw. A few years ago, Janet had basically stopped brushing her teeth because in her words it caused her too much pain. Burton started buying her mouth wash to rinse her mouth with, but she would not brush. During the course of those years, some of her teeth had become decayed. Burton was fully aware of this issue relating to his mom's health; however, Bethany commented on it and stated that decayed teeth can lead to an increase in heart disease and heart attack. Burton just stood there and listened to her; although he was slightly annoyed by her comment.

"Burton, thank you so much for taking us out on your boat today," Bethany said. "I really enjoyed that little outing."

"Sure, no problem," Burton replied. "I enjoyed having you guys out with me today. Mom, did you have fun?"

"Yes, Baby. It was nice," said Janet.

"Burton, Janet appears to have a few teeth that are decaying," said Bethany.

"Yea, I know," replied Burton.

"You really should take her to the dentist to have that looked at," said Bethany.

"She had been to the dentist," replied Burton.

"What did they say about it?" asked Bethany.

"The only thing they could do at this point is pull her teeth and fit her for some dentures," said Burton.

"I don't want any dentures," said Janet.

"As she indicated, she doesn't want to have her teeth pulled," Burton said. "You know she has TMJ, and a not long ago she was fitted for an orthotic to help her jaw realign so that she won't experience so much pain. She says that she can't brush her teeth because the toothbrush rubbing against her teeth causes her pain. Also removing her teeth might make the problem worse. Not sure it would make it worse, but it might, at least that's what her dentist said. Besides she doesn't want her teeth removed."

"That's not good," said Bethany.

"No, it's not but there's a lot of other factors that have contributed to her tooth decay and the only thing that could be done at this point would be to pull her teeth," Burton said. "She doesn't want them removed and her dentist doesn't think it's a good idea either."

"Decaying teeth can cause heart disease and heart attacks," said Bethany.

"I've never heard that," Burton said feeling a little as if he were being put on the spot about something, he had little control over.

"You might want to take her back to the dentist and have him take another look," Bethany replied. "Because she has a few teeth that look pretty bad."

"Yea," Burton replied. "Hey, I got to go to the office for a little while. I've got a few things I need to do before it gets too late. I'll see you guys a little later."

"Bye, Burton," Janet said. "See you when you get back."

"Okay, Mom," Burton replied. "I shouldn't be gone too long."

"We'll be right here," said Bethany.

"See you guys in a minute," said Burton as he closed the door behind him on his way out.

"Jeannie I sure did have a nice time out there on Burton's boat," Bethany said. "Wasn't that fun?"

"Yes, it was," Janet said.

"Why don't we have a glass of wine and relax," said Bethany.

"Okay," replied Janet.

"Jeannie, I'm so happy to see you," Bethany said. "It has been a while since I've been to Mobile. Much too long if I may say so myself."

"You know I've been wanting to ask you something?"

"What, Jeannie," Bethany said. "Ask me anything?"

"Well, I've been wondering," said Janet.

"What," said Bethany.

"Who is your father?" asked Janet.

"My father," Bethany replied. "My father is Angle B. Owens."

"Angle B. Owens?" asked Janet.

"Yes Angle B. Owens is my father," Bethany said. "My father is your father. We have the same father and his name was Angle."

"So, you're telling me that Angle B. Owens is your father," said Janet.

"Yes," replied Bethany.

"I'll be damned," Janet said. "Isn't that some shit."

"What do you mean by that, Jeannie?" asked Bethany.

"Angle B. Owens is your father?" said Janet.

"That's what I said," replied Bethany.

"All these years I thought my dad was a kind and decent man," Janet said. "And come to find out I got a bitch for a sister."

"Our father was a kind, decent man," Bethany said. "We have been sisters for over seventy years."

"We've been sisters for that long," Janet said. "Then why am I just finding out about you?"

"Jeannie are you serious," said Bethany.

"I'm as serious as a heart attack," said Janet.

"You didn't just find out about me," Bethany said. "You knew about me the day I was born big sister."

"I've known about you since the day you were born," Janet said. "I don't think so."

"Jeannie, we grew up in the same house and we have the same mama and papa," said Bethany.

"I grew up at 1013 S. 12th Street in Wilmington, North Carolina," said Janet.

"I grew up in the same house Jeannie," Bethany said. "You don't remember me?"

"I don't remember you growing up there," said Janet.

"That's where I grew up too and I certainly remember you," said Bethany.

"What did you say your name was again?" asked Janet.

"My name is Bethany," said Bethany.

"Bethany," replied Janet.

"Yes, Bethany," answered Bethany.

"That name sounds familiar," Janet said. "Can't say I remember you from 1013 though."

"Sweetheart you must be getting tired," said Bethany.

"Didn't you say you were going to fix us a glass of wine," said Janet.

"Yes, I did say I was going to fix us a glass of wine," replied Bethany.

"Well, what are you waiting for," Janet replied. "I'm thirsty."

"Okay, one glass of wine coming up for you sister," said Bethany.

The following morning Janet appeared to remember who Bethany was. Bethany remained there in Mobile with Janet for another day before she caught her return flight to home. The remainder of her visit was alright, and Janet appeared to be happy her sister had come to visit her. There was no drama between them, and it did not appear that Bethany had come with any hidden agendas.

Burton was convinced that Bethany had come out of concern and a desire to visit with her sister Janet. It had been over five years since any of her family had visited her. Of course, some of her family members would not have been allowed in the house, because Burton had lost all trust in them. However, Burton sensed that Janet was very pleased that Bethany had come to visit her, and he hoped her visit uplifted Janet's spirits to some degree.

The next few days and months went by relatively fast. They followed their daily routine; however, Mae indicated to Burton that some mornings when Janet would come to the door it took a considerable amount of time for Janet to figure out how to open the door. She asked Burton if he could figure out another way for her to get into the house when she came to work. Burton did not want to give her a key and usually, he did not hear the doorbell ring in the morning when she arrived at work.

Mae said when she would ring the doorbell, Janet would come to the door and would often stand there rubbing the door and the wall next to the door instead of using the key around her neck to open the door. She told Burton that one morning she had been outside almost two hours before Janet finally figured out how to open the door. Burton informed Mae that he would take what she said into consideration and try to work something out so she could get in the house when she got to work.

The Memorial Day weekend had arrived. The long hot and humid days of summer were about to arrive. Burton was off work for the long weekend. He had invited his friend Sandy over to the house. Janet, Burton, and Sandy were in the kitchen where Burton was preparing a pot of spaghetti. Janet was in a relatively good mood as she stood over in the far edge of the kitchen sweeping the floor.

Burton was there at the stove cooking and Sandy was seated at the table talking with Burton while he cooked. It was about 5 o'clock and still daylight outside. Janet stopped her sweeping and lay the broom against the wall. She stepped down into the Florida Room and went out the back door. Burton saw his mom go out the back door and thought nothing of it. He continued to stir and season his sauce. The spaghetti was almost ready, and he was hungry.

As soon as Janet went outside the door she stepped on the bottom part of her housecoat and lost her balance. She fell striking her head on the handle of a water faucet which was located at the edge of the back porch. A piece of the faucet handle was broken, leaving a jagged edge protruding upward. This is what Janet hit her head on when she fell. A very short period of time elapsed, perhaps less than two minutes before Janet stepped back inside the door. Her face was completely bloody. She was holding her hand up to her forehead and there was blood everywhere.

Burton looked up from the pot of spaghetti and he could not believe his eyes. The blood on her face was as red as the spaghetti sauce in his pot. It had happened so fast, and at first, Burton was not completely sure how it happened. It looked as if someone had hit Janet in the head. He ran to his mom and looked outside to see if anyone was out there. There was no one on the back porch or in the yard.

He asked Sandy to wet a paper towel and bring it to him. She was equally surprised by what had happened because it all happened so fast and was quite unexpected. Sandy took some paper towels from the roll there on the table and moistened it with water and brought it to Burton, so he could wipe his mom's face. There was so much blood coming from Janet's forehead, it appeared the injury was severe, and Janet would definitely need medical attention. Burton turned the stove off. He and Sandy helped Janet into the truck, and they drove her to the emergency room.

Janet was presented to the emergency room. When the ER staff saw all the blood which appeared to be coming from her forehead, they took her straight to the back. Once Janet was back in the examining room at the ER, Burton asked for something he could use to wipe the blood off his mother's forehead. Once Burton was able to wipe the majority of the blood from around the wound, he was able to see that the cut was bad but not quite as bad as he originally thought.

However, she still had a large gash on her forehead that was approximately two inches long and there was still blood oozing out of it. Burton took some gauze and applied a little pressure to the wound. Janet was conscious and alert. Although she was obviously hurting from the injury, she did not appear to be in any serious pain.

Finally, the emergency room physician Dr. Rousso peeped his head in the door. He came into the examining room and took a look at the open cut on Janet's forehead. He requested sutures so that he could suture the cut. Dr. Rousso also stated that he wanted to take an x-ray of Janet's head and skull to make sure that she had not fractured her skull. Janet was very cordial to Dr. Rousso. Despite her injury, she appeared to be in stable condition overall. The doctor asked Janet what had happened to her head, but she was unable to articulate or recall how she had hurt herself.

Burton explained to Dr. Rousso that he thought Janet had fallen on the back porch and hit something. He was not altogether sure how it happened because he had not seen what happened; however, he was pretty sure she had fallen and hit her head on the faucet handle just outside the back door of her house. Sandy who was also there in the examining room with Janet and Burton indicated that Mrs. LeFlore had gone out the back door and came back inside the door in what seemed like a matter of seconds, with blood gushing out of her forehead.

Dr. Rousso gave her a few shots of Lidocaine around the wound and started suturing Janet's head. After about twenty minutes he was finished putting in the stitches. Her ex-ray did not suggest there was anything significant pertaining to a skull fracture or any internal problems related to the fall. After about Three hours Janet was finally discharged from the ER and went home. By now they were all starving since they had not eaten dinner. Sandy agreed to go back to the house and help Burton get his mom fed and settled into bed.

Burton gave Janet her dinner and her medicine for the evening. By now it was close to 9 o'clock. They all ate the spaghetti that Burton had prepared. Shortly after dinner, Janet went to bed. What a day, Burton thought to himself. He was glad that Janet was alright because earlier that night after she fell when he first saw her, he did not know what to think. Truthfully, he thought his mom was injured much worse than it actually turned out to be. He was relieved as he put her to bed that night. He sat there with Janet on the side of the bed and said a little prayer with her before leaving her room.

Janet's injury healed and she did not appear to have any other related problems as a result of her fall. About a week later, Burton took her over to Dr. Bell's office so that he could remove the stitches. After removing the stitches from Janet's head, Bell gave Janet a brief checkup and asked her how she was feeling. She indicated to him that she was feeling perfectly fine.

He asked her if she had experienced any headaches or dizziness. Janet stated that she had not suffered from any headaches. Burton, who was also there with Janet, affirmed that Janet appeared to be doing alright the last few days and had not complained of having any headaches or dizziness.

After the appointment with Dr. Bell, Burton took Janet to a nearby Mexican restaurant to get something to eat. Today was Tuesday which meant the restaurant was having dollar tacos for Taco Tuesday. Since Janet did not get out of the house often, he would always use something like an outing to the doctor to let Janet ride with him for a little while and usually he would take her somewhere to have a bite to eat. He enjoyed spending this time with his mom and getting her out of the house.

When they got to the house, Mae had gone for the day. Besides a few sink baths, Janet had not had a bath in the tub in practically a week because she was not supposed to get her stitches wet. As soon as Burton got his mom to the house, he told her it was time for her to take a bath. He went into the bathroom, ran her bath water and filled the tub with liquid soap. That way he could give her a washrag and let her use the soap in the bathwater to bathe herself. It was easier than trying to get her to keep up with a bar of soap while bathing.

"Mom, I've got your bath water ready," Burton said. "Come in here and let's get you in the tub."

"I don't want to take a bath right now," said Janet.

"You haven't bathed in the tub in several days," replied Burton. "Your stitches are out now. You need to get in this tub."

"I've had two baths today already," said Janet.

"Mom, you have not had two baths today," said Burton.

"I don't feel like taking a bath right now I told you," argued Janet.

"Mom, I've got your water ready now," Burton said. "Come on before it gets cold."

"I'm not taking a bath, now leave me alone," said Janet.

"Mom, I need you to get in the bathtub and take a bath," Burton replied. "You haven't had a bath in a few days, and you need a bath. You need to sit in the tub and soak for a little while. A hot tub of water can be good for the body and soul."

"I'm scared I might fall," said Janet.

"I'll help you and make sure you don't fall," Burton said. "Don't I always help you and try to make sure you get in there without falling."

Once Janet got into the bathroom, Burton helped her to take off her clothes. He noticed her Depends had a considerable amount of urine in them and dropped to the floor as soon as he tugged at the elastic waist. He helped her take the rest of her clothes off and placed them on the vanity.

By now Burton had become accustomed to undressing his mother and helping her into the tub.

At first, he felt very uncomfortable about helping Janet to disrobe and seeing her naked; however, over the years he had become used to it and had just accepted it as part of what he had to do in order to care for his mother at this point in her life. He directed her to step into the tub while he held her by the arm to make sure she did not slip and fall.

Another lesson Burton learned with Janet, is that sometimes caregivers can be overbearing and treat their loved ones as if they are unable to do anything when there are many things a person with Alzheimer's can still do for themselves. A caregiver must encourage and allow the person to be as self-sufficient and do as many things on their own as they are capable of doing.

For instance, Janet needed assistance undressing and getting in and out of the bathtub. She legitimately feared that she might slip and fall and hurt herself which created a great deal of reluctance on her part to even take a bath. Janet always resisted and argued with Burton every time he even mentioned the idea of her getting into the bathtub for a bath. However, once she was in the tub and felt safe, she was perfectly satisfied. Burton could then give her a washrag and she would bathe herself.

"Now doesn't that feel better," Burton said. "I bet you feel like a new person already." Janet did not reply. She sat there quietly in the tub bathing herself and enjoying the warm water. Burton left her there in the bathroom to go and find her a change of clothes. He found her something to wear and brought it back into the bathroom and placed it on the vanity, taking her dirty clothes and the saturated diaper. He threw the Depend into the garbage and put her clothes in the laundry room for Mae to wash. A few minutes later Janet said she was ready to get out. Burton helped her out of the tub and dressed her.

Sandy asked Burton if he would bring Janet by her house so that she and her mother could talk. Both of them were concerned about the fact that their mothers were somewhat isolated and did not have much interaction with other people. Burton had brought Janet by there on one or two other occasions to visit with Mattie Lou and the two of them seemed to get along. They would usually talk and laugh among themselves and seemed genuinely appreciative to be in the presence of another elderly person.

Burton told Sandy he would bring Janet by there on a Saturday afternoon. Mattie Lou remembered her and appeared to be glad to see Janet. Janet also remembered Mattie Lou and appeared equally happy to see her again. Janet sat down on the sofa next to where Mattie Lou was seated, and they started to small talk. Mattie Lou likes to watch television and she would sit quietly and watch television for a great part of the day;

Janet, however, did not have the patience for television and rarely watched it. Usually, if Burton or anyone else was in the house watching television Janet would watch for a brief period of time and then start asking questions or move on to something else. However, she listened to Mattie Lou trying to explain to her what was happening in the television program she had been watching. It appeared that both of them just enjoyed each other's company.

Burton decided that he wanted to take them all to dinner. He asked Sandy if her mom would go with them to dinner. Sandy asked Mattie Lou if she wanted to go and she said yes. Janet and Burton waited while she went with her mother into her room to help her put on something to wear. They all loaded into his truck and drove over to Daphne and had dinner at a local seafood restaurant. They shared an enjoyable dinner and ride to and from the restaurant.

Janet sat in the back with Mattie Lou and she did not get angry with or try and call anybody any names. The four of them ate a nice meal and everything went well. Both Janet and Mattie Lou were mannerable and behaved. They sat and ate their dinner and talked to each other. After they had finished, Burton paid the bill and he took Sandy and her mother home. He and Janet continued on to the house for the evening.

The following week, Burton's Mardi Gras organization had a cabaret. Burton belonged to the Midnight Mystics which was one of the many Mardi Gras associations in Mobile. Burton decided to take Janet to the cabaret. Sometimes he felt so sorry for Janet because she was becoming increasingly more confined to the house. He was always busy with work and did not always have time to take Janet anywhere, so he thought it would be a good idea to take her to the cabaret.

The Mystics had a nice turnout for the cabaret. As soon as Burton got Janet to the party, he noticed that she was happy to be at a party and to be around some people. There was food, music, libations, and dancing. He fixed Janet a plate and got her a soda. She sat there at the table eating and rocking her head to the music. There's no telling how long it had been since Janet had been to a party.

It made Burton feel good to see his mother enjoying herself or having an opportunity to be in the company of other people for a change. Burton prepared himself a plate and fixed himself a drink. He sat at the table with Janet while they ate. The entire time Janet kept swaying her head back and forth as she rocked to the music. About the time she had finished eating her food, Burton's friend from grade school, Alexis Towner came over and escorted her out onto the dance floor. Alexis was Burton's lifelong friend and knew Janet very well since she had been like a second mother to him back in the day.

Alexis stayed out on the dance floor with Janet for almost half an hour. Janet loved every minute of the dancing. It had been years since she danced to some music. Alexis performed his signature dance and Janet danced right along. She was enjoying herself immensely. Burton really appreciated his friend inviting his mom to dance. It brought a lot of joy to Burton's heart to see Janet having a good time and he was glad that he had brought her out that night.

CHAPTER TWO

Not long after her husband Beck passed in 2001, Janet started having problems with the Internal Revenue Service. Now, in 2012, Janet had not managed to completely resolve those issues. Every year it appeared they were saying that Janet owed a fairly large sum of money, and she had little if any deductions to claim. Burton decided that he would try and enter into an Offer in Compromise with the IRS to see if he could get Janet's debt settled. He had spent a considerable amount of time working with their accountant to get this together on her behalf. They hoped it would work out because with penalties and interest the IRS was attempting to collect in excess of Two Hundred Thousand Dollars from her.

Burton left his office with the paperwork in a file to take to Janet so she could review it and sign it. He found Janet at home without her glasses as usual. Even though her glasses helped her vision, at this point she refused to wear them for any period of time. She frequently lost them. He presented her with the Offer and Compromise as he explained to her what he was trying to do as far as negotiating a reduction in the debt she owed to the IRS. Janet listened to her son as he looked around for her glasses so she could glance over the documents. He put her glasses on her face to enable her to see a little better. Then he tried to locate a pen so she could sign it.

He gave Janet the pen and showed her the line where her signature was required. Burton pointed to the line where she needed to sign, and Janet's eyes followed his finger to where he was pointing on the piece of paper on the table before her. He then directed her hand to where the line was located on the page. Janet started writing very slowly and her signature started to drift up the page and away from the line. She was struggling to write her name. Burton observed that her signature, which she had signed a thousand times over the course of her lifetime, had now become difficult for her to write. She was regressing neurologically, and it was noticeable in the fact that she struggled to sign her own name.

Janet was slowly succumbing to Alzheimer's and dementia. As the days passed one by one and turned into weeks, months and years Janet was starting to suffer more severe cognitive impairment and ability to function. She was now totally incontinent and had to wear diapers which needed changing three or four times a day if not more sometimes. She stopped with all the sweeping and instead would sometimes sit quietly for hours rubbing the surface of a table or bedspread or whatever might catch her attention at any given point in time. Sometimes if there were objects on the table or surface where she would be rubbing at the time, she would knock those objects onto the floor with little concern, other than she needed to keep passing her fingers across the counter in a repetitive motion.

Burton still struggled sometimes to understand and comprehend what was taking place before his very own eyes with regard to his mother. Janet had been a fiercely independent and hard-working woman with a tremendous amount of drive. Now she was the same determined woman; although, there were instances now where she struggled to maintain her independence as Alzheimer's was slowly causing her to regress. Janet was always an incredibly beautiful, reliable, kind and devoted wife, mother, grandmother, sister, daughter and friend. Only now her husband was gone, much of her family had turned their backs on her. Most of her friends were either dead or not concerned with her.

A brilliant and vibrant woman who had always been the answer and rarely the problem; however, her memory loss had practically taken over every aspect of her life. Janet had been a loving and selfless mother to her two boys. At this point, one of her son's was gone and; although, she had not forgotten Burton sometimes she became mistaken as to what their relationship was.

Burton's brother Champ had passed away almost twenty years ago, and it was just him there trying to comprehend and make sense of everything going on with their mom. Sometimes he wished his brother was still around, at least he would have had some help with Janet. However, he wondered if he and his brother might have butted heads about how they felt their mother should be cared for.

There were times when watching his mother deteriorate mentally was difficult for him. He wondered how his brother Champ would have handled going through the various stages of Alzheimer's with their mom.

He watched her go from being able to drive to not wanting to drive for fear that she might get lost. Burton had observed how her relationship with her family members, particularly her sisters erode into nothing. Along with the increased amount of confusion as to time and place as she struggled to try and comprehend her own reality. This condition was affecting her in other ways not only with regard to her memory.

It was affecting almost every aspect of her daily existence. At this point, she was becoming increasingly incontinent. Memory plays a tremendous role in a person's life and their ability to thrive, function and survive. Burton did not know what to expect from day to day or what might come next. However, he resolved to be there for his mother step by step and to take life one day at a time with her.

All of these thoughts ran through his head as he now stood there watching Janet struggling to sign her name to a document. A little old lady who had worked and paid her taxes all of her life. Now she was unable to go back to work and basically living on a fixed income, the IRS was going after her for a fairly substantial amount of money. Somehow all of this seemed inherently unfair that someone so wholesome and good, had lived her life and given the very best she had to give to everyone she came in contact with over the years. Surely old age and death are inevitable for anyone who lives, but it seemed that Alzheimer's was slowly taking away her life and the IRS was going to take the rest.

Routine was important and Burton tried to keep Janet on a daily regimen and schedule. He tried to get home about the same time every day to give her medicine and make sure she had her dinner. These things became increasingly important as the Alzheimer's progressed. Sometime when he would get a little off schedule, he literally feared that he might come home to the unexpected. For instance, one day he was running about two hours late coming home from work.

When he arrived home, he discovered that Janet had had a bowel movement leaving a trail of droppings all the way down the hallway leading to her room. She was soiled and her diaper was saturated with urine and feces. He had to clean his mom, change her, get her into the tub for a bath and clean up the mess she had made in the hallway. More than likely if Burton had been able to maintain his usual schedule with Janet, he would not have encountered what he did when he arrived home that evening.

As Burton watched the progression of Alzheimer's in his mother over the years, it appeared that she was moving into the final stages. Her cognitive ability was becoming increasingly worse and now some of her motor skills were starting to be affected. Although Janet was still very active, her hyperactivity made it more difficult to manage her. However, she had slowed down considerably. She did not sweep and mop as much, instead, she would sit on the side of the bed for hours and rub her hand along the surface of the bedspread or she would sit and rub her hands across the table. Janet still enjoyed going outside and being in the yard, but she started to spend less time outside and more time in the house. Burton eventually took the house key from her since he was increasingly fearful that his mom would go outside and wander off somewhere.

Another afternoon he got home from work after Mae had left and found his mother seated in the flower bed. She was wearing a gown as she often wore when she was around the house. Burton had brought her a number of gowns that were comfortable gowns, but not nightgowns. Janet was in the middle of the flower bed. She was dirty as she could be. Janet was sitting there clawing at the dirt with her fingers and toes as if her hands and feet were rakes. Janet seemed completely unconcerned that anything would crawl on her. There were snakes in the yard, possums and other animals, but Janet had no fear of anything like that. She continued to claw at the dirt with her fingers. The bottoms of her fingernails were full of dirt.

On this day, tears came to Burton's eyes when he saw his mom sitting there in the flower bed clawing the dirt. He did not know what he could do to help his mother, make her happy or make her understand that she should not be seated in the flowerbed clawing at the dirt. He helped her up. Her hands, legs, and feet were filthy. He took her into the bathroom and started to take off her clothes. As usual, she strongly resisted taking a bath. Burton ran her bathwater. When Janet finally got into the bathtub the bathwater was full of dirt and almost black worse than a child's bath water that had been playing outside all day.

Mae had started to hide the brooms and mops because she needed a good broom and mop to clean the house; however, she failed to realize that the broom and mops were part of Janet's activity. He wondered if Janet had sat on the ground and started clawing the dirt because she was unable to find a broom to sweep with, or was it something more. Was it simply that Janet was getting worse? The Alzheimer's had become like a horrible mystery unfolding and manifesting itself in an array of different ways on a regular and consistent basis. Slowly but surely, Janet was starting to succumb to this Alzheimer's.

A few days later Janet found the broom. Burton had gone away from the house for a moment and he received a phone call from one of the neighbors stating that Janet was outside sweeping the street again. The neighbor indicated that the police were down at the end of the street talking to her. They were not certain if everything was okay, but they thought he needed to come home right away. Burton rushed home. He found Janet at the end of the street in front of the house.

The police were there trying to figure out what was going on with her. The police indicated they had seen Janet in the street and wondered if she was alright. Burton explained to them that Janet suffered from Alzheimer's and that occasionally she would wander out onto the street to try and sweep up the pine straw that fell from the pine trees in their front yard. He thanked the officers for checking on Janet.

The officers suggested that he might want to try and keep her from coming into the street. He stated to them that he tried but that occasionally she came out into the street anyway. He thanked them once again, before taking Janet up the driveway and back into the house.

"Mom, you have got to stop going out into the street like that," said Burton.

"Why? It's my street and I can go out there any time I get ready," replied Janet.

"Do you want them to take you away from me?" Burton asked. "Is that what you want?"

"They're not going to tell me what to do," said Janet.

"This could really get ugly," Burton said. "I'm so worried about you, Mom."

"I'm a thousand years old, and I didn't get this old by being stupid," said Janet.

"I do everything I can to try and make sure you're okay and taken care of," Burton said. "I do everything I can possibly do. I'm as good to you as I know how to be."

"You're a good son Burton," Janet said. "I appreciate you so much. Everything you do."

"But you don't understand, if you continue to go out into the street and sweeping the street like that, and if the police see you or the neighbors complain about it. A situation could be created that might not work out too favorably. I want you at home with me, not in a facility," said Burton.

"I want to be home with you, Baby," said Janet.

"You're not acting like it," Burton replied. "If you keep going out into the street like that, they're probably going to take you away from me. So, you've got to be careful and not go out there anymore."

"Well, what can I do then," Janet said. "Seems like everything I do is wrong."

"You can do a whole lot of things, Mom," Burton said. "Just going out into the street with that broom to sweep is not one of them. How about that. And you're not wearing your shoes again. You can't be outside without your shoes. I keep telling you, you're going to catch a cold."

"I've never had a cold," Janet said. "You know I don't catch colds. Never had a cold in my life."

"The first cold you have, maybe your last one," said Burton.

"I've never had a cold in my life," replied Janet.

"I just want what's best for you, just like you always wanted what was best for me," Burton said. "I'm not trying to make life unhappy for you. I just want what's best for you. I love you. You're in my care, and I want you to stay in my care because you're my mom, and I don't think there's anybody out there who can do a better job taking care of you than me. But you've got to work with me, and not against me."

"I'll work with you, Baby," Janet said. "I'll work with you."

"You've got to listen to me when I'm talking to you and try to remember certain things that we discuss because it's in your best interest that I say some of the things I say to you. Like when I tell you please don't go out into the street with that broom and start sweeping the cul de sac."

"Okay, okay I won't sweep out in the street," said Janet.

"Promise?" asked Burton.

"I promise," said Janet.

"Thank you," replied Burton as he gave Janet a hug.

About a week later, Sandy approached Burton and stated that her mother had some medical bills that she had not been able to pay. She said they were afraid the creditors might file liens against her house and possibly try to take their home. Burton suggested that they might want to put her name on the deed to the house. Burton stated they could not levy on her mom's house for her bill if someone else name was on the deed. He told Sandy she assumed the primary responsibility of caring for her mom, so her mother would probably want to leave the house to her anyway. Sandy asked Burton if he would come by the house and discuss this with Madea. Burton agreed and told her he would stop by her house later that evening when he got off work.

"How are you doing, Ms. Mattie Lou?" said Burton.

"I'm as well as can be expected," Mattie Lou said. "How are you?"

"I'm good," Burton said. "Sandy asked me to come by here and talk with you about something."

"What you want to talk about?" asked Mattie Lou.

"She was telling me that you had some medical bills and that some of your family is worried they might try and levy on your house," Burton said. "One way you could try and protect your house is to do a deed putting one of your children's names on it. That way it would be more difficult for any creditors of yours to go after your home. Is that something you think you want to do?"

"Say I got some medical bills?" Mattie Lou replied. "Well, whose name could I put on the house?"

"Why don't you put Sandy's name on the house," said Burton.

"Sandy?" Mattie Lou said. "I don't know about that, you talking about her," she said pointing at Sandy with a grin on her face.

"What's wrong with me?" asked Sandy.

"Sandy is the one who stays here with you and helps you the most," Burton said. "I'm not trying to tell you what to do, I'm trying to make you aware of options you might have to protect your house."

"How would we do something like that?" asked Mattie Lou.

"Well, I can call a friend who owns a title company and have him draw up the deed giving you a life estate in the house and putting one of your children on the deed with you, and you sign it," said Burton.

"Call him," said Mattie Lou.

"Why don't you discuss it with your family first and then let me know," Burton said. "I'm more than happy to help you if that's what you want to do."

"Alright then," said Mattie Lou.

The discussion was waged within Sandy's family and they decided to get the deed drawn up with Sandy's name on it. Sandy contacted Burton and stated it was permissible to get the new deed drawn up to the house and Madea was willing to sign it. Burton called the title company and requested they draw up the deed.

Mattie Lou gave Burton the money for the deed to be drawn up. The document was prepared. Burton met Sandy at her house with a notary where they presented the deed to Mattie Lou. Mattie Lou took a pen and signed her name. They took the deed and recorded it with the clerk of the probate court.

It appeared that everything was a done deal until Burton got a phone call about two weeks later. He was at home around the house watching television when his phone rang. It was Sandy's number, Burton thought that was odd since Sandy was at his house helping him change and bathe Janet. Burton answered the call and he heard Mattie Lou's voice on the other end. She was angry as she raised her voice at Burton over the phone.

"Hello," said Burton.

"Is this LeFlore?" said Mattie Lou.

"Yes," replied Burton. "Ms. Mattie Lou, is everything alright?"

"I want my damn house back!" Mattie Lou said. "You hear me, you give me my house back right now."

"Say what, your house?" said Burton.

"I don't care how handsome you are," Mattie Lou said. "Think you're so damn good looking. You give me my house back," Mattie Lou said. "I'm telling you. Do you hear what I'm telling you?"

"Nobody's got your house besides you Ms. Mattie Lou," Burton said. "It's your house. I'm not trying to take your house. You said that you wanted to put Sandy's name on the house and that is all we did."

"Motherfucker, don't make me have to come looking for you," said Mattie Lou.

"Mam, I don't know what you're talking about," Burton said. "How did you get my number? Do you want to talk to Sandy?"

"No, I don't need to talk to her. I want my house back!" Mattie Lou said. "And you better give me my damn house like I told you."

"Sandy, this is your mom on the phone," Burton said. "Ms. Mattie Lou, please understand that I didn't take your house and I would never do anything like that. You signed a deed putting your daughter's name on your house and that is what you said you wanted to do."

"Alright Pretty Rickey," Mattie Lou said. "You better get me back my house oooohhh. Don't make me have to tell you again."

"Here, here's Sandy," Burton said. "You talk to her. Mam, I'm not trying to take your house."

"Madea," said Sandy.

"You're in on all this Sandy so I'm telling you now," Mattie Lou said as she started to cry. "Y'all better give me my papers to my house."

"I'll be home in a minute, Madea," Sandy said. "We'll talk then."

Burton decided he would take Janet to the hairdresser so that she could get her hair done. Mary Morris had been doing Janet's hair for many years. Burton could remember Janet going to Mary back when he was very little. She would go there and get her hair done and Burton would play with her son Ken way back in the day. Janet had continued to use her throughout the years. Burton made an appointment with Mary, and got Janet ready to take her over there for her visit.

When they arrived at Mary's, Janet stayed there waiting for a few minutes. However, shortly after Burton left and went back to work, Mary called him on his cell phone. Burton was worried that something was wrong given the fact that he expected Janet to be there at the beautician's for at least an hour or two. He answered the phone. Mary was on the other end. He was concerned and hoped that Janet was not being rude or acting out of place.

"Burton," said Mary.

"Yes, is everything alright?" Burton asked. "Mom is being nice today, isn't she?"

"Yes, she's always as sweet as she can be," Mary said. "But I don't know if I'm going to be able to do her hair this afternoon."

"I thought you said this would be a good time to bring her," Burton said. "I really was hoping she could get her hair done today, it's been a while since she's had it done, and I'm not sure when I might be able to bring her back over there. Did something come up?"

"Well, no," Mary said. "I was ready to do her hair. It's just that."

"What's wrong?" asked Burton.

"I think your mom may have had a little accident," Mary said. "I really think you need to come and check on her."

"An accident," Burton said. "Alright, I'll be right there."

"Okay we'll be here waiting for you," said Mary.

It was very embarrassing for Janet. Burton got Janet into the truck. He was concerned because he really wanted for Janet to get her hair done and he was not sure if and when he might have time to bring her again. He asked Mary if she could still do Janet's hair if he was able to get her home, clean her up and bring her back in a timely manner. Mary assured him that she would still do Janet's hair if he could get her back within an hour. Burton took Janet with him in the truck and they went to the house.

Burton cleaned his mom up, and made her take a bath. He then gave her a fresh pair of Depends and a pair of fresh clothes to wear. As soon as he was finished getting his mom together, he called Mary to ask if she could still do her hair appointment. Mary said she would be there waiting if he could bring Janet on now. They got back into the truck and went back to her shop, where Janet finally was able to get her hair done.

As Burton left Janet at the beauty parlor for the second time, he thought about how he used to visit the beauty parlor with his mother when he was a child. A lot of time, and a lot of years had transpired since then. Here he was with Janet at the same place getting her hair done after all these years. However, a lot had changed over the years. Janet was now incontinent and along with the dementia she suffered from, incontinence was becoming another significant factor which was starting to affect her daily life. She and her beautician Mary had been very good friends over the years, and now Mary was calling to say she could not do Janet's hair because she had pooped on herself.

Incontinence had now become another factor in Janet's life which would result in her being further isolated and unable to function in the everyday world. It was also an issue that meant Burton was having to incorporate the unpleasant aspect of having to change his mom when Mae was not around to do it for him. However, as he matured and become more accustomed to taking care of his mother as her condition advanced, he took the situation in stride and handled it well, so Janet finally got her hair done.

    Later that evening Burton received a call from his friend Sandy stating that Mattie Lou had fallen on the floor. She asked if he could come and help her because she was unable to get her off the floor by herself. Although Burton had no problem with helping Sandy, he was reluctant to go over to the house because of the way she had talked to him a few days prior about giving her back her house.

    He decided to go over and help Sandy with her mom because Sandy was there for him quite frequently when he needed help with Janet. She had been there for him despite some of the names Janet had called her or some of the psychotic episodes Janet had involving Sandy. Burton rushed over to Sandy's house to find Mattie Lou laying in the middle of the hallway unable to get off the floor. Mattie Lou was not fat, but she was a big-boned lady and she was not a lightweight by any means. Burton was able to pick her up off the floor and help her to the side of the bed. She seemed relieved to be off the floor. Once Burton got her off the floor, Sandy took over from that point getting her ready for bed.

    Just like taking care of a child, there is rarely a dull moment when taking care of a parent with Alzheimer's. Unfortunately, many of those moments are sad. Whereas with a child, the child is growing, exploring and becoming more independent with each passing day and witnessing a child grow and mature can be a joyful experience. With an aging adult, the adult is regressing and becoming less independent. Often it is difficult for loved ones to see the person they looked up to and admired so much over the years experiencing one setback after another. Adults on the other hand, often do not give up their independence easily and often there is conflict and confusion which is not always a happy situation either.

Burton would bring Janet something to eat every evening when he came home from work. He would give her medicine, feed her, make sure she was dry and help her to bed. This was part of his daily routine and he tried to stick to it. Life was easier that way.

This was also time he always spent with Janet every day. Usually, after she would eat and take her medicine, she would be ready to go to bed. Although, Burton always loved his mother dearly, somehow now he felt a deeper love and appreciation for her. Obviously, she was getting older and the likely hood that she might not be around much longer was a factor; however, it seemed that since she needed him more and depended on him for practically everything, their bond had become deeper. There is no bond in this world like the bond between a mother and a child. Burton was no longer her child; he was a grown man and still very much her son.

Over the last few years, he had developed more empathy for her; the wonderful life she had lived; the tremendous example she and his dad had set for him and he accepted her as she now was. There was no way he would let her down. Even though it was not always easy, she had always been there for him and he knew he had to be there for her no matter what.

As he hugged Janet good night, he thought back to that morning a few years ago when he had gone downstairs to get a drink of water. He had awakened that morning, hungover and tired just wanting to go into the kitchen and get some water and return right back to his bed. When he went downstairs on this morning, he was startled by Janet who he thought was still asleep. His mother was standing in the doorway of her bedroom which was adjacent to the kitchen.

Janet was standing there with a huge smile on her face and her arms outstretched for him. She was so happy to see him. Burton had looked over at her standing there, finished getting his water and left her standing there with her arms outstretched. He did not hug her or even say good morning.

He turned and walked away and went upstairs to his bedroom and went back to bed. Burton felt like such a jerk later on when he thought about that moment. How could he have just walked away and not even acknowledged her? In her eyes, he saw nothing but joy in her heart that morning. She saw him and it was as if she had seen her happiness and wanted to embrace it. He had shared many hugs with Janet. Somehow, he knew he would always regret missing that one hug.

A few months later, one of Janet's friends and former colleagues at Bishop State Community College. Dr. Yvonne Kennedy who had risen in the ranks at Bishop State from instructor to president of the college. Yvonne Kennedy was also an Alabama State Legislator. Upon her death, her legislative seat was vacant. Burton decided to run for the position. There were a number of other people who also ran for the seat. Burton knew very little about political campaigns. He planned to run as a Democrat but was not certain about when the deadline was to qualify, so he missed the deadline and ran as an Independent candidate. Burton's work schedule was hectic, and he had to get close to five hundred signatures on a petition to get his name on the ballot.

He asked Mae if she would start staying at the house with Janet and be there with her round the clock. Mae had moved out of her house and was staying with family members, so she agreed. From that point, Mae basically moved into Janet's home. Burton spent an increasing amount of time away from the house. Either he was working or out getting signatures on his petition. Burton started to put an increasing amount of responsibility on Mae as his focus changed from taking care of Janet in the evenings to doing other things. He would leave early and come home late and was very often gone on the weekends also. Weekends were another time Burton usually spent caring for Janet without any help or assistance. As the next few weeks went by, Mae was there at the house with Janet most of the time and Burton was gone.

CHAPTER THREE

It was Mardi Gras Monday, 2013 and time for Burton's annual Mardi Gras party at his office. Every year the parade ran right by his office on Lexington Avenue. Monday and Tuesday Burton and his friends would always do a tremendous amount of food, have a good time and watch the parade. Burton always liked to take Janet along with him. It was always a great time to get her out of the house and let her have some enjoyment. The forecast for today was a little wet, but as the day progressed it cleared up.

Janet attended the parade. Burton found her a broom and let her sweep the sidewalk for a little while. Janet ate chicken, fish, hamburgers and hot dogs and drank some sodas. She caught moon pies, beads and candy. Everyone had a good time and certainly Janet enjoyed herself tremendously.

On Mardi Gras day, it was raining. Although Burton still tried to urge her to come to the office with him for the parade. She said she did not want to go in the rain and decided to stay home. Burton went on leaving her at the house but it continued to rain. Janet stayed at home and Mae also stayed there with Janet. It continued to rain for the majority of the day into the evening. It was a rainy Mardi Gras day for sure which soon came to a lackluster end like every Mardi Gras. The following Ash Wednesday Burton went back to work and life went on as usual. He was still involved with his campaign and busy work schedule. Mae was still there with Janet in the house and Burton trusted that Mae was caring for Janet properly. The following Thursday after Mardi Gras, Burton found Janet balled up in a knot in her bed. Janet was in excruciating pain.

"Mom, are you okay?" said Burton.

"I'm hurting," said Janet balled up in a fetal position.

"Where does it hurt?" Burton asked. "Does your leg hurt?"

"Yes," said Janet.

"Do you think I need to take you to the hospital?" asked Burton.

"No, I'll be alright," said Janet.

"Why are you balled up like that?" Burton asked. "Does your stomach hurt?"

"Yes," said Janet.

"What else hurts?" asked Burton.

"My side hurts," Janet said.

"Did you fall?" asked Burton.

"I don't know," said Janet.

"Maybe we should go to the hospital," said Burton.

"I don't want to go to the hospital right now," Janet said. "I'll be alright."

"Well, if you don't feel any better tomorrow we're going to the hospital," said Burton.

"Okay," replied Janet.

"Take your medicine," Burton said. "Here's something to drink. Can you drink this for me?"

Janet untied herself from the ball she had immersed herself in and tried to take the glass of juice in her hand. However, Burton noticed she was struggling to hold it, so he grasped the glass in his hand and guided it to her mouth. He had to place the medicine in her mouth as well. She drank the juice and swallowed her medication. Burton tried to assist Janet in obtaining a comfortable position to lay in. After observing Janet and talking with her for a few minutes, Burton was of the impression that Janet may have fallen and broken or fractured a bone. He wondered if Mae knew anything about her having fallen, because he was convinced that she had fallen and hurt herself in some way. He sat there on the side of the bed with Janet for a few more moments. Afterward he went to have a talk with Mavis.

"Mae, do you have any idea what's wrong with my mom?" asked Burton.

"She hasn't been feeling well today," said Mae.

"Did she fall?" asked Burton.

"Not that I know of," replied Mae.

"Are you sure," Burton said. "Because she acts like she got a broken or fractured bone. Then she's saying her stomach hurts too."

"I don't know, she's been up and about most of the day," Mae said. "She just got like that a little while ago."

"And you're sure she didn't fall or anything like that," said Burton.

"No Burton I ain't seen her fall," Mae said. "She's been up and around the house most of the day and then she went in there and laid down. Don't you think I would have called you if I thought something was wrong with your mama."

"What did she have to eat today?" asked Burton.

"She ate good today," said Mae.

"I told you about giving her those noodles all the time," Burton said. "They have no nutritional value."

"Well, that's not all she eats," Mae said. "I cook whatever you bring in the house."

"You say she didn't fall though," said Burton.

"Not that I know of," replied Mae.

"You sure about that, because she's acting as if she fell and hurt something," said Burton.

"I'm sure," said Mae.

"Somethings not right with her," Burton replied. "If she's not any better by tomorrow, I'm going to have to take her to the hospital."

Needless to say, by the following day Janet was not feeling any better. She refused to eat anything and lay in bed the majority of the day still balled up in a knot like she was in serious pain. Burton spoke with Mae before leaving work. She indicated that Janet was doing any better than the night before. Burton called Dr. Hunte and told him that he thought something was wrong with Janet and he thought he might need to take her to the hospital. Hunte assured Burton that he and Dr. Bell would attend to her if she had to be admitted. Burton called an ambulance to meet him at the house. He wanted to take Janet to the hospital with no further delay. When Burton arrived at the house the ambulance was not far behind. Janet was there in the bed pretty much like she had been the night before and pretty much the entire day. The ambulance arrived and they took Janet to the Mobile Infirmary emergency room.

Dr. Rousso was on duty that Friday night. He was the same doctor who had attended to Janet when she fell and busted her head open on the water faucet. Burton told Dr. Rousso that he thought Janet may have a fractured bone or something; although, he was not certain. After observing Janet and her movements and indications of where her pain was coming from, Dr. Rousso also surmised Janet might have fallen or hurt herself in some way. He ordered some ex-rays which all came back suggesting she had no broken bones or fractures. Dr. Rousso ran some further tests which later indicated that Janet had a urinary tract infection. After several hours in the emergency room, Janet was finally admitted to the hospital for treatment of the urinary tract infection.

A simple urinary tract infection seemed easy enough to cure. Janet was in an intense amount of pain from the infection. Just two days before Janet had been perfectly fine, at the Mardi Gras enjoying herself immensely and now she was in the hospital with a urinary tract infection. Little did Burton know that a urinary tract infection would be the point where Janet would take a severe turn for the worse.

Janet remained in the hospital for approximately ten days while she was being treated for the urinary tract infection. During those ten days she was labeled a fall risk and for the most part hospital staff tried to keep her in the bed. Although Janet was steady on her feet and ambulatory every one of the nursing staff would tell her not to get out of bed and try to keep her from getting up. When the hospital staff was not in the room Mae constantly reminded her to stay in bed.

After a few days in the hospital Janet started to develop small bed sores on both sides of her bottom. When Burton asked about the small sores, he was told they were giving her antibiotics and the sores would more than likely clear up quickly. Otherwise, Janet was doing well and did not appear to be having any more problems related to the urinary tract infection. She was soon to be discharged. One afternoon while Burton was there visiting with Janet, one of the nurses entered her room.

"Mrs. LeFlore, it's time for me to check these IV's. How are you doing? You feeling better?" asked Nurse Kim.

"I'm fine," Janet said. "Thank you."

"Mom, I think they'll be letting you come home in a few days," Burton said. "Isn't that right?"

"That sure would be nice, I know you must be ready to go home Mrs. LeFlore," said the nurse.

"Yes," replied Janet.

"I would never have thought you would be in the hospital for almost ten days for a urinary tract infection," said Burton.

"Oh yea. Some UT infections can be very serious in elderly people," Nurse Kim said. "Especially people who suffer with Alzheimer's and dementia. That's why she has been on continuous intravenous antibiotics ever since she got here and that's been almost a week now."

"Oh really," said Burton.

"Now that doesn't have to be the case here with regard to Mrs. LeFlore," Nurse Kim said. "But there are many instances when in elderly people they just don't react well to it."

"Well, she seems to be doing fine," Burton asked. "Aren't you, Mom?"

"Yes. I feel much better now, Baby," said Janet.

"I'm a little concerned about those small sores on her behind," said Burton.

"Have you talked with her doctor?" asked the nurse.

"Just briefly I spoke with him about it," said Burton.

"They ought to get better in a few days." said Nurse Kim.

"I hope so," replied Burton.

Janet was released from the hospital. Burton picked her up at the patient discharge area. Janet was brought out to his truck in a wheelchair. Mae accompanied her and brought her belongings. Burton opened the door and he assisted Janet in getting into the vehicle. She stood and stepped up into the truck with relative ease. They drove to the house and Janet was able to walk perfectly fine from the truck to the house. Once inside Janet went into her room. Burton brought her things into her room and welcomed her back home. The nurse from the home healthcare agency stopped by not long after they had arrived back at the house. She wanted to evaluate Janet and have Burton fill out some paperwork so that she could be admitted to their care.

After sitting down with the home health nurse, Burton had to leave the house. He was still involved in a rather lackluster campaign for the Alabama State Legislature as an Independent candidate. He had just about managed to get all of the signatures he needed to get on the ballot. However, he still had more signatures to get and the deadline for him to have this in to the Alabama Secretary of State was drawing near. He had given a few interviews to the media and put out some yard signs in the district, but he did little else in furtherance of his campaign. Janet's being ill had further thrown him off course.

A few days after Janet had arrived back home from the hospital, she cut her foot while walking around her bedroom. Mae had given her a glass of juice earlier in the day and had not removed the glass after Janet was finished. Janet had knocked the glass of the table and broken it on the floor. He found Mavis on the sofa fast asleep. He found Janet seated on the floor of her bedroom near the door. Her foot had been bleeding. When she realized she was bleeding she sat down on the floor and started rubbing her hand in the blood. There was a short trial of blood and fingertips as she had been seated there for a period of time rubbing her hands in the blood from her foot.

Burton quickly got a paper towel to wipe Janet's foot. He saw the piece of glass in her foot and he was able to pull the piece of glass out of her foot. She still continued to rub her hands in the blood that was smeared across the wooden bamboo floor in her bedroom. Burton helped her up off the floor and took her to the bathroom to wipe the blood off her hand. Janet was extremely confused on this particular night. Burton took her to sit on the side of her bed. He encouraged her to sit there while he got her medicine.

"Mae, what are you doing?" asked Burton.

"I had nodded off for a minute," Mae said. "I was tired."

"My mom cut her foot," Burton said. "There's blood all over the floor in her bedroom."

"Burton, I thought your mama was in bed," Mae said. "She was laying down in the bed when I laid down on the sofa and fell asleep."

"Well, she's not asleep," Burton said. "She cut her foot on a piece of glass."

"I'm sorry," Mae said. "I'll be right there."

"Can you get the mop and clean that blood off the floor," Burton said. "She's been sitting there rubbing her hands in it."

"All your mama seem to do is rub now a days," Mae said. "She's always rubbing. She rubs everything."

"She's been rubbing her hands in the blood from her foot, and I need you to get it up for me if you can," Burton said. "I'm trying to give her medicine."

"Is her foot cut bad?" asked Mae.

"It's not too bad but there's blood all over the floor," said Burton.

"I'll get it up," Mae said. "Just give me a minute. Here I come."

"I'd greatly appreciate it," said Burton.

"I didn't mean to fall asleep," Mae said. "It's just that I was exhausted."

"Mae, if you could just help me get the blood up off the floor, I would greatly appreciate it," Burton said. "There's also some broken glass on the floor. I would appreciate it if you could get that up too. You may have to stop giving her water or juice in a glass. You might have to start giving her drinks in a plastic cup instead."

Burton proceeded to give Janet her medicine and dressed her foot with some alcohol before putting a bandage on it. Mae mopped the blood off the floor and swept up the glass. It was starting to seem like Janet was getting worse since Mae had been staying there at the house. Prior to Mae starting to live at Janet's house, Burton had taken responsibility for her care during the evening and night.

Although Janet was aging and logically her condition was getting progressively worse, it seemed to Burton that Janet had been declining at a quicker rate since Mae had started to remain there overnight and he had placed more responsibility of Janet on her shoulders while he was out working and doing campaign related activities. Although Burton was glad that Mae had been willing to stay there at the house with Janet, and he did not have to worry about running home so quickly every day. He wondered if Mae was the proper blame for Janet's decline or was it just the onset of her disease.

Overall, Janet's demeanor and behavior after coming back from the hospital this time was a little different. She was not as active as she used to be. Janet started spending more time in bed than she usually did. She started talking less and asking fewer questions. Her motor skills were starting to become affected. She had undergone a change drastic enough to make Burton think that there might still be something going on with her. Perhaps the UTI had not been completely cured.

Burton wanted to assume that perhaps she still might have a urinary tract infection than to believe that maybe the Alzheimer's was progressing. It was extremely difficult for Burton to accept the fact that Janet was getting worse. For several years now, Janet had been suffering, not so much from physical ailments because she had enjoyed excellent health for the majority of her life. However, she had become increasingly impaired mentally as the days went by. Burton was starting to believe that Alzheimer's caused more pain and discomfort for a person's loved one than it causes the individual affected by it. It affects practically everyone that person comes in contact with but it's not contagious.

Needless to say, Burton did not run a nearly effective or competitive campaign for the legislative seat and did not win the election. He did not know anything about running a campaign and he did not try to find out. He was also inundated with work and taking care of Janet. He thought the few signs he put out and the newspaper articles about the election and his campaign would be enough to win. The first thing Burton failed to realize in his inexperience was that this was a special election and a lot of voters don't even go the polls during an election that's not a general election. On the night of his defeat for the legislative seat a friend of Burton's had come to join him at the house to watch the election results. After the results were announced, he and his friend Arthur got into a discussion.

"Burton, if I were you, I wouldn't even worry about this little legislative seat," Art said. "If I were you, I would run for Congress."

"Congress?" said Burton.

"Yea man, with your name in this community, you should be able to win," said Art.

"You're crazy man, I don't know what the hell you've been smoking," replied Burton.

"Burt I'm serious," Art said. "You can say whatever you want, but I personally think you should consider it."

"Whatever man," Burton said. "Maybe I should consider jumping off a cliff too."

"I think you should consider it," Art said. "You can say whatever. If you ask me you need to run for Congress."

"Well, that's quite a compliment Art," Burton said. "I appreciate your words of encouragement and motivation. And I approve that message."

"You think I'm bullshitting," Art continued. "You don't even need to think about the state legislature, when you should really be somewhere like Washington."

"Right now, I'm a washed-up political operative," said Burton.

"You've got time," Art said. "Do some homework on this thing and when your time comes run for Congress dude."

"I hear you," Burton replied. "If I run then I guess you're going to be my campaign manager."

"I would if you asked me," Art said. "Although you might want to get someone a little more experienced than me, but I would manage your campaign."

"Okay I'm going to keep that in mind," said Burton.

"Man, you act like this is some kind of joke or something," Art said. "I'm serious."

"Okay, alright," said Burton.

"Burton, you need to give it some thought," said Art.

"I said I would," Burton responded. "And I hear what you're saying."

"Just give it some serious thought," said Art.

Despite the fact that Burton knew full well he did not wage any sort of campaign for that legislative seat, he was still a little devastated that he did not come close to winning. Two days after the election he was seated in his office, thinking about it. Burton decided to take a trip to the elections office to gather whatever information and statistics about the district and the previous election he could find. He certainly had to admit to himself that perhaps he had not done his homework and had not put forth the enough effort. In addition, his running as an Independent may have also played a role in the outcome. He went to the elections office and was asking them about the information he wanted, when the elections officer announced to him that Congressman Joe Bonner had announced that he was vacating his seat to take a job at the University of Alabama.

After the conversation with his friend Art a few days prior, he could not believe his ears. Here he was in the election office talking with the County Elections officer when the news was released. Given the conversation with Art and now the extreme coincidence that he was there with the elections manager who told him about the Congressional seat which was about to become vacant. Burton went back to his office wondering if maybe he might need to put his name in the hat for that seat. After all what did he have to lose.

Meanwhile, Janet was also a major concern. Janet was simply not her old self. There were home health nurses coming in to see her three times a week. Burton decided he would take her back to the hospital to make sure she was not still suffering from a urinary tract infection, since he had also heard sometimes when elderly people have UT infection their behavior changes. Janet was exhibiting and displaying a marked indication of behavior swings. At any rate, Burton thought it would be best to take her back to the hospital and let them run some tests on her.

Janet was admitted back to the hospital; however, they found no signs of any sort of infection in her body urinary or otherwise. She was admitted but she was only admitted for observation. Her diagnosis was, "Failure to Thrive." Burton was not even aware that she was only admitted for observation, and was not being treated for anything. He was glad to find out they thought nothing was wrong with her but valued his opinion about his mother's health enough to admit her to the hospital and make sure everything was alright instead of sending her home. While she was in the hospital for over Ten days, they refused to allow her to get up at all or walk around.

Every time she would even think about getting out of bed she was quickly shoved back into the bed. For the entire time she was in the hospital she was labeled a fall risk, even though technically she was not a fall risk. During those days in the hospital laying in bed, the small sores that she had on her backside started to get larger. The sores were not huge they definitely got a little larger over the few days she was in the hospital. It was about the same time that Burton realized that sores were getting bigger when he was informed that Janet was only there for observation and was not being treated for the sores or anything else. Janet was diagnosed as failing to thrive.

Burton had become increasingly involved in the new campaign he had managed to thrust himself into. By now he had hired some consultants to coach him on how to run his campaign and how to raise money for his campaign. He was more actively involved in raising money, not to mention his regular work in his business. All along, Janet did not appear to be improving much at all. Although, at the same time she was fine, it was just becoming obvious to Burton there were some changes going on with Janet. She was becoming more detached and it was certainly unusual for her to stay in bed for long periods of time unless she was asleep. She was becoming less active and less inquisitive about things going on around her and in her life.

On the day she was scheduled to be released from the hospital, Burton picked her up at the patient discharge area. A patient transport person brought Janet out to his truck in a wheelchair. He helped her into the truck. Mae got into the back seat carrying the items they had at the hospital. Janet stood to her feet and stepped into the truck which was rather high off the ground. She stepped up onto the running board and then into the truck where Burton helped her get seated. From the hospital he drove Janet home. On the way to the house Janet started to rub her right hand along the dashboard of the truck. Burton took her hand in his for a moment while they drove and slowly guided her hand back down toward her lap. She quickly returned her hand to the dashboard and continued to rub its surface.

He decided he would let her rub the dashboard if that was what she wanted to do. He was just glad she was coming home and hoped he would see some continued improvement when she returned home. They drove into the driveway and Burton walked around to the passenger side of the truck. He opened the door for Mae and Janet. Mae hopped out of the car and Burton opened the door so that she could take their things inside. He then returned to the truck to help Janet in the house. He took Janet's arm and encouraged her to step out of the truck. Janet stepped out of the truck assisted by Burton. He closed the door behind them and proceeded to help her down the steps leading to the back door.

Janet slowly took about four steps forward and all of a sudden, she stopped dead in her tracks. Burton encouraged her to continue on so they could get inside. She would not take another step. She leaned slowly in Burton's direction. He had his arm around her so she did not fall. Burton straightened her up and again encouraged her to walk inside. Janet could not take another step. It was almost as though her legs were frozen and locked.

Burton continued to try and get her to walk with him but she simply would not take another step. After Burton had tugged, pushed, pulled and pleaded with Janet to walk and take another step, she just stood there holding on to Burton. He called Mae and asked her to bring him a chair from inside. He was able to get Janet seated in a chair. They were still outside. At this point, Burton had to figure out how he was going to get Janet into the house.

He picked Janet up in the chair and carried both her and the chair into the house. Once inside he was able to pick Janet up in his arms and carry her to her bed. He helped her to change her clothes. He also checked her Depends to make sure she was clean. It was then he examined the soars on her butt cheeks again. He wondered why she was getting those lesions on her rear end. Since Burton had become increasingly busy with his business and campaign he had been paying less and less attention to his mother Janet and what was really going on with her.

One thing that he had not really noticed was that Janet was spending an increasing amount of time in bed. Almost twenty days total she spent in the hospital they would not allow her to get out of bed. Then when she was at home, she was spending more time in bed and not getting up and walking around. Janet was starting to develop bed sores and it started to happen so quickly.

The next day Burton got in from work and asked Mae if Janet had been out of the bed at all today. Mae said that she had tried to get her up out of the bed but she said she did not want to. Mae did however say the home health nurses had been by earlier today and wanted to talk with him about certain aspects of Janet's care. He went into Janet's room and saw her lying there on the bed watching television. He went over to the side of the bed and gave Janet a hug. She appeared to be happy to see him.

He pulled the cover back and noticed that the home health nurses had put bandages over both sores on both sides of her bottom. Janet was resting and comfortable. The home health people had bathed Janet so she was clean, her hair was combed and she looked nice. She smiled and extended her arms out to Burton. Burton leaned into her and gave her a big hug. He asked her how she was doing and Janet said she was fine. She continued to smile. She was in good spirits today.

"Hi, Baby," said Janet.

"Mom, how are you feeling?" asked Burton.

"I'm okay," replied Janet.

"You're not hurting anywhere?" asked Burton.

"No," said Janet.

"You've been in bed all day," Burton said. "Do you want to get up and walk around for a few minutes?"

"Not really," Janet said. "Not right now."

"I noticed you've been spending a lot of time in bed," Burton said. "Why don't you want to get up and ambulate a little bit?"

"I'm afraid," said Janet.

"Afraid of what?" asked Burton.

"Afraid I'll fall," said Janet.

"Mom, you have always been agile and steady on your feet," Burton said. "Why would you be scared you're going to fall all of a sudden."

"Just scared I'll fall," said Janet.

"I can walk with you and make sure you don't fall until you feel like you're steady on your feet," said Burton.

"Maybe later," said Janet.

"You can sit in the chair for a while and watch television," said Burton.

"Not right now," Janet said. "I'm fine."

"Are you hungry?" Burton asked. "Do you want a little something to eat."

"Maybe a little bite," said Janet.

"Let me go in the kitchen and fix you something," Burton said. "Better yet you can come into the kitchen and sit at the table and eat."

"Not now," said Janet.

"Would you mind taking your medicine for me?" asked Burton as he propped Janet up in the bed and handed Janet the medicine. She tried to put it to her mouth but dropped it in the bed. Burton picked the medicine up off the bed and tried again. "Okay, Mom, open mouth," he said as Janet opened her mouth and he placed a pill inside of Janet's mouth. Burton put the glass of water to her mouth and she took a drink. He placed another pill in her mouth and she took another swallow. By the third pill she did not swallow all of the way. So, he gave her another swallow of water. He gave her the last pill and she barely was able to swallow it but she did. Janet humbly and lovingly looked Burton in the eye.

"Alright. Well, I'll go and fix you something. I'll be right back," said Burton.

"Thanks, Baby," replied Janet as Burton went into the kitchen to fix her a little something to eat. Burton brought home a plate from Morrison's with some cream spinach, sweet potatoes and chopped steak. He places some small portions on a small plate for Janet and took it into the room for her. He handed her the plate and the fork. He placed her in position so she would be seated up and could swallow her food. She took the fork and got some sweet potatoes and put it to her mouth. He could tell she was struggling a little but she held the food and continued to feed herself. He watched as Janet ate her food.

He was worried about Janet because he saw her undergoing some changes that he did not understand. He hoped that he would somehow have more luck at getting her out of the bed over the next few days. However, on the other hand he thought that if she persisted in not walking and remained reluctant to get out of bed, then he would have to get her a wheelchair so she could get around a little better. It hurt Burton to see his mom in bed all of the time and not wanting to get up. Not to mention the sores were getting larger. One thing he knew for sure, it was completely out of character for her. Perhaps like most things with Janet at this point it was just the Alzheimer's taking its course.

One morning about two weeks later Mae went into Janet's room to give her a bath and change her Depends. She was able to get Janet to sit on the side of the bed for her. The first thing she did was clean Janet as she tried to avoid the two bandages on each side of her buttocks. One bed soar was about twice the size as the other since Janet was laying mostly on her left side. After changing her, Mae helped her to take off her robe and was about to put on a new one. She left Janet seated there on the side of the bed and turned around to get the other gown out of the drawer. When Mae turned around, Janet lunged forward off the side of the bed and fell onto the floor. She tried to get her up but was unable to so she ran upstairs and awoke Burton. She said Janet had fallen on the floor.

Burton rushed downstairs and found Janet on the floor of her bedroom. Janet was completely naked besides the Depends which she wore. Janet was in distress as she lay there on the floor flailing her body in one spot. She wanted to get off the floor but she could not get her nerves and muscles to cooperate with her mind. Burton was still very concerned about the bed sores that Janet had. Burton could not understand why Janet was developing these sores and they just continued to get increasingly worse. He did not understand why it was happening or what he could do to stop it. He took her back to the hospital again, where he requested that they treat her for the sores. They admitted her and started giving her antibiotics intravenously. This time she stayed in the hospital for approximately a week. He found Janet in slightly better spirits now, but she still was not getting out of bed much at all.

All during this time, Burton was becoming increasingly busy with his campaign for Congress. He was busy making phone calls to potential donors, sending out pledge cards, doing interviews and attending forums with the other candidates. Burton was much more active and proactive in this campaign even though he was running for Congress in a district where no Democrat had been elected since the year of his birth in 1965. He was facing an uphill climb in his campaign and he was facing an uphill climb where his mother's health and care was concerned. He often talked about healthcare during his campaign and often he wanted to discuss his desire to see something done on the federal level to boost money for research into this devastating condition known as Alzheimer's and dementia. However, he was afraid to let word get out to the general public that he was caring for an elderly mother with Alzheimer's.

During the morning hours, he had done an interview with a local news station at Unity Point near Downtown Mobile. After the interview he, went to the hospital to visit Janet. Right about the time Burton arrived at the hospital, the news story he had done earlier that day was about to air. Burton went past the front desk and up the elevator onto the fourth floor where Janet was receiving care. Burton walked into Janet's room. He saw Mavis seated there in the seat next to her bed and Janet there in bed eating her lunch.

"Hi, Mom. How are you?" asked Burton.

"I'm fine, Baby," Janet said. "How are you?"

"I'm good," Burton replied. "I see there getting some antibiotics in you."

"Hi, Burton," said Mae.

"Hey, Mae," Burton said. "You want to take a break for a little while. I'll be up here with her."

"No, I'm fine," Mae said. "We've just been sitting here watching TV."

"How's she been doing?" asked Burton.

"She's been doing pretty good today," Mae said. "She had a big breakfast and she's eating again. So, she has been eating good today."

"Hey, look. There's the interview I did earlier today for the news," Burton said. "Turn that up. Mom, do you see your son on TV?"

"That's you?" said Janet.

"Yea, Mom, doesn't that look like me?" asked Burton.

"Yea, I guess," said Janet.

"I'm running for Congress in for the Alabama District 1 seat," Burton said. "Do you remember me telling you that."

"You're running for something?" Janet asked. "What are you running for?"

"He's running for Congress Janet," Mae said. "He's on TV."

"I see him," said Mae.

"So how are you feeling today?" asked Burton.

"Mrs. LeFlore, we need to take your blood pressure," said the CNA as she entered the room "How are y'all doing?"

"This is Mrs. LeFlore's son Burton, Mr. LeFlore," said Mae.

"Hi, Mr. LeFlore," said Cindy the CNA.

"Hi," Burton said. "So, you're the one coming in here checking on my mom. It's nice to meet you."

"Yes," Cindy said. "Hey, aren't you that guy who's running for office?"

"Maybe," Burton said. "Maybe not. It depends on what guy you're talking about."

"Yea you're Mr. LeFlore," Cindy said. "What are you running for? You're running for something because there were some people talking about voting for you just the other day."

"I'm running for Congress," Burton said. That may be what you're talking about."

"Yea. I thought that was you," Cindy said. "Mrs. LeFlore give me your arm so we can take your blood pressure."

"It's nice to meet you," said Burton.

"You too," Cindy said. "I'll be back to check on you in about two hours Mrs. LeFlore," Cindy said. "I hope you win your election."

"Appreciate that," Burton said. "I hope you'll get out and vote."

"Oh, I will," said Cindy.

"Can you ask her nurse to come down here for a minute," said Burton.

"Sure," said Cindy.

"I miss you, Mom," Burton said. "I need you to hurry up and get better so we can go home."

"Is this my house?" Janet asked. "Where is home or am I going to stay here?"

"Home is 2216," said Burton.

"2216," said Janet.

"Yes 2216 Rue de LeFlore," said Burton.

"That's where I'm going?" said Janet.

"As soon as you get out of the hospital," Burton said. "Trying to get you better and figure out what's going on with these soars on your behind. But as soon as we get through with the antibiotics and your care here. We're going home. I miss you and I want you to come home."

"I want to go home," said Janet as Dr. Bell came into her room.

"Dr. Bell, how are you," said Burton.

"Fine, thanks for asking," said Bell. "How are you, and how are you Mrs. LeFlore?"

"Tired and weary, yet trying to keep on," said Janet.

"Well, we all must keep on keeping on," said Dr. Bell.

"How's she doing?" Burton asked Bell. "Those soars don't appear to be healing up much at all."

"Well, Mrs. LeFlore is receiving antibiotics and it should help them to heal," Bell said. "If they don't start to heal then the only other alternative would be surgery."

"Surgery," Burton said. "What kind of surgery."

"Plastic surgery to remove the decubitus ulcer," said Dr. Bell.

"Do you think they're going to get any better?" Burton said. "Because they seem to be getting worse by the day."

"I can't say Burton," Bell said. "Only time will tell. But they should get better, that's why we're giving her the antibiotics to see if that will help to clear them up."

"Okay," said Burton.

"We'll just have to keep any eye on it and play it by ear," replied Dr. Bell.

"You know I would like to talk with you about my campaign for Congress," Burton said. "Is there a good time when I might be able to contact you to talk about my campaign?"

"Just give me a call," Bell said. "I'd be glad to talk with you about your campaign."

"Okay," Burton said. "I'll call you tomorrow."

"Give me a call," Dr. Bell said. "Mrs. LeFlore, I'll be by a little later to check on you."

"Thanks, Dr. Bell," said Burton.

"You're quite welcome," Bell said. "I'll be looking forward to hearing from you."

"Don't worry. I'll be making the call," said Burton.

"See you later," said Bell as he made his way to his next patient.

"Thanks. I look forward to speaking with you," said Burton.

When Janet was discharged from the hospital this time, Burton had to lift her from the wheelchair into his truck. When they got home, he used a wheelchair that he had gotten for her and brought her into the house. After transporting her from the car basically to the bed, he laid Janet in her bed. As he sat there with Janet on the side of the bed he started wonder how and why Janet was seemingly taking a serious decline in her health.

Now not only was she mentally compromised by the onset of Alzheimer's, she was becoming physically compromised. He realized Janet was spending almost all of her time in bed now, but this was a sharp contrast to how Janet had been all of her life since she had given birth to him many years prior. Janet had always been extremely active. She did not exercise much, but one would have to understand the mindset of most depression babies who did not worry so much about exercise. The mentality of most depression babies was that you could get your exercise at work.

Janet was still relatively alert and somewhat inquisitive. She just seemed to lack the desire to move around or was it that she had forgotten how to walk and move around. Had Janet become physically unable to ambulate due to neurological reasons. Was it a combination of things that caused her to become more vegetative. Burton could not help but wonder why Janet seemed to be declining more quickly since Mae had moved into the house.

He was spending less time caring for her. He certainly did not want to blame Mae for the simple fact that nature and old age might be taking its course where Janet was concerned; however, it did appear odd to him that since he had been spending less time around and relying more on Mavis to care for Janet that she was declining more rapidly. He greatly appreciated Mae being there for Janet and for him. Perhaps he just wanted someone to blame for what was happening to Janet.

As he sat there with Janet he thought back to when he was a very young boy and used to drive over the bay with Grandma Teah to the nursing home in Daphne to visit her sister Sadie. Sadie suffered from Alzheimer's and she was practically bed ridden and rarely talked. They used to call people like Sadie senile back then. Those images of his great aunt always stuck in his mind. As a child it was hard for him to understand old age and Sadie's condition.

However, he struggled to comprehend what he saw when he went with his grandmother to visit Sadie. Now over forty years later, he was now sitting in Janet's room on her bedside and she was starting to look a lot like Sadie. Janet was becoming confined to the bed and her decubitus did not appear to have improved despite her having been on antibiotics.

CHAPTER FOUR

About a month and a half later, Mother's Day arrived. Janet was not feeling well. Burton had been very busy with his campaign. Although, on Mother's Day he gave Mavis the day off and put everything aside to spend the entire day with Janet. He had purchased her a big bouquet of one dozen roses and went into her room that morning when he awoke. Burton found her in bed. Burton put the roses on her night stand and wished her a Happy Mother's Day. She thanked him for the flowers. He encouraged her to get up and she did not express any interest in getting out of bed. However, Burton insisted that he wanted her to get out of bed for Mother's Day.

He brought the wheelchair around to her side of the bed and lifted her out of bed into the wheelchair. Janet did not like the wheelchair and she frowned with discontent about being placed in the chair. It also appeared that when she sat down in the chair that her sores were hurting her worse. The home health nurses had been coming by three times a week to check on her. When Burton would arrive home in the evening, he was very concerned about the decubitus, but he was reluctant to pull the bandages and look at it for fear he would not be able to secure or refasten the bandages. Since the home health nurses did not say anything to him about it, he just assumed they were getting better. However, this afternoon Burton did check the decubitus and they appeared to be getting larger. Not only were they getting larger but now they were covered by scab tissue.

Janet sat there in the wheelchair slumped over. Burton took her into the kitchen and asked her if she wanted something to eat. He fed her something but she would not eat. When Janet would not eat the food on her own, he tried to feed her, but she still would not eat. Finally, after several attempts she took a small bite of food and barely chewed it. She stopped chewing and started holding the food in her mouth. Burton noticed she was not chewing so he encouraged her to chew the food. She would not chew anymore. Concerned that she might swallow the unchewed food, he tried to get her to spit it out. After some degree of convincing she eventually spit the food out of her mouth. Burton was becoming increasingly worried that Janet was not feeling well. He tried to get her to talk to him but she would not say much of anything. Janet just continued to stay there slumped over in her chair. Also, she looked extremely pale.

It was a beautiful Sunday on this Mother's Day and Burton wondered if taking her outside would brighten her day some. He knew how much Janet loved being outside and the day was stunning. Burton took Janet outside on the front porch. He studied her closely to see if there was any change in her demeanor or mood. Janet hardly raised her head to look around. She just sat there slumped over and looking desolate and melancholy. The bright sun on this incredible May morning did not brighten her face in any way.

She remained in the same or similar condition for the remainder of their time outside. The Dogwood trees that she had transported from Wilmington to Mobile and planted in the front yard where blooming. A sprig from Mamma's Dogwood tree in the back yard of 1013 S. 12th Street. The Dogwood was in full bloom on this magnificent springtime day, everything was in full bloom but Janet. She was frail, weak, and pale. Her Azaleas were also in full bloom. It was an incredible day but Janet was obviously not doing incredibly.

"Mom, what's wrong?" asked Burton. Janet did not reply. "It's Mother's Day, are you having a good Mother's Day?" Janet nodded her head in the affirmative; however, her sullen nod was not very convincing to Burton. "Do you want to stay outside for a little while longer," Burton said. "Or maybe we can go back in the house." Janet continued to sit there relatively silent and non-responsive. "Mom, it's Mother's Day. You're not going to talk to me. You're not talking to me?" Janet said not a word.

"Looks like we might be spending Mother's Day at the hospital," Burton said. "Do you think we need to take you to the hospital?" Janet raised her head and dropped it back down. "Maybe we should go back inside." Janet just sat there. She heard Burton but could not reply. "You won't eat anything, you're not talking to me, what's going on sweetheart? I'm here and I don't know what to do. I've done and I try to do everything I can and all I can do. What is going on with you, Mom?" Janet continued to sit there with her head bowed. She would look up occasionally but it was obvious to Burton that his mom was in some sort of distress. They had spent a lot of time at the Hospital in the last few months, and unfortunately even that had not brought much of any improvement in her condition or mental state.

"You think maybe we should go back inside?" Janet continued to sit there relatively non-responsive. "Yes," said Janet. "That's about the first thing you've said to me all day." Everything that was going on with Janet was beyond his comprehension. Burton was not sure if his mom was ill; or if his mom had not slept well the night before; or if she no longer had the will to live; or if she had no idea who he was; or if she was in pain; or if she was suffering; or if she was in need of medical care; or if he took her to the Hospital again after having been there several times before. Let's back it up, he knew she was suffering in some way, only he was trying to understand how. Burton tried hard to be unselfish and step outside of his own suffering and pain and try to wrap his mind around Janet's circumstances.

The entire experience was exhaustive for her and for Burton. It reminded him of the day his mother told him that she had discovered a little old lady who Dr. Bishop had asked her to go and see. Janet found her having been seated in her lazy boy chair having fallen and sustained an injury. Ms. Aundre Johnson had been seated there in that chair for over two days. She had urinated and defecated on herself and Janet had empathy for her. Aundre had been a janitor and Bishop State. The same institution that Janet held a Chemistry professorship. From the moment Janet visited Aundre until the time she died, Janet agreed to take care of her.

Janet consulted Beck about getting her medical care. She found housing for Aundre in a housing community for senior citizens, she visited her, Janet purchased groceries for her and made that her bills were paid. Janet embraced Aundre from day one, and she pledged to take care of her no matter what. A lady who she hardly knew who had been a janitor at the same institution she held a position as Chemistry teacher. Janet had little more than laid her eyes on this woman at work on a few occasions and now she had decided to take her on as someone who she was going to be responsible for.

Burton always admired and sought to understand Janet's selflessness and her desire and ability to give her very best of herself to everyone she encountered. She was an Alpha female married to an Alpha male. Together they had been an Alpha couple. They had been the caretakers and the providers. Janet had no problem giving back, she had no problem sharing, she was able to have empathy and concern for someone besides herself. Aundre Johnson sparked a flame in her heart to help and serve.

"Be the best you can be," Janet always used to say. She truly tried to give her best to everyone she came in contact with. From the first day she encountered Aundre there in her home complaining of an injury, drenched in her own urine and feces begging for help and compassion. Janet took up this woman that she did not know, and had never met in her life, and she cared for her even thought there was nothing financially she could possibly gain. There was nothing in it for her other than she knew she would be caring for someone in need. She had looked out for an old lady who had no one, no husband, no children, just her, just her, an old, lonely, confused, sickly, injured, hurting, suffering, ailing, incontinent, unable to move or walk around, dazed, confused, disoriented, in need of medical care, in need of aid, in need of assistance, remorseful, dejected, feeling neglecting, unloved, misunderstood.

An old lady holding on to what little life she had left. A humble and hard-working woman who had worked as a Janitor at the same junior college where she taught organic and inorganic chemistry. Although, Aundre just suffered from old age, not Alzheimer's. Like many people who are for the most part on their own, she was just in need of help, assistance and care. She could remember what you said and what might have happened the day before, she could not get around like she used to be able to and she needed help and assistance in living her daily life.

Now Janet had become old. As he sat there with Janet on Mother's Day desperately trying to do something or say something that would make her happy and brighten her day, he reflected on how Janet used to take care of Aundre. He realized how selfless and giving she had been all of her life. She had served her family and the ones she had done the most for had turned their backs on her. She had served her husband who had been dead now for over twelve years. She had served her children and lost her oldest son who had been gone for almost twenty years. She had served her students.

She had practiced random acts of kindness to people she did not even know. Burton thought how blessed he was to have had Janet as a mother. Now he knew there was no way he could ever turn his back on her because she had never, and would have never turned her back on him for any reason. Janet had truly lived a life of unselfish service and duty to so many people who had been blessed to come into her presence. Burton was inspired by Janet's exemplary life. She had truly led by example.

Burton thought about what an incredible woman his mother had been throughout the years. He realized she had set a wonderful example for him and that at this point in her life, she needed him to display some of the characteristics she had demonstrated during his lifetime. Mainly the characteristic of love and compassion for others. At this point, she needed all of the love and compassion he had to give. Caring for her was becoming increasingly difficult as she underwent physical changes.

He had not read much or studied much about Alzheimer's; however, he had been living with it now for seven or eight years. He did understand that there were stages to this disease and Janet was definitely in the advanced or what might be considered the final stages of the disease. It was like the Alzheimer's was slowly stripping her of everything. Alzheimer's was slowly taking away her life and her ability to live and function. He wondered if it was old age or if Alzheimer's had simply stripped her of everything. Had she not slept the night before he thought to himself.

After bringing her back inside, he found a brush and brushed her hair. It appeared that when he brushed her hair it was soothing to her; however, her mood did not change. Burton decided not to take her to the Hospital on Mother's Day, instead he was going to spend some more time with her and give her some Seroquel early and let her get to bed early tonight. He would let her get a good night sleep and see how she was feeling tomorrow. The home health nurses were scheduled to come to visit her tomorrow. Perhaps they could check her out when they came.

He tried to get Janet to eat something but she still would not eat. He gave Janet her medicine early and put her to bed. She fell asleep relatively quickly and slept well throughout the night. Burton checked in on her several times and she appeared to be sleeping very well. He hoped that her behavior today had been a result of her not having much sleep, but somehow. he was worried about Janet and felt there was a strong possibility it was more than her needing a good night rest. Burton was fairly certain that Janet was ill but he felt it was safe to wait until Monday to see how she was doing tomorrow.

The next day he checked on Janet before he went to work and she was still resting. A few hours later the home health nurses arrived at the house. Mae let them in and they went into the room to see Janet. They took her blood pressure and her temperature. The nurse noted that Janet's temperature was elevated. They removed the bandage on her right side and measured the decubitus on her right side. The soar on her right side was smaller than the soar on her left side. The took a measurement and a photograph. They then bandaged her back up. They took off the bandage on her left side which was larger. They took a measurement and then a photograph of it. Finally, they bandaged her left side. The soars had an odor and even though the nurse noticed the odor and her elevated temperature, she did not bother to contact Burton to discuss anything pertaining to Janet.

Burton assumed the home health nurse would contact him if she thought Janet might need further medical attention after she had evaluated her during her visit to the house. When Burton did not hear anything from the home health nurse, he thought that must have been a good sign that she did not think something might be wrong with her or that she might need to be evaluated by a doctor. Later that evening when he returned home, Mae was seated there in a chair in the kitchen.

"Mae, did the home health nurses come today?" asked Burton.

"Yea. They came," said Mae.

"What did they have to say?" asked Burton.

"Nothing," Mae said. "They said she had a little temperature."

"Oh yea," Burton said. "Did they say she might need to be seen by a doctor?"

"No," Mae said. "They checked her like they always do and changed her bandages and left."

"How's she been doing today?" asked Burton.

"She hasn't eaten much, but she just been in the bed," said Mae.

When Burton walked into Janet's room, the first thing he noticed was that Janet's had one of her arms outstretched. She did not say anything when Burton entered but she saw him and she glanced up at him. Her face was still pale and it was clearly noticeable to Burton that Janet was in distress. She was in serious distress. There was no doubt in his mind that something was wrong with Janet. There could be no further delay in getting her to the hospital. He immediately took out his phone and called for an ambulance to come transport Janet to the Emergency Room. It was obvious to him that she was in need of medical care and at this point he could not understand why the home health care nurses had not called him and expressed any concern.

The ambulance arrived relatively quickly, and before long Janet was hoisted onto the gurney and taken out the front door to the awaiting transport unit. Burton told them to take her to Mobile Infirmary. Burton followed the ambulance in his truck. Within five minutes there had arrived at the entrance to the Emergency Room. Janet was taken in to the back. Burton was asked to wait just a few minutes before he would be allowed to join her.

The hospital staff drew some blood from Janet's arm. They had some difficulty finding a vein to draw the blood. Janet was having some difficulty breathing so they put her on oxygen in an attempt to stabilize her while they awaited the test results from the lab. After further review of Janet, the doctor decided she needed to be intubated. They immediately took steps to do so. Burton asked if it was alright for him to go into the examining room with her but they requested that he wait a little while longer. Burton tried to explain to them that his mother suffered from Alzheimer's and might be scared or confused and he need to be by her side. By the time Burton was allowed to go into the room where Janet was being treated, she had been intubated. The Hospital staff acted a little strange as they took him into the ER, it was like there was something he needed to know but they did not tell him.

He was a little alarmed to find Janet on a ventilator. Suddenly, he understood why the personnel he had come in contact with prior to entering her room had seemed to be acting shady and keeping something from him. More than likely they had had experiences in the past where family members find their loved one on a ventilator and panic or become emotional. Although, Burton was surprised to find Janet on a vent, he was fully cognizant of the fact that Janet was in serious condition when she left the house and for that matter had been just as serious the day before on Mother's Day. It had also been clearly obvious that Janet had gone from bad on Mother's Day to worse the following Monday. Yes, he was shocked and a little rattled by this, but he was just happy that Janet was receiving some treatment for whatever was going on with her. He walked over to her and took her hand in his hand.

Janet's hand was a little cold, but when she felt his hand squeezing hers, she squeezed his hand. "Hi, I'm Dr. Anderson," Anderson said. "Are you Mrs. LeFlore's son?"

"Yes," said Burton.

"We had to intubate her," Dr. Anderson said. "She was having some difficulty breathing."

"What's the problem?" asked Burton.

"Lab tests indicate she's septic," said Dr. Anderson.

"Septic?" asked Burton.

"Yes, she had Septicemia," said Dr. Anderson.

"Septicemia," Burton said. "What's that?"

"She has bacteria in her blood stream and it appears that she's about to go into septic shock," Dr. Anderson said. "Septicemia can eventually cause a person's organs to shut down. So, we're going to treat her."

"Her organs are going to shut down?" asked Burton.

"Hopefully, we're going to be able to start treating her before that starts to happen," Anderson said. "Looks like she got to the hospital in time, but she is definitely septic. I noticed she has some decubitus and they're infected. How long has she had those sores?"

"Maybe two or three months," said Burton.

"Two or three months huh," said Anderson.

"Yea she's been in the Hospital during that time," Burton said. "I just had her here a month ago and they treated her with antibiotics and I thought they were getting better. The home health care people come and check on her three times a week. They hadn't said anything about the soars getting worse. I thought they were getting better."

"When they start getting infected, they have an odor," Dr. Anderson said. "They have a bit of an odor and her blood work clearly indicates she had bacteria in her blood stream obviously caused by those sores on her behind."

"She started developing those soars and they are just getting worse and worse," said Burton. "She's going to be admitted to the Intensive Care Unit," Anderson said. "We're waiting on them to call us and tell us they've got a bed ready for her."

"Intensive care?" said Burton.

"Yes, this is serious," Dr. Anderson said. "Mrs. LeFlore is in critical condition."

"How long do you think she will be on the ventilator?" asked Burton.

"If we can get her stabilized and get rid of the bacteria in her system," Dr. Anderson said. "Hopefully, we'll start to see some improvement and she shouldn't be on respiration for too long."

"I knew I should have brought her to the hospital yesterday," said Burton.

"There's no point in saying that," Anderson said. "She's here now and we're doing everything we can to get her through this, but at this point she is considered to be in critical condition."

"Thanks," said Burton.

"It shouldn't be long," Dr. Anderson said. "They'll be taking her upstairs in a few minutes."   Just as Dr. Anderson had said, it was not more than Thirty minutes before they came to get Janet and transported her up to the intensive care unit. Burton went with her into ICU. When she arrived there, the nurse on duty that night needed to get some personal history and Janet. Burton spoke with him about her health history and she inputted the information he provided into her patient file. Janet had been placed on IV's and she was breathing with the aid of the ventilator. An additional tube had been placed down her nose to deliver nutrients into her system. Janet was there in the intensive care unit and the rules and regulations in the unit were different from the regulations in other part of the hospital. First of all, no one was allowed to stay in the room with the patient overnight. The intensive care unit also had specific hours when family and friends could visit a patient. This was problematic for Burton, because he wanted someone to be with Janet the majority of the time when she was in the hospital. Usually, Mae stayed there in the hospital with her but now they were saying it was not possible.

They encouraged Burton to return home and come back during the regularly scheduled visiting hours. He looked at Janet hooked up to a ventilator in the ICU and could not help but to feel a sense of desperation. This was serious, and there was no denying that Janet had seriously taken a turn for the worse during the last few months. With repeated hospitalizations she was suffering one setback after another. Burton took Janet's hand once again, and she squeezed his hand tightly again. With his other hand, he stroked her hair. The one thing that scared Burton was how fast all of this had happened. One day they were at Mardi Gras having a good time, eating, drinking and having a good time and then all of a suddenly a few days later she was balled up in pain. Ever since the Urinary Tract infection and the onset of those soars on her behind, Janet had experienced a severe decline.

Burton was so distraught about his mother that he posted a request on Facebook for prayers for his mom. Suddenly people started posting replies praying for Janet to have a speedy recovery. Burton knew there was nothing more he could do now than put it in God's hands.

All of the responses he received on social media gave him hope in a time of desperation. He finally got a chance to speak with Janet's primary physician Dr. Bell the next morning. Bell basically reiterated what Dr. Anderson had already said. He stated that Janet was septic and that she had bacteria in her blood system. Although she was on the ventilator, he said he thought they would be able to take her off the vent in no more than two days. Although it looked bleak, Bell was optimistic that he thought Janet would recover.

Bell also said he thought they may need to put Janet on a feeding tube. He said they were concerned she might not be able to take in enough nutrition orally anymore to heal the soars and that she would receive nutrition into her system better through a feeding tube. Burton could not believe his ears. Now Janet would be on a feeding tube receiving artificial nutrition and that was if she managed to survive all of this. Bell asked Burton if he would be willing to consent to allow Janet to undergo the procedure which he said was very simple. Burton asked if the feeding tube would be temporary or permanent. Bell indicated that more than likely the feeding tube would be permanent.

Burton asked Bell to give him a chance to think about it, but assured him that he wanted to do whatever was in Janet's best interest to keep her alive and well. He stated to the doctor that he did not want to make such a decision without giving it some thought. He remembered how on several occasion over the last few months had been struggling to feed herself and having a difficult time chewing and swallowing. He thought about the few times when she would chew her food and hold it in her mouth without swallowing it. There had been some discussion about her not receiving adequate nutrition and that providing her with nutrition a different way might help to heal the soars she had on her rear end.

Burton said more than likely he would have no problem with inserting the feeding tube if it would help. Burton thought back several years to when his dad had been placed on a feeding tube. He remembered thinking how a relatively large man like Beck was going to be able to survive on a feeding tube, needless to say Beck did not live more than about two weeks after that. However, Burton had heard about people who had lived for years on a feeding tube. He wondered if Janet would fare well on a feeding tube and how that would possibly work out for her.

The doctors had insinuated and talked about her nutrition and made correlations to the soars she was developing. There had been instances where Janet was holding food in her mouth, not eating, displaying difficulty eating and sometimes a reluctance to swallow over the last year. Perhaps the feeding tube was the solution, but he still was not sure.

The following morning Burton went to the hospital to visit Janet not really knowing what to expect. He went to her bedside. She was still on the ventilator as she lay there with her eyes closed. Burton removed the protective mitten from her hand and grasped it in his. Janet opened her eyes and looked him directly in his eyes as if to say, it may not look so good now, but I got this, and I'm getting better. She gripped his hand firmly and looked him straight in the eyes. There was a look of determination and resolve in her eyes. She did not speak a word because the tube from the vent was down her throat, but she spoke very clearly with her eyes. As far as Burton was concerned, it was definitely a good sign. Perhaps all of his prayers and the prayers of his friends where helping.

One of the ICU nurses stopped by to check on Janet. Burton asked her how his mom was doing. Nurse Debra indicated to Burton that she was now in stable condition and the doctor thought they would be able to take her off the ventilator in a day or so. She indicated the concern at this point, was whether or not he was going to give the authorization for them to do the procedure to place Janet on a feeding tube. Nurse Debra told Burton that she did not think Janet would live much longer if they did not equip her with a feeding tube.

"You're Mrs. LeFlore's son?" said Debra.

"Yes, I'm Burton," Burton said. 'I'm her son."

"I'm Debra," Debra said. "I'm her nurse for today."

"How's she been doing today?" asked Burton.

"Her condition is listed as stable right now," Debra said. "She's a pretty sick little lady right now, but they were saying this morning they thought she would be able to breath on her own and should be taking her off the vent in a day or so."

"Thank goodness," said Burton.

"I think the main thing they're concerned about now is whether or not you are going to consent to allow them to place the feeding tube."

"Yea I've been giving it some thought," Burton said. "I just don't want to do that if it's not absolutely necessary."

"Mrs. LeFlore's probably not going to live much longer without it," Debra said. "Those wounds that she has are infected. When they get infected there's an odor. As soon as I walked in the door this morning, I could smell it from all the way across the unit. I had to clean them this morning, and I think it was kind of painful for her. But in reference to your question about the feeding tube, she's not going to be able to get enough nutrition otherwise. That's probably why she's developed those sores. Has she stopped getting around much?"

"She doesn't get around as much as she used to," Burton said. "And she's been in and out of the hospital for the last, well ever since February she been in and out of the Hospital."

"Those soars aren't going to get any better unless she gets the proper nutrition given the fact that she is less active than she used to be."

"You're saying that putting her on a feeding tube might help?" said Burton.

"You've discussed it with her doctor," Nurse Debra said. "That's just my opinion."

"I certainly want nothing but what's best for her," said Burton.

"I knew your dad very well," Nurse Debra said.

"Really? You knew my dad," replied Burton.

"Yes Dr. LeFlore was a well-respected physician here at Mobile Infirmary. We worked together for many years before I started working in the ICU. How long has he been gone now?"

"It's been about twelve years now," said Burton.

"Dr. LeFlore was a fine man," Debra said. "And he was so funny. He had a real sense of humor. I remember one joke he used to tell, he'd say Debra, 'why was six afraid of seven, because he eight nine," she said with a chuckle. 'I sure do miss Dr. LeFlore."

"Yea he did love to laugh and tell jokes," Burton said. "We miss him too."

"He was very serious when it came to his patients," Debra said. "And he wouldn't hesitate to raise hell if he didn't feel like we were doing what we were supposed to do when it came to one of his patients. But he always liked to keep us laughing when he could."

"He was quite the practical joker too," Burton said. "I'll never forget the time my grandmother was cooking a raccoon and he told me it was the next-door neighbor's dog, and that was just one of many."

"As far as your Ms. LeFlore goes," Debra said. "While I've been here today, all of her vital signs have been stable. The tube from the vent is probably a little uncomfortable for her. She was tugging at it earlier. That's why we had to put those mittens on her hands."

"Yes, I was intending to ask you about those," said Burton.

"We put those on her hands to keep her from pulling the tube out of her mouth," said Debra.

"Has she had a temp?" asked Burton.

"Her temperature is close to normal," said the nurse.

"That's good to hear," Burton said.

"When I got here, I gripped her hand and she held my hand tightly and looked me straight in my eyes and I knew she was trying to tell me something. But she didn't have to say it, I knew exactly what she wanted to say. She's a fighter. That's for sure. She's not ready to give up. I hope you guys will take real good care of her."

"Don't you worry," Debra said. "I'm going to take special care of Mrs. LeFlore. I've been here in the ICU for over ten years. I take my job very seriously, and I have a lot of experience at what I do. Now sometimes it doesn't matter what we do, it's in God's hands. Death is a part of life, and only the good Lord makes the final call with regard to whether or not it's somebody's time. But while your mother is here in my care, I'm going to do my best to make sure she's taken care of properly and you can rest assured of that."

"You knew my dad, and I appreciate you mentioning him and sharing your memories of him. I appreciate everything you're doing for her," Burton said. "I'm not ready to lose her yet."

"You're running for something aren't you?" Debra said. "You're running for some office, aren't you?" asked Debra.

"Yea," Burton said. "Yes, I'm in the race for that District 01 Congressional seat."

"Good luck with that," said Debra.

"If I can manage to rally some support in this community and this district which is comprised of six counties, I might have a chance at winning."

"And all that stuff between those Republicans," said Nurse Debra.

"Yea it's been quite a dog and pony show on their side," said Burton.

"I saw you in the debate with the other two candidates," Debra said. "I was impressed. You made some very good points. Those two guys are like dumb and dumber."

"We'll see on election day," Burton said. "I certainly would appreciate your support."

After giving it further thought, Burton decided that given her current condition, perhaps the feeding tube would make it easier for her to get the adequate amount of nutrition she needed since she might not be able to get it through eating food orally. He just wanted Janet to get better. He just wanted her to live and be as healthy as she could possibly be at this point in her life. Nutrition is one of the keys to good health, so Burton decided to call Bell and let him know that it would be alright to perform the procedure to put in the feeding tube.

Little did Burton know this was the beginning of a long period of hospitalization for Janet. The doctors were able to stabilize her and get her on the road to recovering from septicemia. She was expected to recover, but the simple fact remained she had almost gone into septic shock. Janet was on the verge of death. She almost died. Had she not been brought to the Hospital when she was, it is improbable that she would have lived another twenty-four hours. She would have to continue antibiotics for many more days. However, she was taken off the ventilator and started to breathe on her own within three days. As soon as she got off the ventilator, her primary physician scheduled the surgery to put in the feeding tube.

After coming off the ventilator and the feeding tube was put in her stomach, she was evaluated for the LTAC which is the long-term acute care unit of the hospital for patients who are critically ill and potentially suffer from complex medical conditions involving multiple parts of their body or organ system failure. She was admitted to the LTAC unit when she left the ICU. Her doctors had also decided that Janet should undergo plastic surgery to remove the infected tissue from her butt cheeks. This was surgery they felt she would need to have in order to avoid becoming reinfected.

Janet left the ICU and was transported to the LTAC unit for further care and medical attention. Although she had improved significantly, she was hardly in the clear. As plans were made to have Janet undergo surgery to remove the infected tissue from her bottom area, Janet started her transition to being fed from a tube through a hole leading into her stomach, pumped by a machine which delivered formula into her system artificially.

Janet also started to vegetate and lay in one position continuously. It started to become necessary for her to be manually turned every two hours. She would just lay in one position. She was totally responsive in other ways but she did not ambulate in bed, she would simply remain in one position until she was moved.

She was now completely incontinent, catheterized, and immobile. Janet was basically in a persisted vegetative state. She would communicate on occasion and respond to questions and other stimuli around her, but for the most part she was totally in need of care, supervision and round the clock attention. Once she was in the LTAC unit Burton brought Mae over to the hospital to stay in the room with her and be with her at all times. Janet was placed on an air mattress to cause less pressure to her infected soft tissue areas.

Janet needed constant maintenance and attention to the feeding tube which became an integral part of her sustenance. She was catheterized and would soil herself without any thought of maintaining her hygiene. The question was becoming increasingly evident that Janet was in the clutch of needing round the clock care and supervision. At this point, it was not easy to know or understand exactly how much of what was going on around her she fully comprehended or was capable of recalling or appreciating to the extent of being totally aware.

The days in the LTAC went by one after another. Janet did experience significant improvement but clearly her threshold of mobility, responsiveness, discernment, perception, cognizance and overall well-being was in question. Overall, she was in stable condition physically at her current state of being. However, her condition had advanced. Burton wondered if the changes his mom was experiencing were neurological, physical, psychological, and mentally. Certainly, all of the above. Although, most significantly and importantly, while Janet was being treated and cared for in the LTAC unit, he was still in denial about the level of care that would be required when she came home.

The sad and disheartening thing was that all of this had happened very quickly. It was sudden and seemed to have occurred over a few weeks. Three months ago, Janet had been at the Mardi Gras parade walking around, eating, drinking soda, and catching moon pies and beads thrown from the floats. She had a urinary tract infection a few days afterward. Now just a short time later she had been in and out of the hospital; she had developed septicemia; she had spent several days on a ventilator; she had stopped ambulating; her legs were slightly contracted; she had developed bed sores, and she was on a feeding tube. Her range of motion was significantly diminished. How could all of this have happened so fast Burton thought to himself.

Burton had to come to grips with the fact that his mother Janet Owens LeFlore was in the final stages of a complex and debilitating disease. Her current problems and complications were simply a condition subsequent to what was really the crux of the matter, Alzheimer's, dementia and old age. Over these last few years Burton had watched Janet exhibit the signs and symptoms. Janet had struggled to remember the simplest things and it got progressively worse to the point where she had forgotten how to go the bathroom on her own.

She was a woman who had lived an exemplary life. A person who had loved and taken care of him through thick and thin ever since he had arrived on this planet earth. He was not sure how he was going to do it, but he was determined that he was going to care for his mom no matter what.

The next issue was the infection she had sustained as a result of the bed sores. Despite everything, they had been getting larger and larger. Burton was surprised because he had actually thought they were getting better. He wondered why the home health nurses had not said anything to him about it. They were coming by to check on Janet regularly and since they had not mentioned to him that the sores were getting worse, he just assumed they were improving. He also did not understand why they had not said anything to him when they came in earlier that day and examined her. When he found her at home that evening before he called the ambulance, she was clearly in distress and had an elevated temperature. It seemed to Burton they would have suggested to him that Janet might be in need of medical attention, but they did not. Her sores were infected and as the nurse in the ICU told him they smelled. After giving it some thought, Burton decided not to use that agency anymore when Janet returned home.

Janet's doctors started talking to him about Janet having surgery to remove the infected tissue from her rear. A plastic surgeon was consulted and he evaluated Janet for surgery. The month of May was coming to an end, and Burton's son Bryceton was scheduled to graduate from high school. Although he was inundated with everything going on at the hospital with Janet, he knew he could not miss his son's graduation. After Janet's evaluation with the plastic surgeon, he discussed it with Burton and it was decided that Janet would have the surgery. Burton then found out they had scheduled the surgery for the same day as Bryceton's graduation.

Burton felt a little conflicted. He did not want to be away if Janet was going to have such serious surgery; however, there was no possible way he was not going to be there for his son's graduation. Since Burton and Candace has separated several years ago. She moved to Mississippi, there were a lot of things Burton had missed in his children's lives. Burton had filed for divorce almost three years ago and they were still in court having gotten no closer to the actual divorce than he was when he first filed in 2010.

The relationship between he and Candace had become somewhat strained, primarily because Candace refused to allow the children to come and visit with Burton or to stay with him. She had also done everything she could to try and convince the judge not to allow him to have joint custody or regularly scheduled visits with the kids. She was clearly doing this in an attempt to try and hurt him.

Burton had been a good and loving father. He had also provided for them during the entire time. She had not worked in years, and she still was not working. Burton had given her money for the kids and she had never had to try and take him to court to get him to provide money for his children. She was usually cordial if he went to visit them, but she absolutely refused to allow him to spend any time around the boys unless she was also present. At first Burton tried to go to visit them fairly regularly, but started to find it insulting that she tried to insist that he could only see his children on her terms. This angered Burton immensely so as time went on the visits became less frequent. For a fairly substantial period of time, Burton had no help with Janet on the weekends.

"Hey, don't forget to bring the car with you when you come to Bryceton's graduation," Candace said. "He wants a jeep."

"I'm not going to be bringing a car with me to the graduation," Burton said. "You know, practically every day you call me asking for money, and talking about what the kids need. And that's cool because the kids do need stuff. I don't mind doing for my kids. But in all these years, you have not once picked up the phone and asked me when I was coming to get my kids."

"Bryceton wants a car so you better get out to the dealership and get him one," said Candace.

"How many times do I have to tell you my mom is in the hospital," Burton said. "Bryceton doesn't even have a driver's license yet, because you won't let him drive. He needs to get his license and learn how to drive first," Burton said.

"He's going to be really disappointed if you don't get him a car," said Candace.

"After he graduates, he can come over here for a few weeks before he goes to college and we can get his driver's license and see about getting him a car," said Burton.

"I don't think that's going to happen," said Candace.

"Really, and why is that," Burton said. "Because you're a selfish, self-centered bitch," Burton said. "Bryceton is an adult now and he doesn't need your permission to come and visit me."

"Bryceton doesn't want to come and visit you," replied Candace.

"You don't speak for him or any of my boys," Burton said. "You can pretend all you want I love them very much and they certainly need their dad in more ways than just to send them money."

"You won't even buy your son a car," Candace said. "

"I haven't had time to go and look at any cars, my mom is in the hospital. My mom is in the hospital. She is seriously ill, and you don't even have the decency to bring the boys over here to see her. You won't even bring them over here to see her."

"I got to go," Candace said. "Talk with you later. Don't show up without that car."

Burton could not believe that his life had come to this. Here he was struggling to take care of his mother with little help, in divorce court for over two and a half years and rarely seeing his children. It would probably lift Janet's spirits so much if she could see her grandchildren. He had tried on several occasions to ask Candace if she would bring the kids to see Janet in the hospital during these last few times; however, she basically refused to bring them to see her.

It was a beautiful late spring day in Mobile, Alabama. Despite all of the chaos Burton was feeling in his heart the warmth of the sunny blue southern sky which managed to put him back at peace. He had no control over the fact that Janet's condition was advancing. All he could do was to do his best to make sure she was cared for. Nothing had changed between him and Candace and more than likely would never change.

He was not going to be able to buy Bryceton a car before his graduation. Even though he did not want to be out of town when Janet had her surgery, there was not much he could do anyway. He had to be there for his son's graduation. There was no way he was going to miss it. The springtime air caused him to take a moment and pause to clear his head and acquire his resolve. A moment to give thanks to God for all the blessings in his life.

He took a second in his day, as he left his office to go back to the hospital to check on Janet, that he had so much to be thankful for, if nothing more than to witness the wonderful day that the Lord had allowed him to still be among the living. Despite everything Janet was also still with the living and she needed him now more than ever. He was thankful for all of the days that Janet had been there for him and now she needed him. His son Bryceton had earned a scholarship to Ole Miss and was about to go to college. All of his children were doing well. He realized then on his way to the Hospital to see Janet that he would have to put his faith in God and trust in the Lord and wait for the Lord.

"Hey, Mom," Burton said as he entered her room on the LTAC unit. "How is my sweetheart today?"

"Hi Burton," said Janet.

"Wow that's the first thing you've said to me in a few days," Burton said. "Can I have a hug. Are you feeling a little better today?"

"Yes," Janet said. "I'm better."

"You've been really ill, Mom," Burton said. "You had me scared there for a minute. I'm so glad you're feeling better today. You know Bryceton is going to be graduating from high school in a few days."

"Bryceton," said Janet.

"Yes, my son Bryceton," Burton said. "Your grandson is graduating from high school."

"Nice," said Janet.

"That is nice isn't it," Burton said. "He's got a scholarship to Ole Miss. It looks like he's moving to Oxford, Mississippi in the fall. And we got to get you better so you can come home."

"Home, where is home?" said Janet.

"Home is right around the corner," Burton said. "Where you're going to be going when you get better and get your strength and get out of here. Mae has Dr. Bell been by here today?"

"He came by early this morning," said Mae.

"What did he say," said Burton.

"He said they were going to take her to surgery," said Mae.

"I'm going to have to go to my son's graduation and it looks like it's been scheduled for the same day as her surgery so I'm going to need you to be here at the hospital while I'm gone."

"Sure Burton, I'll be here with Janet not a problem," Mae said. "I'm always here with her anyway."

"I need to be sure," Burton said. "And I need to make sure you're here and that you keep me notified if there is anything you think I may need to know."

"You go and see your son graduate," Mae said. "I'll be right here with her. You don't need to worry."

"Mom, we're about to have another graduate in the family," said Burton.

"Congratulations," Janet said. "I, I'm hungry."

"You're hungry," Burton replied looking over at the pump which was connected to the feeding tube. "How does this thing work? It's not on, why isn't it on? Where is her nurse?" he asked as he reached for the intercom on the side of the bed.

"Yes," said a voice on the other end.

"Can you send Mrs. LeFlore's nurse down here," Burton said. "I need to talk with her about something."

"Someone will be right there," said the voice.

"She says she's hungry," Burton said. "Why is this thing not on?"

"They said they only give it to her for so many hours per day," said Mae.

"You wanted to see me," said Nurse Louise.

"Yes, first of all, I wanted to ask you how she was doing," Burton said. "Secondly I was wondering why this pump is off and my mom is saying she's hungry."

"She just recently got the feeding tube," Nurse Louise said. "All of this is a bit of a transition for her, but it's just about time to turn it back on. We don't want her to be hungry. She's so precious."

"I appreciate that," Burton said. "This is a bit of a transition for all of us. Although, my dad was on a feeding tube for a few days before he died, and I remember a little about how they work, but this is, can you please just turn it back on. She says she's hungry. She hasn't said much to me in the last few days."

"Yes, I can turn it back on," said the nurse.

"Thank you," Burton said. "I would greatly appreciate it."

"Okay we got it back on," the nurse replied. "She has been doing well today. Bless her heart."

Janet for the most part languished in bed all day and all night. She was catheterized and incontinent. She would lay in one position and not move from that position. She would only move her hands to stroke her hair or to rub in the area of her hips. She would talk and communicate, but sometimes she would not respond or offer any words. Janet was still in a considerable amount of pain and discomfort. She was debilitated and about to undergo surgery. It is uncertain if she had much memory or recollection of anything at this point. It is hard to comprehend if she was even aware of her own existence or the extent thereof. She still recognized people around her. Janet would still have her say; however, she was "failing to thrive," as she was now classified and characterized in her medical records, among a number of other things.

   Every day, Janet lived in that hospital room in the LTAC unit where she was bathed, wiped, poked, examined, changed, rotated, adjusted and monitored on a continuous and round the clock basis. Janet had showed improvement, but it was clear that she would probably never get up out of her bed again. She was transitioning in many ways. Although it was difficult for Burton at times, he knew all he could do was his duty that was best and leave unto the Lord the rest. Nobody lives forever. Janet was suffering immensely in her struggle to survive. Burton knew his Mother Janet very well and he knew that she must not have been very happy like she was, or had she lost all cognizance, recollection and understanding of what might make her happy or discontent.

   Janet was now connected to a feeding tube, her quality of life was severely diminished along with her ability to comprehend, understand and now most recently, her ability to move. There was not much more she had to hold onto other than her love of life itself. Burton showed her a lot of love. Probably had it not been for him Janet would have been dead a long time ago. She would have died and gone to eternity with her husband Beck. However, she was still alive and semi kicking, simply surviving.

   Despite everything the Alzheimer's had taken away from her, she still possessed tremendous strength, fortitude, courage and most importantly the will to survive. Janet remained quite a woman intent on continuing to live. The worst of the storm was over, and now it was just time for her to continue to recover and adjust to the feeding tube. Not to mention the surgery she was scheduled to undergo to remove the infected scabs she had. The area of infected tissue was continuing to spread so there was no other option than to allow the doctors to perform the surgery on Janet.

There appeared to be no other alternative. Burton hoped this would serve as a way to finally stop the spread of her bed sores. Little did he know there was pretty much no likelihood after the surgery that the wounds would ever heal. Hospital staff said there was a strong chance the wounds from the surgery would regenerate; however, it was not fully communicated there was a clear and present danger the wounds would never fully heal. More than likely Janet would have to live with the wounds that would not fully heal for the remainder of her life. Burton thought about how he saw pictures of young sexy women on the internet with tattoos on their hip and leg. The plastic surgeon was about to carve a piece of her buttocks, pretty much like somebody would cut themselves a piece of steak.

Although Burton was undaunted in his decision to allow them to perform the plastic surgery to remove the infected scar tissue; he only wanted to do whatever was best for her. Burton wanted to do whatever would make it better for Janet. He was not certain, but he wanted to make shore Janet received the best healthcare she could possibly get. Perhaps the finish line was inevitable, the time had come for him to man up and deal with this thing face to face. Janet was dying, she was dying a slow death right before his very own eyes. She was his mom. He loved her with all his heart. There is nothing more he wanted than for her to be the same lady who had given birth to him and raised him. However, he realized finally, she was that same lady. Now it was his turn.

The day arrived for Bruceton's graduation and for Janet to have her surgery to remove the infected tissue. Burton got up early and went by the hospital to see about Janet and make sure everything was alright with her before he left. He informed the staff there at the hospital that he would be away for a few hours, but if they needed to reach him for any reason to please call him on his cell phone. Right about the time he was about to leave they were preparing to take Janet to surgery. Janet had been moved from her room to an area down in the Operating Room. They allowed Burton to go back and spend a few minutes with her before he left for Mississippi. He took Janet by the hand and said a prayer. He asked her how she was doing, and told her that she was about to have surgery in a little while. Janet was still alert and awake as Burton kissed her goodbye and told her that he was going to Bryceton's graduation and he would be back later on that night.

It hurt Burton's heart to have to leave Janet in there by herself. Although, the surgery she was scheduled to have was serious, there were no indications the surgery was life threatening. He left the hospital and got into his truck. Burton sat there for a moment and thought about Janet. He wondered if she understood or comprehended everything that was going on at the time, or was she simply oblivious.

I know she knew when she was not feeling well and had indicated to him the other day she felt better. He wondered if she was afraid, bewildered, confused or if she felt unloved. Certainly, there was no way she could feel unloved, since he showed her plenty of love. However, he could not get into her mind and know what was going on inside her head. All he could do at this point was put it in God's hands. Maintain hope for the best. He hoped this surgery would help to get her back on the road to wellness.

Burton made it to the graduation ceremony about an hour before Bryceton was scheduled to walk across that stage and accept his diploma. He met up with Bryceton, and his younger boys He had a moment to congratulate Bryceton before he joined the rest of his class for the graduation ceremony.

The graduation was held outdoors at the school stadium. The ceremony started as the senior class of Bay High School walked out onto the field and took their seats. It was a joyful moment to see Bryceton go up there and get his diploma. The graduation lasted about an hour until the last of the students were called onto the stage to get their diplomas. Burton was so happy for Bryceton. He was glad to see Breaghan, Bridge and Brooke.

After the graduation ceremony he invited the kids to dinner. He asked them where they wanted to go and have a graduation dinner for Bryce. They named a restaurant that Burton had never heard of on South Beach Boulevard. A few minutes later Burton met the kids and Candace at the restaurant where they wanted to eat. They had dinner. This was the first time Burton had sat down and eaten with his children in over a year. It was somewhat of a bittersweet moment, because Burton was glad to see his boys. However, he was still worried about Janet. At any rate he had not gotten any disturbing phone calls from Mobile. He was fairly certain that Janet was alright and her surgery had gone well.

"Congratulations Bryce on your graduation from high school," Burton said. "I'm so proud of you son. I'm proud of all you guys."

"Thanks Dad," Bryce said. "I appreciate that."

"Everyone raise your glasses and let's have toast," Burton said as they all lifted their glasses. "Cheers to Bryceton and congratulations on your scholarship to Ole Miss."

"Cheers to Bryceton," said the other boys as they all clinked their glasses.

"This is a pretty nice restaurant you guys chose today," said Burton.

"We've never eaten here," Brooke said. "But we've been wanting to eat here for a while."

"The food here is pretty good," said Bridge.

"The food is good," Burton said. "This was a good choice guys."

"It's good to see you Dad," said Bryce.

"It's good to see you too, all of you," Burton said. "It was good to see you walk across that stage and get your diploma. So that's two down and one, two, three more to go."

"Thanks for coming," said Bryce.

"You know I wasn't going to miss your graduation," Burton said. "Your grandmother had surgery today."

"I see you didn't bring the car," said Candace.

"Please don't start," Burton said. "I'm trying to have a nice dinner with the kids. Don't start. Bryceton do you have your driver's license yet?"

"No," said Bryce.

"Did you take drivers ed?" asked Burton.

"No," said Bryce.

"You didn't take drivers ed," Burton replied. "Why didn't you take drivers education?"

"I don't know," Bryceton said. "It wasn't a requirement."

"So basically, you don't know how to drive yet?" Burton said. "I guess I'm going to have to teach you how to drive, and then we'll work on getting you a car. I can't believe you didn't take drivers education."

"I'm not sure if they even offered drivers education," said Bryce.

"Practically every high school in America offers drivers education," said Burton.

"How is grandmother doing?" asked Breaghan.

"She had surgery today," Burton said. "And she hasn't been doing to well. She's been in the Hospital for a month now. It would be nice if you guys would come and visit her. She hasn't been doing well at all these last few weeks."

"Does Mae still work there?" asked Bridge.

"Yes, Mae is still there," Burton said. "She's been helping me with your grandmother."   "That's probably part of the problem Dad," Breaghan said. "Look who you have taking care of grandmother."

"You mean Mae," Burton said. "You think so?"

"Yea Mae," Breaghan said. "Grandma Janet used to always say Mae was lazy."

"You may have a point Breaghan," Burton said. "I have been kind of thinking about that same thing myself lately."

"So, what's wrong with grandmother?" asked Brooke.

"She developed Septicemia," said Burton.

"Septicemia," Bryce said. "What's septicemia?"

"Yea she almost went into septic shock where your organs start to shut down," Burton said. "She has been very sick. They even had to put her on a ventilator for a few days."

"Will you tell Grandma that I said hello, and I hope she feels better," said Bridge.

"I will tell her, but it would be nice if you could tell her yourself," Burton said. "I really want you guys to come and visit her, you probably can't imagine how happy she would be to see you guys."

"When can we come?" asked Brooke.

"Anytime," Burton said. "I've been trying to arrange it with your mom. When do you think would be a good time for them to come and visit their grandmother in the hospital?"

"Um I don't know," Candace said. "Maybe when you get the car we can ride over and pick it up."

"No, I asked you when would be a good time for you to bring the boys over to Mobile so they can visit with their grandmother. She's been very ill."

"Let me think about it and I'll let you know."

"You know this is Bryceton's graduation and I'm not going to allow you to make me angry or start an argument, so why you just do that," Burton said. "She had surgery today."

"Why'd she have to have surgery?" asked Bridge.

"Yea why did she have surgery?" asked Brooke.

"She had plastic surgery to remove some infected skin tissue from her body that's been causing bacteria to get into her bloodstream," said Burton.

"Sounds serious," Bryceton said. "Is she going to be alright?"

"I hope so," Burton said. "She is so proud of you. I told her you were graduating today and she was so happy for you. This is your day, congratulations son."

"Thanks Dad," said Bryce.

"I love you," Burton said. "I love all of you guys."

"Yea. If he loved you, he would send y'all some money," said Candace.

"Are you serious?" Burton said before he paused and regained his composure. "Hey, guys. I'm going to have to be getting back pretty soon. Looks like everyone enjoyed their dinner. I certainly did."

"Yea it was good," said Breaghan.

"Yea thanks Dad," said Bridge.

"Don't even mention it," Burton said. "We got a graduate in the house."

"It's good to see you Dad," said Brooke.

"Even better to see you," said Burton.

"Congratulations Bryce," said Brooke.

"Way to go, Bryceton," said Breaghan.

"And Breaghan you're about to start high school this year, that is tremendous, you'll be a freshman. How does it feel to be a soon to be high school kid?"

"I think it'll be good," said Breaghan.

"It certainly will be," said Burton as the waiter brought over the check. He signed the check and they gathered their things and left the restaurant.

CHAPTER FIVE

Meanwhile Janet was back in her hospital room following the surgery. She was sedated and resting. Janet was experiencing a lot of pain in the areas where the tissue had been removed. She was now connected to a device called a wound vac. The wound vac provided suction to the areas where they had just operated in an effort to cause the skin to fuse back together. Now she had two gaping holes on both sides of her behind.

Three of Janet's fingers on her right hand had contracted. She retained use of her index finger which usually remained in a pointed position and her thumb, but for the most part the remaining three fingers on that hand were contracted and stayed bent inward toward her palm. Her left hand was still fully extended and she had complete use of her left hand. The medicine and anesthesia had her fairly incoherent as she slept uncomfortably with the two wound vacs affixed to her rear end. Mae sat in the chair next to her bed watching television.

Burton was winding up his visit with the kids and Bryceton's graduation. He asked them to walk out to his truck because he had something to give them. He had bought them a Play Station for Christmas, but had not seen them until now. He wanted to give it to them before he left. They walked down South Beach to the parking lot where Burton's truck was parked. He hugged them and gave them the gaming device. He said goodbye to the boys and headed on back to Mobile. As he was driving, he wondered how Janet was doing. He had not heard from anybody at the hospital so in this case no news must have been good news.

However, at the same time he had no idea what to expect when he got back to the hospital. By the same token, he was glad to have been able to spend some well needed time with his children. It was a clear and starry night along Interstate 10 as Burton drove back to Mobile. The weather was warm and there was a moderate amount of traffic on the highway as Burton crossed the Alabama state line. Burton was able to get back to Mobile in about an hour. When he got back to the city, he immediately went to the hospital to check on Janet.

He found her in her room on the LTAC unit resting soundly. One of the CNA's was in the room making sure she was turned. Mae was in the chair next to her bed still watching television. One of the first thing Burton noticed was the tubes connected to a device near the bed, the tubes were connected at the other end to Janet on both sides of her hips. She was connected to IV's and tubes. Burton wished there was something he could do to stop her suffering. However, he was also thankful to still have Janet here on earth. He clearly felt that Janet continued to have the will to live, and he hoped that God was not going to take her away from him yet. He asked the CNA if he could get the nurse for him after finished. Burton said hi to Janet. She opened her eyes, glanced at him and went back to sleep. He hoped this surgery would help with those sores and stop her from having anymore infection.

That night when Burton left the hospital, he went by a nearby gas station to get gas. He saw a young lady at the cashier. She was dressed in her work clothes. Based on what she was wearing Burton surmised that she was probably employed as a CNA or healthcare related field. Burton asked her what kind of work she did and she stated she was a CNA. Burton asked her if she would be interested in working for him on the side, because his mom was in the hospital and when she returned home, she was going to need a person trained to do this type of work. She explained that she had a full-time job but might be interested in some part time work. Burton gave her his business card. He took her phone number and asked her to contact him if she was interested. The young lady named Jayla, said she would be sure and call him to discuss it further.

About two days later Burton received a phone call from a lady who identified herself as Lacey. Lacey said she had heard that he was looking for someone to help him with his mother. Burton said that he was looking for help with his mother and inquired as to how she heard about the position. The lady on the other end said her daughter had told her about it. Burton affirmed that her daughter was correct in that he was looking for someone to help him with Janet and he would like to talk with her. Burton asked her when she would be able to come by his office for an interview, and she said she was flexible because she was not currently working and needed a job. Burton told her his mom would probably be in the hospital about another month and a half after she left there and went for twenty-one days of rehab in a nursing facility, but that he would like to talk with her the following day. The following day Lacey came to Burton's office to meet him and discuss the position.

"I'm Lacey Morgan," Lacey said. "It's nice to meet you."

"Burton LeFlore," Burton said. "Thanks for coming."

"My daughter gave me your card and she said you were looking for someone to help you with your mother," said Lacey.

"Yes, I'm going to need some help with her," Burton said. "So, you're a CNA?"

"Yes, I'm a CNA," Lacey said. "I've worked at a number of nursing homes in the city."

"Have you ever done private duty care," said Burton.

"Yes," said Lacey.

"My mother is on a feeding tube, and she is bedridden, she has to be turned every two hours no less than four hours, she's on a catheter and she has to be changed as needed," Burton said. "She also has two wounds that need to be dressed and changed about twice a day. Do you have any experience doing that type of work?"

"Yes, I've worked with patients with feeding tubes and I have done wound care," Lacey said. "I worked at Allen Memorial for over three years, and I've done pretty much everything in the patient care area from bathing, to changing, to turning, to wound care, and feeding tubes."

"Not that I'm going to hold this against you, but for someone with such extensive experience," Burton said. "Why aren't you currently employed?"

"Well about a year ago, I got a felony on my record," said Lacey.

"A felony," said Burton.

"It was something between me and this guy that I used to date," Lacey said. "I'm on probation right now, and no nursing homes or hospitals will allow me to work there with a felony."

"Can you provide me with some information and documentation about that?" asked Burton. "Yes, I can get that for you," Lacey said. "By the way this is a copy of my resume."

"Is that it?" asked Burton.

"What?" asked Lacey.

"Is there anything else in your background or history that I should know about?" asked Burton.

"No, I've never been arrested before in my life before then," Lacey said. "That was just some dumb shit between me and some dude I probably should have never been messing with anyway. But besides that issue my record is clean."

"Can you get me a police report which will verify what you're saying?" asked Burton.

"Yes, I would be happy to," Lacey said. "Hey. Can I ask you a question? Aren't you that guy who's running for some office or something?"

"I'm running for Congress," said Burton.

"Congress, oh wow," Lacey said. "That's um, that's in Washington."

"Yea and I have no idea how I'm going to do a job in Washington with everything going on with my mom right now."

"That's really impressive," Lacey said. "I've seen you on the news a few times. I thought that was you."

"I'm looking for someone full time, which would probably entail at least eight hours a day," said Burton.

"You're talking about say from eight to four," said Lacey.

"Yea. That's about what I'm talking about," said Burton.

"Not a problem," said Lacey.

"At any rate, I would like for you to come and meet my mom," Burton said. "She's going to be in the hospital for a while longer and then she's supposed to do twenty-one days of rehab at a nursing home. She won't be coming home for a while longer. Why don't you get that stuff I asked about? Let me look over your resume and let's talk in a few days."

"I'll get to work on that. I look forward to talking with you in a few days," said Lacey.

"Yes, it was very nice to meet you," Burton said. "Please get that documentation for me and let's talk further."

Burton concluded the interview and Lacey promised to follow up with him in a few days when she had the information he had requested. He thought Lacey was nice and hoped what she said about her past record was true. The only thing was, Burton saw a lot of stuff going on at the hospital and a lot of things being done and things that needing to be done for Janet. There were multiple staff members doing the work. Although Janet was going to be in the hospital and in the nursing home for a few more weeks, Burton was seriously in denial about how he was going to be able to take care of Janet at home.

Besides having just spoken with Lacey and one or two other people about possibly helping him in some respects on a part time basis, Burton was in no way shape or form prepared to embark on the undertaking of making sure Janet was cared for at home. He knew that he did not want her in a nursing home. However, in all reality he also had no idea how much it was going to cost him to keep Janet at home. It seemed to him like in the state of Alabama it was cheaper to put your loved one in a nursing home than it was to care for them at home.

A few days later Burton ironically got a call from his cousin Ivan LeFlore, who is a plastic surgeon. Ivan told Burton that he was visiting his sister in Pensacola and wanted to know if he could come over to Mobile with his wife for a day or two. Burton was pleased to hear Ivan's voice and welcomed him to Mobile. Burton had spoken with Ivan about two months previous about his campaign for Congress and he had graciously donated a Thousand Dollars to the cause which Burton greatly appreciated. Ivan was Burton's second cousin on his dad's side of the family. He was Ray's older brother. How wonderful Burton thought to himself. He had not seen Ivan in a while, and now he could consult him about this surgery that Janet had just undergone about a week prior. Burton explained to Ivan that Janet was in the hospital, but he would very much like for him and his wife to come to Mobile and visit.

Ivan and his wife drove over the next day. They arrived in the afternoon and Burton took off work a little early to meet them at the house. When the arrived Burton asked them if they wanted to and have some oysters at Wintzell's Oyster House. Burton told them they could not really say they had been to Mobile, Alabama if they had not eaten at Wintzell's. So, they went to Wenzell's and had a great meal.

Afterward Burton dropped them off at the house to get settled in and he went to the hospital to see Janet. He found her in pretty much the same fashion she had been in for the last few days. She was still on the wound vacs and still in an incredible amount of pain from the surgery. Later that night Burton returned home and fellowships with his cousin.

The next day Burton went to work and Ivan and his wife went out to explore the city of Mobile a little. Burton called Sandy and asked her if she would go by the hospital with him and wash and jell Janet's hair. He indicated that his cousin was in town with his wife. Burton said he wanted her to look nice when they saw her. He picked Sandy up from her house and then they went by the hospital where Sandy gave her a little makeover. Burton was still at the hospital with Janet when Ivan called and said they had been all over and were wondering when he would be able to meet up with them. Burton indicated that he was at the hospital but that he could come and meet them but he wanted them to come by the hospital and visit with Janet.

Burton went over with Sandy to the house and picked them up, and they went straight back to the hospital. Sandy had dolled Janet up a little so she would look nice when Ivan and his wife visited with her. Burton dropped Ivan, his wife and Sandy off at the front entrance. He parked the car and joined them at the front entrance by the reception desk. They proceeded up to Janet's room and Burton followed.

On the way up in the elevator Sandy expressed to Ivan that she felt Burton was paying Mae to take care of Janet and, that in her opinion, Mae could do a better job. Sandy stated to them that she had talked with Burton about it on several occasions and even asked if he would hire her to help with Janet, but that Burton continued to allow Mae to remain. Sandy mentioned that Mae neglected to do little things like clip Janet's fingernails which were getting long, and that occasionally Janet would scratch herself. She also stated that although she did not mind doing it for Burton, but that he asked her to come and do things for Janet that she felt Mae should be doing, since she was being paid. Sandy asked Ivan if he would possibly talk with him about this since it seemed that Burton respected his opinion.

They continued to talk as they strolled down the hallway to the LTAC unit. Burton was not far behind. They arrived in Janet's room a brief moment before Burton. Mae was curled up in the chair next to the bed asleep. When everyone came into the room to see Janet, Mae was a little startled as she was awakened. Janet was laying there in the bed on her side. Her hair looked very nice and Sandy had done a good job sprucing her up. Janet recognized Ivens and was glad to have him and his wife come to visit her; however, the introduction between Ivens and Mae was somewhat awkward.

"Janet how are you?" asked Ivan.

"Hi," said Janet.

"It's me Ivan," Ivan said. "Do you remember me?"

"Yes," said Janet.

"She's talking this afternoon," Burton said. "She hasn't said much the last day or two. She must be happy to see you guys."

"She' so precious," Ivan's wife said. "Janet you're still so beautiful."

"Thank you," said Janet.

"This is Mae," Burton said. "She helps me with my mom. Mae this is my cousin Ivan and his wife. They're here for a few days visiting."

"It's nice to meet you," Mae said. "Sorry I had dozed off for a minute."

"Likewise," said Ivan.

"Mom, are you happy to see Ivan and his wife," asked Burton.

"Yes," replied Janet.

"You're talking to me today," Burton said. "That's wonderful."

"Janet your fingernails are so long," said Ivan's wife.

"Yea they are pretty long," Ivan said. "Mae you probably need to cut her nails."

"I'm not going to cut them," Mae said. "I'm afraid I might cut her finger. It would probably be better if one of the nurses did it."

"Why would one of the nurses need to do it," Ivan said. "You're her caretaker, aren't you?"

"Yes, but I'm not very good at clipping nails," said Mae.

"Burton if you bring the nail clippers," Sandy said. "I'll clip them for her."

"I think the nail clippers are already here," Burton said. "I'll look through her things in that bag over there. If not, I'll bring them tomorrow, because her nails do need to be clipped."

"Here they are," said Mae as she pulled them out of Janet's bag and handed them to Sandy.

"Oh good," Sandy said. "Mrs. LeFlore will you let me clip your nails for you."

"Okay," said Janet.

"Give me your hand," said Sandy.

"Janet you're just as sweet as you can be," said Ivan's wife.

"They still have her hooked up to the wound vac," said Ivan.

"Yes, I think she's going to be on the wound vac up until the time she comes home," said Burton.

"That wound vac should help to pull the tissue together so that hopefully it will heal," said Ivan. "Hopefully," Burton said. "Why do you say hopefully?"

"She had surgery to move infected decubitus," Ivan said. "At your mother's age and given the fact that she is not very active at this point, there is a strong chance they may never heal all the way."

"You mean to tell me she could have those wounds on her behind indefinitely," Burton said. "I was under the impression they would heal eventually."

"They might but then again they might not," Ivan replied. "You probably need to talk with them about removing those boots off her feet too. I can't believe they're still using those things down here. They've been banned from use in hospitals in Maryland."

"Why is that?" asked Burton.

"Because they can cause the same type of soars around the feet and ankles in patients if they wear them too long," said Ivan.

"I certainly don't want her to start getting soars on her feet," Burton said as he started to remove the boots from Janet's feet.

"There you go, Mrs. LeFlore," Sandy said. "I think I got those nails cut for you, so you won't be scratching yourself."

"Thanks, Sandy," said Burton.

"Mom, I'm going to take Ivan and his wife to get something to eat," Burton said. "I promise you I'll come back by and check on you again before I go to bed tonight."

"Okay, Baby," said Janet.

"Janet, it has been so nice to see you," said Ivan's wife.

"Nice to see you," said Janet trying to smile.

"Janet, it has indeed been a pleasure," Ivan said. "I pray that you will continue to recover and regain your strength."

"Thank you," said Janet.

"Okay, Mom. I'll be back in a little while after we eat," said Burton.

Burton left Janet's room accompanied by Ivan, his wife and Sandy. They walked back down the hallway to the elevator. They had dinner at Felix's Fish Camp located on the Causeway. After a relatively enjoyable dinner, they drove back to Mobile. Burton dropped Sandy off and they continued on to the house. When they arrived at home, Ivan told Burton there was something he wanted to talk with him about. Burton thought it was odd they had been talking most of the afternoon, and then when they got home, he stated he wanted to talk with him about something. Burton curiously wondered what it could be, since he had ample time during the course of the evening to say anything he had to say. Ivan placed his hand on Burton's shoulder and looked him in the eye.

"You need to fire that lady," said Ivan.

"Who are you talking about?" said Burton.

"That lady," Ivan said. "What's her name, Mae. You need to fire her right now. You need to go back over to that Hospital tonight, this very moment and fire her. Tell her get out of your mother's room."

"You think so," said Burton.

"Yes, I think so," Ivan said. "That lady is killing your mother. You need to get her away from Janet."

"I do feel that she's not going to be able to do the things my mom is going to need done when she comes home, and I have been looking for somebody else to help me with her," said Burton.

"Do you hear what I'm saying to you Burton," Ivan said. "That lady isn't worth a shit. She's killing your mother. You need to go over to the Hospital and fire her right now. Burton, I have been a physician for many years and my wife is a nurse. Those bed sores your mother has. She wouldn't have them if she was doing what she's supposed to be doing."

"Burton, we even asked her about clipping Janet's fingernails and she said she didn't know how," Suzan said. "What grown woman doesn't know how to clip fingernails."

"Do you want me to go and tell her she's fired," said Ivan.

"Perhaps you're right, Ivan," said Burton.

"Perhaps I'm right," Ivan said. "You need to get that woman away from your mother, and you need to do it now."

"I appreciate your concern, but I'm not going to fire her until I've found a replacement," Burton said. "I don't want my mom there in that Infirmary room alone, and that is really what I'm paying her to do right now, is just to be there in the room with her. She has been staying there round the clock with her since she's been in the LTAC unit."

"You're paying this woman grand theft money just to sit there in the room with your mom and she can't even cut her fingernails," Ivans said.

"I wouldn't say I was paying her grand theft money," Burton said. "I have interviewed another lady and I'm considering hiring her to help me when Janet comes home."

"Hire Sandy to help you," Ivan said. "She said she would help you."

"Sandy does help me with my mom a lot, but I'm not sure if she can do the job either."

"I really need someone with some training and experience," Burton said. "Actually, Mae has been with me for a while, and I agree she doesn't have the training and experience to do the things that need to be done to care for my mom."

"Burton, that's your mother, and I can't tell you what to do," Ivan said. "You're an intelligent guy, and I know you care about Janet."

"Yes. It is so obvious that you care about Janet," said Susan.

"Well right now I need someone to be there in the room with her," Burton said. "I don't want her to be alone at the hospital without anyone there. I can't be there all the time."

"What difference does it make," said Ivan.

"As a nurse who works at a hospital," Susan said. "She's not alone. The staff will take good care of her."

"Why do you feel like you need this woman to be there with her," said Ivan.

"Because somebody could walk in her room and punch her in the face and she couldn't tell me who did it or what had happened," Burton said. "I've got to have someone there with her. I feel a lot more comfortable that way."

"Burton I can't be a party to this," Ivan said. "I know you don't plan to let this lady come back and continue working for you to care for your mom. I'm not trying to be critical, but she is doing your mom no good whatsoever. She is killing Janet. You need to fire her, and if you allow her to keep working with your mom, I guarantee you she's not going to live much longer."

"Like I said," Burton replied. "I just interviewed a new person with training and experience, and I intend to interview a few more people and make a decision before she comes home. I don't plan on Mae being part of the equation when mom comes home."

"If you ask me you need to cut her out of the equation now," Ivan said. "Preferably tonight if you ask me, but ultimately Janet is your mother and it's your decision. But if you want Janet to have any sort of life expectancy from this point, you need to get rid of that lady."

 Shortly afterward Ivan and Susan went to bed. They left early the next morning without hardly even saying goodbye. Burton had been glad to see them, and just their presence had lifted his spirits somewhat, just to have them around for a few days. However, Burton had experienced the criticism that usually follows when disinterested people come into the picture. It never seems to fail. People come for a day or two and then want to start making split second judgments and evaluations of the situation.

 Burton was no stranger to this. He had experienced it numerous times over the last few years where family members and friends come around. Burton was doing everything he could for Janet and everything he could to make sure she was cared for. Perhaps there was some truth to what Ivan was saying, Burton had been thinking practically the same thing himself for the last few months. But he was not ready to let Mae go yet, because she was still serving a purpose. What Ivan had said in such a blunt and quip manner was somewhat true but it simply was not as easy as going to the hospital and telling Mae she was fired.

Mae had been working with him for some time now. She had been loyal and dependable. It was clearly obvious that Mae did not have the training, the ability or the consistency to perform most of the duties Janet would require when she arrived home from the hospital. Burton was no fool, he already knew this. He had already had his own concerns that Mae was incompetent and completely unable to continue serving as Janet's caretaker.

Burton already had his concerns about how much Janet had declined so quickly when Mae actually started working as a live in, and he stopped providing the majority of her care in the evenings. He had hired her as a housekeeper and to prepare meals for Janet over seven years ago. It was clear the ball game had changed where Janet's care was concerned and Mae was not a good choice going forward.

Throughout the entire day Ivan's words resonated in Burton's mind. In a way it angered Burton that his attitude was so condescending, and that he appeared to base his entire opinion on such a brief encounter. However, he knew that Ivan meant well. He also appreciated the Thousand Dollars Ivan had donated to his campaign. He felt that Ivan's comments were made strictly out of concern for Janet, and her well-being. It just frustrated him that so many people tend to want to walk into the situation and start making quick judgments about what's going on or what needs to go on, and usually their point of view is not formulated based on a total knowledge of all the facts. Ivan's mother also suffered from Alzheimer's' and Ivan's brother Jim had been her primary caregiver.

Perhaps this reminded him of his own mother who suffered from Alzheimer's and he felt a little guilt. All the same Burton did not like the way the message had come across; however, he could not deny there was some truth in the message. Burton called his cousin Ivan later that afternoon and they talked for a while. Burton told him that he was going to hire someone else to care for Janet. Ivan said they had made it back to Pensacola and had gotten a room on the beach for their last night in the area, and he had enjoyed his visit to Mobile. He still hoped Burton would get rid of Mae. Burton thanked Ivan for coming and thanked him again for the campaign contribution and assured him he was going to take care of it.

As Janet got closer to being released from the hospital, Burton was still not prepared for her to come home and still had no idea exactly how he was going to care for her once she returned. Lacey contacted him, and indicated she had the paperwork and documentation he had requested. They agreed to meet again, this time he told her to meet him at the house. Lacey agreed and he gave her directions how to get there. About an hour later, Burton arrived at the house and Lacey got there a few minutes later. She presented him with the documents he had asked to see, and to his surprise her record was clean despite the one charge which stemmed from a domestic situation. It was pretty much as she had indicated and Burton was somewhat relieved. He was becoming more interested in hiring her now and knew he would need to make a decision soon. Burton asked Lacey if she could possibly stay overnight sometime and she said that would be possible.

Lacey confided in Burton that she was a recovering Alcoholic and that she had been clean and sober for two years now. She said she could be available for work whenever he needed her, but that she would let him know in advance that she regularly attended AA meetings and would need for him to be understanding about her needing and wanting to go to her meetings which she usually attended in the evenings. She stated that she was drug free and did not use any drugs and that furthermore, she was on probation and had to report regularly to her probation officer. Other than that, there was no reason why she could not do the job he needed her to do. They also discussed compensation.

Burton hoped that he would not lose her interest in the position. He said that he would be willing to pay her by the week instead of by the hour. Burton offered her Two Hundred Dollars a week. She frowned a little when he said that, but she still appeared to be interested. She said she needed a job and she needed the money because she had been out of work for a while.

Burton told Lacey that he had a one or two other people that he intended to interview but in actuality he had not lined anyone else up yet for an interview. The more he talked with Lacey, he started to feel that she might be a good person for the job. Despite a few personal problems she had going on in her life, she had the qualifications and but for the blemish on her record, she would probably be working at a nursing home or other healthcare facility caring for patients in the same or similar circumstances as Janet. After they talked a while longer, Burton said he wanted for Lacey to meet his mother. He said he would like to arrange for her to come by the Nursing Home to meet her in a week or so, since Janet was scheduled to be released from the Hospital to the Nursing Home the next day.

Burton had gone around to several nursing homes in the area and spoken with a number of the directors at the various facilities. After having visited about five different places, he decided that he was going to entrust Azalea Manor to care for Janet during the remainder of her twenty- one day of rehabilitation. Azalea Manor boasted that they had one of the best rehab programs in town. Burton toured the facility and met a few of the employees. He decided to allow Janet to be released to them because it was close to the house, he had a good feeling about the place when he visited, it was clean, they said their rehabilitation program was exceptional and they stated they had staff who had training in using the wound vacs which Janet was still connected to. They even showed him the room where Janet would be staying if he decided to entrust them with her care. The room they said they would give her was right next to the nursing station. They assured Burton they would provide Janet with the best possible care.

    The decision was made and Burton notified the hospital that when they released Janet, they were to release her to Azalea Manor Nursing Home. He also notified the nursing home that he was going to bring Janet there and requested they work with the Hospital to insure a smooth transition from the Hospital to their facility. The wheels were now in motion and Burton felt like he had made a good decision to take her to Azalea Gardens. While all of this was going on with Janet, Burton was still busy with work and his campaign for Congress. He tried hard to juggle work, campaigning and making sure they were taking care of Janet.

    Janet was transported by ambulance from Mobile Infirmary Hospital to Azalea Manor for her twenty- one days of rehabilitation. She would need to complete before she was scheduled to go home. Burton met with the staff at the Nursing Home to handle all of the necessary paperwork for Janet to be admitted to their facility.

    The staff also began their evaluation of her for the rehab she would be receiving. Burton requested they do some aggressive rehabilitation especially to Janet's legs which were becoming more contracted. At this point her legs had become bent at the hip and her knees were starting to want to remain in a bent position also. This worried Burton, but they said they were unsure if there was anything they could do. They suggested that most of her rehab would be limited to her current range of motion. They did however, place Janet on her back and brought out an A shaped object which was fitted with a base and placed it between her thighs and lower legs. Burton was not sure what this was going to accomplish but at least they were trying something, since they said her knees where practically locked in that position. It was not recommended to pull her legs or attempt to make them extend because it might cause her severe pain or injury.

They agreed to allow Mae to stay there at the nursing home with Janet for the first night or two but no longer after that. The nursing home indicated they did not allow people to stay with their loved ones overnight in the nursing home. However, they would make an exception for one or two nights but that was all. Burton agreed that he would not have a problem with their rule as long as he felt comfortable that Janet was being cared for properly. They assured him they would do their very best to provide her with the highest level of patient care. Mae had gone to the facility with Janet, and was prepared to stay there with her. Burton appreciated Mae's willingness to stay with her, but he explained to her that the nursing home was only going to allow her to stay with her overnight for a few days.

People, including Janet, could say whatever they wanted about Mae, but she had been a loyal employee over the years. Janet's care had gotten beyond her capability, but she did care about Janet and she had spent a lot of nights in the Hospital with her. She had been devoted to Janet and her job working there with Burton. Many days her employment with the LeFlore's was not easy because Janet was often cranky and downright rude to her frequently calling her a host of derogatory names and epithets.

"Oh, I didn't know you were still here," said Mary the CNA on duty that night.

"Yes, I don't think we've met," said Mae.

"I'm Mary," said Mary. "I'm Mrs. LeFlore's CNA for the night."

"I'm Mae and—," said Mae.

"I was just wondering because they said her son was up here earlier but he left," Mary said. "Are you a relative of hers?"

"No," Mae said. "I'm her caregiver."

"Her caregiver," Mary said. "Oh, okay I was just wondering because it's almost 1 o'clock in the morning and visiting hours where over a while ago."

"I'm spending the night with her," said Mae.

"They don't allow people to spend the night in patient's rooms and nobody mentioned anything about that to me," Mary said as she turned Janet who was kicking and fighting because she did not want anybody bothering her.

"Mr. LeFlore asked me to stay here for the first few nights with her to make sure she's properly taken care of," said Mae.

"You best believe she's going to be properly taken care of here," Mary said as she peeled back the bandages over Janet's left side. "You're her caregiver. It looks to me like you're the one who hasn't been taking the proper care of her alright."

"I take good care of her," Mae said. "I've been taking care of her, working for Mr. LeFlore for seven or eight years now. I don't think that's fair of you to say that. Mrs. LeFlore just getting old. She's had that Alzheimer's ever since before I even started working for them."

"All I'm trying to say mam is it doesn't matter who you are or how long you've been working for who," Mary said. "And I'm not fin to lose my job over you being here when you're not supposed to be here. We're caring for her now and she's in good hands," said Mary.

"That's nice to know," Mae said. "So, what you want me to leave right now."

"Mam if they said you can stay here tonight then all I need to do is verify it with the nurse manager and everything will be fine," Mary said. "It looks like Mrs. LeFlore is comfortable now. Mrs. LeFlore I'm sorry I didn't mean to wake you. I just had to make sure you were turned to the other side," she said with a smile. "I'll be back in a little while."

The next morning one of the staff members who had just arrived at work came in and asked Mae once again why she was there in the room so early. She indicated once again that she was supposed to stay in the room with Mrs. LeFlore and that she had been given permission to stay there for the first few days. They basically told her at that point that she would not be allowed to stay anymore nights at the facility. They explained that she was more than welcome to stay all day during visiting hours if she wanted but that she would not be allowed to stay another night at the nursing home with Janet. They were also very rude about it, making it perfectly clear that she would not be allowed to stay there. Mae felt extremely unwelcome there and decided that she would discuss it with Burton when he got there.

Mae basically got her things together and called a friend of hers to ask if she could come and stay with her for a few days. Her friend agreed to let her stay there so she called Burton and asked him when she could get paid. She explained that the nursing home staff kept telling her that she could not stay there with Janet and she wanted to stay with Janet but the people there repeatedly told her she could not remain in the room overnight with Janet.

Burton said they told him she could remain there for a few days but he did not want to place her in an uncomfortable situation. She asked if he would mind paying her and if it was okay for her to take a few days off. He agreed to pay her when he came by to visit Janet. Later that evening he met with Mae in the parking lot of Azalea Manor and they had a little talk.

"I spoke with the director and he said that you could stay another night or two," said Burton.

"The people keep coming into the room and they tell me they don't want me there," said Mae. "Someone on the floor did make a comment about it, and it seems they don't really want you to stay in the room with her so I understand," said Burton.

"Can I get paid today?" asked Mae.

"Sure, you can get paid today," Burton replied. "I really appreciate you hanging in there with her. You've been there with her every night at the hospital for almost two and a half months and I appreciate you being there."

"I'll come over in the day and spend time with her during the day," said Mae.

"Okay but you need a few days off," Burton said. "Why don't you take a few days off and then come back."

"I don't mind coming up here during the day, but they haven't been very nice to me since I've been here," said Mae.

"Here's your money," said Burton.

"It seems like you don't need me anymore," replied Mae.

"I appreciate you and everything you have done for me and my mom," said Burton.

"You saying you don't need me anymore?" asked Mae.

"I didn't say that," Burton said. "I don't have anything to do with what the people at the nursing home said."

"You no longer need my services," said Mae.

"Here," Burton said as he paid her. "I'll call you in a few days."

"Okay. I'll talk with you then," said Mae.

Janet's continued rehabilitation lasted for several more weeks at Azalea Manor. One day Burton went into her room. She was laying there rubbing her hand through her hair. She did not say anything to him when he said hello to her, but she looked at him and appeared to be in good spirits. He started to talk with her and she listened but still did not reply. He said to her that she might be coming home soon. Burton asked Janet if she wanted to come home. Janet looked at him and nodded her head, no. Burton replied no in a surprised tone. Burton explained to her that he had been talking with a lady named Lacey who he was strongly considering hiring to help him take care of her. He indicated to Janet that he wanted to bring Lacey by the nursing home to meet her to see how she liked her before he made the final decision.

However, the clock was ticking. In less than ten days, Janet was scheduled to be release from the nursing home. Although he had pretty much decided to hire Lacey. He still did not have solid plan in place for how he intended to take care of Janet once she returned home. Ironically, Janet had just basically told him that she did not want to come home. Perhaps that was a sign that the people at the nursing home were treating her well and making her feel loved and cared for. Burton wanted her to feel loved and cared for when she arrived home. He called Lacey and asked her if she would meet him at Azalea Manor's on the following day to meet Janet. Lacey agreed and they set up a time that would be mutually convenient for both of them.

The following day, Lacey met Burton at Azalea Garden's and he took her up to Janet's room to meet her. Burton introduced Lacey to Janet and explained to her that this was the new lady he was going to hire to take care of her once she returned home. He told Janet that Mavis would not be returning to the house to work anymore one she was released. Lacey was very kind and jovial with Janet. Janet said hello to Lacey and she appeared to be happy to meet her. Lacey spent about an hour in the room with Janet becoming acquainted with her. Lacey seemed to be kind and compassionate.

At this point, now that Burton had an opportunity to see how Lacey related to Janet in person, he was certain that he was going to hire her. He told Lacey that she could start on the day that Janet was scheduled to return home, which was July 21st, which was in approximately a week. Lacey accepted the position and agreed to be available to start work on the day Janet returned home. Burton hoped and prayed that he had made the right decision in hiring Lacey. He had a good feeling about her and she said she was knowledgeable and experienced in all aspects of the care that Janet would need. He figured all he could do at this point was to give her a chance and hope she would be able to do a good job with Janet once she returned to the house. The following day after he introduced Janet to Lacey, he asked Janet if she wanted to come home. This time she nodded yes, in the affirmative.

CHAPTER SIX

The day had finally arrived when Janet was scheduled to be released from Azalea Gardens Nursing Home. Burton was frantic. Janet had not been home now in almost three months and everything had changed with regard to Janet and the level of care she would require. The home health agency had come out to the house about two days prior to her arriving and brought a hospital bed for her. He had to break down her old bed and move it out to accommodate the hospital bed. He also moved a large lazy boy reclining chair into the room so the caregivers and visitors might have somewhere to sit.

Janet also received a delivery of supplies that she would need. The supplies ranged from bed pads; diapers; a pump for her feeding tube with formula and bags; a device to suction her mouth; items for oral care; bandages; gauze and antiseptic, just to name a few.

It was cloudy and rainy on this July day as the ambulance arrived at the rear of the nursing home to pick up Janet and transport her to the house. Burton tried to contact Lacey and let her know that Janet was leaving the nursing home. He expected her to come to the house and start working on Janet's transition back home. He called her number two or three times and got no answer. Burton could not understand why she did not answer, seeing as she said she would be waiting for his call and would be ready to come to work. He started to panic.

Unable to reach Lacey he contacted Sandy and asked her if she could come and help him because Janet was about to be released from the nursing home. Sandy told Burton she would be happy to help him and that she would be waiting for him to come and pick her up. Burton did not discuss his plans to hire Lacey with Sandy.

Truthfully, Sandy knew Janet was going to need an increased amount of care and she was thinking that Burton was going to hire her to help him with Janet. He had told Sandy that he was not planning on having Mae back at the house working anymore.

Julius was already there at home helping Burton get prepared for Janet's arrival. Finally, Lacey returned Burton's call and indicated she was sorry for missing his call but was ready to come to work. Burton asked her if she could pack a bag and stay at the house the first few nights. Lacey said she already had her bag packed and asked if he would come and pick her up.

Burton asked the people at the nursing home and the ambulance driver to give him a few minutes. He jumped in his truck and sped to Lacey's house which was not far. Lacey was living with her godmother at the time, which was not far from Janet's house. He picked Lacey up, took her to the house and went back to Azalea Gardens to tell them it would be okay for them to bring his mother home.

Meanwhile he was so busy and nervous that he practically forgot that he asked Sandy to come and help him. He followed the ambulance to the house. The sky was overcast as Burton transported his mother through the drizzling rain inside to her bedroom. Burton got busy around the house. Lacey put her things into the downstairs back bedroom and right across from Janet's room. Lacey busied herself getting Janet's supplies organized and ready. She also set up Janet's feeding tube.

Sandy called and Burton told her that he had just arrived at the house with Janet and he would come and get her in a little while. Needless to say, Burton spent the remainder of the evening there at the house with Lacey and Julius. He never went to pick up Sandy. Burton had been very busy trying to get on top of this new situation with Janet and her care. He could tell that Lacey was in fact a very knowledgeable about all the aspects of Janet's care. She knew exactly what to do. Lacey started communicating with Janet engaging her and telling Janet that she was there to take care of her and that she was going to be just fine. She got sheets and cover from the laundry room to make sure Janet's bed was as comfortable as possible. Lacey organized Janet's medicine and familiarized herself with how many times a day she would need to take each pill and what each pill was for.

Lacey asked Burton if he had a grinder to break up the medication so that it could be given to her through the feeding tube. She gave Burton a list of things they would need for Burton to get from the pharmacy. She asked him to purchase some cranberry azo because she claimed it was a known natural remedy that would reduce Janet's chances of developing a bladder infection since she was permanently on a catheter.

Burton knew all too well about bladder infections by now and liked the idea of using a natural remedy to help reduce the risk. Janet was still not taking a lot of medication and Burton had stopped giving her Seroquel. He requested the hospital not give her any while she was there. However, she remained on cholesterol medication and had a regular Narco prescription for pain. However, now over the last few months Janet had gone from being an extremely active woman with moderate to severe memory loss to being in a vegetative state. She was now on a feeding tube. Burton would have to learn how to administer the formula in a bag which then drained down a tube into Janet's stomach. The flow of the nutrition was controlled by a machine which made sure the flow of formula was steady and consistent.

Even though Burton had seen the machine in the hospital and the nursing home. He had not actually been trained or taught how to use it. Her medication was also administered through the plastic syringe through her feed tube.

Since her surgery to remove the infected tissue from her rear end, she had been on the wound vac but she was no longer on the wound vacs anymore. She had two wounds on both sides of her hips right about in the same place where some of the younger women like to get tattoo's. The wounds had to remain bandaged and had to be cleaned regularly. Now Burton was of the understanding that the wounds were not expected to ever heal. This involved pouring an antiseptic agent onto her raw exposed tissue and wiping it and packing the wounds with gauze.

Her range of motion had diminished. She no longer moved her legs at all and they were becoming increasingly contracted and stiff. She still had use of her arms and hands. Now that her wounds were starting to heal, they would itch and she wanted scratch them. It was a constant struggle to prevent her from trying to scratch her wounds. Otherwise, she would reach out and grab the rail on the side of the bed or rub her hands through her hair or rub the bedspread in a back-and-forth motion. Once she was placed in a given position, she would remain in that position. She would not attempt to move or reposition her body in any way.

However, Lacey was stepping in with much compassion and experience. She actually sought to bond with Janet. Lacey talked with Janet on a regular basis. She reassured her as she busied herself around Janet's room. Burton gave her a notebook. He said that he needed her to log in everything she did and what time she did it. Burton also wanted her to log in every time she was turned, the approximate time she was turned and what side.

The evening went on and Burton worked closely with Lacey. Burton decided by that point that it probably would not be a good idea for him to bring Sandy into the equation because it might be awkward. Lacey was well on her way and to getting the situation under control with regard to Janet and he realized it would be best to allow her to continue to work undisturbed. He was starting to feel like he had made a good decision in hiring her. He started to feel more comfortable with Lacey there taking care of Janet.

Lacey's daughter Jayla stopped by the house after she got off work and helped her with Janet for a little while. Jayla assured Burton that she would also be available to come and help him on a part time basis if he wanted her too, when she was off work from her job at the nursing home. Slowly Burton was starting to feel like he was actually going to be able to successfully pull this off. He had also met a few other people at the nursing home who said they would be willing to help him with his mom on a part time basis. Lacey was Janet's primary caregiver and in addition, he had potentially five people he could call to come in part time as needed. He was trying his best to get a support system in place for Janet.

After getting Janet organized, Lacey went into the kitchen which was a little messy. She cleaned the kitchen and straightened up her bedroom and proceeded to make herself comfortable in her new job and new role as Janet's caregiver. Burton now felt somewhat relieved. Janet's transition back home had actually gone very smoothly. He was happy with the progress they had made during the evening and he was optimistic that he had found a competent and caring caregiver for Janet. He also felt like he was starting to get a handle on the things he would need to do for Janet if there was no one around to help him.

Burton decided to take Friday off work as well as the rest of the weekend and stay at home with Janet. He wanted to keep an eye on Lacey and further monitor her work performance before he completely turned Janet over to her free and independent of supervision. Janet had Alzheimer's and she was incapacitated. He still had to be careful, and plus he wanted to work closely with Janet as well to further familiarize himself with the aspects of her maintenance and healthcare needs.

Lacey was a relatively young woman, in her early forties. She was an attractive lady, slightly on the plus side. She was very intelligent and articulate. She liked to talk, and although she had been raised in the south and lived up north for a while, she did not have a southern accent. She had now moved into Burton's house to care for his mother. Arguably under different circumstances Lacey might have been someone Burton would have had a slight interest in. However, Burton was resolved that his relationship with this woman was going to be absolutely and purely professional.

There was no chance whatsoever. There would be no sexual harassment; no innuendos; no flirting; no disrespect; no coming on to her; no her coming into his bedroom; no conversations or communications about them handling any other sort of business other than making sure Janet was properly cared for. He had a clear indicator and common sense told him there was no way he was going to try and throw anything into the mix between him and Lacey other than the care of his mom. Anything other than complete professionalism and mutual respect between them would have been a complete disaster. As far as Lacey was concerned, Janet's care was Burton's primary and only concern.

Lacey assured Burton that she would be up with Janet throughout the night and that he could get some rest. She just asked if he would be available in the morning for a few hours so she would be able to get a little sleep. He agreed even though he did not sleep well that night and continued to check on Janet and monitor her.

Janet appeared to be comfortable and doing well as she lay there wide-awake staring at the television. Burton was glad Janet was back home and he hoped she was happy and content. Her quality of life had diminished to practically zero and she suffered severe cognitive issues. Burton realized that his purpose was right there in front of him. There is a certain peace that comes over a person when they realize their true and current purpose and understand that God will make a way.

Burton had arrived at one of his true purposes in life, at least one of them. His mother Janet lay before him, incontinent; catheterized; bed ridden; on a feeding tube; with wounds extending approximately a half inch into the fatty tissue of her flesh; unable to walk; seldom able or unwilling to talk; in constant agonizing and excruciating pain; helpless and inefficacious totally dependent on external sources for her sustenance, care, survival, well-being, movement and upkeep. She had been the most incredible mother any son could ever wish to have. He absolutely and positively had to make sure she was cared for at this point in her life.

The next day Lacey's daughter Jayla stopped by again after work. Lacey asked Burton if it was alright if she went off for a little while to attend her meeting and go to the grocery store to pick up some items she needed. She said her daughter would stay there with Janet while she was gone. Even though he was there at the house, Burton figured he would let Jayla work with Janet for a while and pay her for her time. At this point, he was building relationships and building his support system for his mother. Burton welcomed Jayla. After all, she was the one who had managed to introduce him to Lacey. From that simple evening in early June when Burton had gone to the service station for gas and saw this young lady dressed in her scrubs looking like she had just got off work.

He had given his business card to her asking if she wanted any part time work. But for him meeting Jayla, he may not have met her mother, Lacey. He was so thankful that God had made a way. Out of nowhere, out of the abyss of nothingness, denial and despair, out of a hopeless outlook and unfavorable set of circumstances Burton, through the grace of nothing more than our almighty God, had made a way.

He had trusted in the Lord. There was nothing more he could do at this point. Janet was dying. She was dying a slow, painful and yet painless death. Burton did not know exactly how long his mother Janet was going to remain here on earth with him. He did know for sure she was all he had, besides his five children. He was resolute and steadfast in doing whatever he had to do to take care of his mom.

Regardless of whether that meant his time or resources to make sure she was properly taken care of. Janet was his mother and she had given him everything. She had loved him unconditionally. There was no way he could have wished for a better mother or human being to raise him. It was up to him to make it happen and make it happen exactly like it had to occur and ensure that Janet was comfortable and cared for during her final minutes, days, weeks, months or years. He knew he had to make sure she was taken care of, and he had to accept that there might come a day when he had no other choice than to place her in a nursing home, even though that was in no way shape or form what he wanted or intended to do.

"Hey Burton, Jayla's here," Lacey said. "I need to run off for a minute to my meeting and I'm going to pick up a few things from the grocery store. Mrs. LeFlore's been turned and I changed her. She should be good until I get back but Jayla's here in the meantime."

"That's fine," Burton said. "How long will you be gone?"

"Shouldn't be more than two or three hours," said Lacey.

"OK," Burton said. "Thanks for asking Jayla to come over."

"Yea, she'll turn her and make sure she's good until I get back," said Lacey as she left.

Thank you, Lacey," Burton said. "I'll see you when you get back."

"Mr. LeFlore," Jayla said. "Your mom has been turned, she's clean and her feeding tube is supposed to be off for about the next hour. I'm so tired. I've been up since about six o'clock this morning and had a long day at work. Do you mind if I lay down for a minute?"

"Mom's good," Burton replied. "No problem, Jayla."

"I just want to take a power nap," Jayla said. "All I need is a few minutes of rest and I'll be good. It's been a long day."

"Jayla my casa is su casa," Burton said. "I'll keep an eye on Mom. I appreciate you."

"Thanks," Jayla said. "I feel like I'm about to pass out."

"Thank you for hiring my mom," Jayla said. "I put your card on my nightstand. I clearly told her that I was considering taking a job with you, but she kept talking about she needed a job and she was going to call you. I was interested in taking the job with you, but I do have another full-time job. So now she's working for you and I'm not mad because I know you needed somebody. She wanted and needed a job too, but it's just the way she went about it, like forget me. But I'm glad you got somebody to take care of your mom. I think she'll do good for you and Mrs. LeFlore though."

"So far so good Jayla," Burton said. "Thanks for introducing us. I think things are going to work out with Lacey. I hope they do."

"I'm going to lay down," Jayla said. "If you need me, just call me."

"OK," said Burton as he went back into Janet's room to check on her again.

About an hour went by. Janet was fine, laying there comfortably in her bed in front of the television. Jayla was laying down on the sofa taking a nap. Lacey had not yet returned. Burton had gone up to his room to relax for a minute. He heard the doorbell ring. He got up and went to the back door to see who it was. He had not been expecting Lacey back so soon and he was not expecting any company. Burton had been so busy with Janet and had so many thoughts going through his mind during the last day and a half, he had completely forgotten about Sandy and there she was at his back door.

"Hey Sandy," said Burton as he opened the door and let her inside.

"How is your mom doing?" Sandy said. "I hadn't heard from you. I came over to see if you needed any help with anything."

"She's back there in her room," Burton said. "Why don't you go and say hi to her."

"I put everything on hold yesterday and waited all evening for you to come and get me so I could help you and you never showed up or called me back," said Sandy.

"I'm sorry," Burton replied. "From the time Mom got home yesterday till the time I went to bed; I was busy trying to get her straight."

"But you knew I would have helped you Burton," Sandy said. "I promised you I would help you. All you had to do was come and get me. I was worried about you and you had me waiting for you all that time."

Burton walked back into Janet's room with Sandy. They found Janet there laying in her bed facing the television. Sandy went to the side of the bed and said hello to Janet. Janet looked up at Sandy. Sandy took her by the hand and asked her how she was doing. Sandy asked Janet if she knew who she was. Janet acknowledged that she recognized Sandy and nodded her head as if to say she was doing alright. Burton and Sandy stayed there in the room with Janet for a moment.

Sandy asked Burton again if there was anything he needed for her to do. Burton said everything was fine at this point and there really was nothing he needed any help with at the present time. They went back into the kitchen, where Sandy then saw Jayla there laying on the sofa. Sandy was somewhat surprised to see this young woman laying on Burton's sofa.

Who is that?" asked Sandy.

"That's Lacey's daughter Jayla," Burton said. "She's helping me with my mom for a little while."

"Doesn't look like she's doing any work to me," Sandy said. "Looks to me like she's sleeping on your sofa. Who's Lacey?"

"Lacey is the new lady that I hired to help me with Mom," said Burton. Right about that time, the doorbell rang and it was Lacey returning from running her errands. She was carrying several bags of groceries in her hands.

"Burt," Lacey said. "I went ahead and brought a few things at the grocery store so I'll have something to eat while I'm here."

"Lacey this is my friend Sandy," Burton said. "Sandy this is Lacey, my mother's new caregiver."

"Nice to meet you," said Lacey as she placed the grocery bags on the table.

"Yea you too," replied Sandy with a bewildered expression on her face.

"Sandy has helped me a lot with my mom over the years," Burton said. "And she may be coming in periodically to help if you need a break sometimes. Her mom suffers from Alzheimer's too."

"Very nice to meet you Sandy," Lacey said. "Burt I'm going to put these groceries up and get back to your mom."

"Can I talk with you for a minute," said Sandy.

"Sure," Burton said. He and Sandy walked to the front of the house.

"Can we go outside?" Sandy said. "I want to talk privately without them hearing what I have to say."

"What's up?" asked Burton now that they were outside on the front porch.

"You bastard, you fucking bastard," Sandy said. "All along you been planning to hire this woman to take care of Mrs. LeFlore." Sandy argued as she started to cry. "You just went and got yourself a whole new family. Y'all are just one big happy family huh. You don't need me anymore. You got Miss. Lacey and her daughter layin her stankin ass up on your sofa talking about she's working. Yesterday you called me and asked me to come and help you and I sat there damn near all night worried if everything was alright with your mom, and waiting for you. Now I see why you never came to get me, because you've got Lacey now and she's taking care of your mom. I guess you're fucking her too huh, or is it her daughter you're fucking?"

"What are you talking about," Burton said. "Nobody is fucking anybody. These people are just here to help me with my mom."

"What about me," Sandy said. "All this time I've been helping you with your mom whenever you needed me. As many times as I've told you to just let Mae go because she wasn't worth a shit and hire me to help you with your mom, so your mom would be taken care of right. And you know I needed a job. But after all you just couldn't do that for me. You couldn't help me for once."

"Sandy, I need somebody round the clock," Burton said. "How are you going to do what I need done for my mom when you're still busy taking care of your own mom. Plus, I need somebody with experience and training."

"You could have let me come over here yesterday so I could learn about the things Mrs. LeFlore needs done,"

Sandy said. "Now I see why you never came. Now you're feeding her and buying groceries for her."

"No, she brought those groceries herself," replied Burton.

"She lives here now," Sand said. "You've moved a whole woman into your house, talking about she's going to take care of your mom."

"Yes, she's going to be staying some of the time," said Burton.

"Burton what kind of a fool do you think I am," Sandy said still crying. "You didn't just meet that woman. You've been knowing her. You're fucking her. You and her got a relationship and you've had a relationship with her probably for a while now. So now that your mom's back home and Mae's not coming back you decided to move her in a make it official. I'm so stupid."

"Why are you crying," Burton said. "Will you please stop crying. Sandy, first of all, I appreciate everything you've done so far to help me with my mom. Secondly, just because Lacey's working here doesn't mean that I won't need any help. I'm still going to need your help and you can learn about some of the things she needs done and you can still help me sometimes and I'll pay you."

"What do you need her for?" asked Sandy. "I could do anything your mom needed and she would have been well taken care of. But you just couldn't do that, nope not Sandy. You call me practically any time of the day or night and if you needed help with Mrs. LeFlore, I was there for you. You got Lacey now, forget me."

"I made a decision which I know is in my mother's best interest and that was to hire Lacey," Burton said. "This is about my mom, it's not about you and it's not about your feelings. You don't need to be coming over here questioning me about what I do in my house to take care of my responsibility. Anyway, like I said, you're still taking care of your mom, so how are you going to take care of your mom and my mom too."

"I bet you I could take better care of your mother than that fat ass bitch," replied Sandy.

"Sandy, she's a CNA," argued Burton.

"Oh yea," said Sandy.

"Yes, and she has worked at a number of nursing homes now," Burton replied. "She has a lot of experience."

"Well why isn't she working at any of those nursing homes now," said Sandy.

"That's irrelevant Sandy," Burton replied. "Because she's going to be working here."

"Fuck you too Burton," said Sandy.

"If you were any kind of friend, you wouldn't be taking an attitude like that," said Burton.

"If I was any kind of friend," Sandy replied. "Is that what you said. Any time you ask me to I lay on my back or bend my ass over to satisfy you. If you need me to clean up, I clean your house, your office. Anytime you tell me you need help with your mom, whether that be changing her, combing her hair, fixing her something to eat, bathing or whatever I've been there for you. Your mom has beat me, jumped on me and called me all kinds of bitches and I never said a word because I know she's just like my mother. She doesn't know any better. I still tried to love her because I try to love everybody. And you say I haven't been a friend to you. You say I haven't helped you."

I never said that Sandy," Burton replied. "I got to do what I got to do to make sure Mom has a safe place, a place where she can be adequately cared for and appreciated. The whole game with her has changed now."

"A lot of things have changed, haven't they," said Sandy.

"It's not about you," Burton argued. "I'm sorry you feel the way you do, but it's not about you. This is about what I gotta do. My mom has to be turned every two hours now; she's got to be changed, she's got to have wound care on a regular basis, she's on a feeding tube. I'm going to need your help if you're still willing to help me but I need somebody full time. I know you're not able to do everything I need done for her and take care of your mom at the same time. Get over it. This is what I know I need to do and it really doesn't matter if you like it or not."

"I wish you and Lacey all the happiness," said Sandy before she stormed out to her car and left. "You can have that bitch."

Sandy got in her car and drove off. She was noticeably upset, surprised and disappointed. Burton stood there for a minute thinking about the conversation he just had with her. He really appreciated Sandy and she had been there to help him on many occasions when he needed her. However, he knew that even though her intentions were good to a certain extent, her ideas about helping Burton at this point where misguided and uninformed as to Janet's true needs. He had not discussed his plans to hire Lacey with her. He only discussed that he did not intend to have Mae return after Janet left the hospital, which arguably did give her the impression that he was thinking about hiring her to do the job.

Perhaps there would have been a better way for him to have introduced his plans to her as opposed to the way it all unfolded with her coming to the house thinking he needed help, and all of a sudden, finding Lacey there helping Burton with his mom. However, unfortunately Burton was not in a position right now to be politically correct, overly cordial or creatively tactful to avoid hurting someone's feelings. He had Janet who needed to be cared for. Either he was going to have to set up the proper support system to make her care happen at home. The only other alternative was that he would have to place her in a nursing home. Burton went back into the house, and at that point he encountered Lacey.

"Burt, whatever y'all talk about is your business," Lacey said. "But I heard what she said about my child. Now if she wants to talk about me then that's fine, but she didn't have to make that comment about Jayla. We're just here trying to care for Mrs. LeFlore and all of that is not necessary."

"I'm sorry, what are you talking about?" asked Burton.

"Talking about her stankin ass laying on your sofa," Lacey said. "Why would she make a comment like that about my child. I had hoped this job might work out for me, but maybe I need to just get my stuff and go back home."

"No, no, no," said Burton. "You don't need to do anything of the sort. What are you talking about?"

"I'm on probation," Lacey said. "I can't have anybody coming over here talking crazy to me, because if she talks about my daughter there's no telling what I might do. I just probably need to go."

"That was a misunderstanding between me and her which did pertain to you," Burton said. "But she is going to have to respect my home and you for that matter. I'm not going to allow anyone to come here and harass you while you're doing a job for me. Now just slow down."

"Mrs. LeFlore is so precious, I'm already starting to feel attached to her," said Lacey.

Mamma it doesn't matter what she said about me," Jayla said. "You think you can take good care of Mrs. LeFlore. You said you wanted to take this job. Why would you want to leave because of what she said?"

"I don't want to leave, but I don't need any trouble," Lacey said. "I just don't need any trouble."

"There isn't going to be any trouble," Burton said. "All I need you to do is stay here and keep working your magic with my mom."

As the days turned into weeks Janet continued to languish and grow increasingly feeble and weak. The weeks turned into months and Janet rarely moved from one position. Her range of motion remained in her arms. She would lay before the television which was almost always on. Janet preferred for the television to be on since it was practically the only stimuli she received besides when she had to undergo the extremely painful process of wound care. Her wounds constantly itched and she would frequently rub the areas of her behind where her wounds were located. Lacey and Burton quickly learned they had to keep Janet covered with a thick blanket to keep her from trying to scratch.

They would pull the blanket all of the way underneath her arm or use a pillow so that she could not manage to reach underneath the blanket and start scratching the large area of open flesh on both sides of her buttocks. Janet was healthy within the confines of her current physical and mental condition. She would speak and talk occasionally but sometimes she would not say anything for days. Janet would however respond when people were bothering her or tried to turn her.

Lacey settled in and assumed the role of being Janet's live-in caretaker. Lacey worked around the clock taking care of Janet. She coordinated the visits with the home health nurses. The home health nurses came three times a week. Lacey would go for weeks at a time without asking for a day off. She only asked Burton if he would care for Janet for a few hours during the night so that she could get some sleep.

Each day she would make sure there was formula in Janet's feeding tube as well as her vitamins and medications. She changed her when necessary. Lacey emptied the bag attached to her catheter. She did Janet's wound care. She made sure Janet was turned every two hours and kept a log in Janet's notebook. She changed her sheets and made sure they were clean. Lacey bathed Janet several times a week and made sure her hair was combed. She also coordinated the visits of the home health nurses. The home health nurses came three days a week. She would sometimes take naps during the day or ask Burton to care for his mom for a few hours during the night so she could sleep. Otherwise, Lacey remained vigil about her duty to care for Mrs. LeFlore.

Janet enjoyed having her hair brushed and combed. Janet always like to look nice and prided herself in her appearance. Even though practically everything had changed with regard to her life and existence, the core aspects of Janet's personality and spirit remained the same. She was still a maverick and still a fighter and still wanting to live. Janet was living and she wanted like every other biological being on earth to survive. Despite her decrease of cognitive ability and physical strength had deteriorated, she was still blessed to be alive. Janet was on a road of pain, increased debilitation, frustration, confusion, dementia, Alzheimer's, arthritis and contracting muscles, bones and joints.

Oral sensations are wonderful and amazing. People eat and they enjoy eating. Janet was now deprived of the oral sensation and enjoyment of having tasty food or drink travel through her mouth and into her body. She was now dependent on the feeding tube which ushered nutrition into her stomach on a consistent basis. Occasionally Burton would give her a taste of some ice cream, sorbet or Italian ice but for the most part she did not consume her food orally anymore.

All of her food, nutrients, medicine and whatnot were given to her via a feeding tube. Janet was completely helpless. She was in need of round the clock care and supervision. She was the way her sisters had described her about ten years ago, she was in need. Janet was at the crossroads of her life and death. She was in transition and all Burton could do was to remain there for her and make sure he did whatever she needed to sustain any level of comfort and complacency or care he could provide.

Ironically none of her sisters who claimed to be so concerned about her maintenance and well-being ever called or made an effort to come and visit her. Actually, her sister Bethany did try and call once right after Janet arrived back home from the hospital, but Lacey told her that she would have to speak with Burton and see if it was alright for her to speak with Janet. From that point, they stopped relying on the house phone and relied more on their cell phones However, for the most part her brother Peter would call occasionally and ask about Janet, but her other sisters did not call at all. They failed to even call and ask how Janet was doing or inquire about her well-being at all.

Burton managed to straighten things out with his friend Sandy who did not say much more about his decision to hire Lacey. It was a while before he even thought about bringing her or inviting her back over to the house. On one occasion Sandy had been doing some work for Burton cleaning one of his rental houses. On the way to take Sandy home that night, he needed to go by his house to get something. This time he invited her inside to come and see his mom. Sandy came inside with Burton. Lacey was seated on the sofa watching television. Burton left Sandy in the kitchen while he went upstairs to get his coat. Right about the time he got upstairs to his room he heard Lacey talking to Sandy in an indignant tone of voice.

"Why are you looking at me!" Lacey exclaimed. "Stop looking at me."

"Excuse me," said Sandy.

"You heard me," Lacey replied. "I said stop looking at me."

"Excuse me," said Sandy.

"You heard me," Lacey replied. "I said stop looking at me."

"I wasn't looking at you," Sandy said. "You don't have anything I want to look at."

"Good then," Lacey said. "So don't look at me then."

"Burton can you please hurry up, your whatever she is, has a bit of an attitude tonight," said Sandy.

"Just don't stand here staring at me," said Lacey.

"Well Burton said I should apologize to you," Sandy continued. "So, I got to thinking about it, and I decided I would be a bigger woman. Even though it's hard to be the bigger woman because you're a pretty big girl. I want to apologize. I shouldn't have made that comment about your daughter."

"You're right, you shouldn't have," Lacey said. "But I accept your apology."

"I try to be nice to everyone and everybody," said Sandy.

"Alright I got my coat," Burton said. "Come in here and say hi to Mom."

"Okay well I'll talk with you some other time," said Sandy.

"Sure," Lacey said. "It's just about time for me to turn her again. What time is it?"

"I'll turn her," Burton said. "How long has it been since you last turned her?"

"About an hour and fort-five minutes ago," Lacey said. "I wrote it down there in her notebook."

"I'll go in there and turn her now," said Burton.

"Thanks," replied Lacey.

"Mom how are you doing?" asked Burton.

"Hey there Mrs. LeFlore," Sandy said. "I haven't seen you in a while. How have you been doing?" she asked.

"Hi," said Janet.

Janet lay there in bed looking up at the two of them standing there at her bedside. She did perk up a little and smile at Sandy. Even though she did not say much else except hello. Janet glanced right into Sandy's eyes and acknowledged both of them. She seemed content and happy for the moment. She was clean, her hair was combed and tied in a pony tail. Janet had not had her hair colored since forever and it was not completely gray with steaks of silver. Burton pulled back the cover and checked her diapers to make sure she was clean down there. She was not soiled and her bandages were fresh. He took Janet by the legs with his right arm and below her neck with his other arm and lifted Janet. He asked Sandy to get a bed pad from the table near the bed and remove the one on the bed. Sandy quickly removed the pad in the bed and replaced it with the new pad. Burton then turned Janet into her right side.

As soon as he placed her on the right side, before he could get the cover back over her, she started reaching for the area of her body where her wounds were located. Burton caught her hand before she was able to reach it and pulled the cover up beneath her arm and then placed a pillow between her legs and another small pillow under her arm.

He checked Janet's feeding tube and made sure she was not laying on the tube and it was not obstructed in any way. She started rubbing her blanket again and once again appeared to be content and satisfied. Burton stayed there in the room with Janet for a few more minutes before leaving to take Sandy home. On the way out he told Sandy that he still needed some help with his mom sometimes and that he always appreciated her help in the past. They drove on to her house and he paid her for helping him clean the house and he dropped her off.

Over the weeks Lacey had been there in Janet's home working. She had grown to know and understand Janet. She communicated with Janet and talked to her. She started calling her mamma. Lacey was a very compassionate caregiver and she had started to get attached to Mrs. LeFlore. She had a comfortable room there in the house near Janet's room and she had not gone back home to her godmother's where she had been living, except to get the rest of her things and for a brief visit one day when she had been off work. Lacey had jumped right in and dedicated herself to Janet's care. Lacey was doing an incredible job. Janet was coming to know her and trust her in her own way. Lacey also started to become quite protective of Janet. Janet was helpless and Lacey took a watchful eye to her at all times. One morning Lacey got up to turn Janet, she was hungry so she put a sausage in a pot of water and went in to see what was going on with Janet.

"Good morning, Mamma," Lacey said. "You doing alright. I'm sorry I overslept a few minutes but I'm here. Did you have a bowel movement," Lacey said as she checked Janet's diaper. "Oh, my goodness. Let's get that changed right now," she said as she unfastened her diaper and started to wipe her. "No Mamma don't fight with me. That's not nice. I'm trying to get you changed," said Lacey as she rolled up the bed pad and wiped her clean trying to make sure her bandages did not get soiled. "Let me get this new clean one on you and get you turned now. Why are you still trying to fight me? I'm almost finished. I'm almost finished. Mamma I'm tired too, I just want to get you clean and get this pad out from underneath you," Lacey continued as she pulled back the covers and checked Janet's ankles. "It's going to get you straight and let you go back to watching television, and I'm going to go back to bed and lay down for a few more minutes."

Burton was also staring to take a very active role in Janet's care. He was still campaigning and busy with work, but he put in time with Janet. He gave Lacey breaks, and he would stay up at night while Lacey slept and turn Janet at least two or three times before he went to bed. Besides work and running his campaign which kept him extremely busy, he was busy with his mother Janet whenever he was home. Up until this point Lacey's daughter Jayla had also been filling in during the evenings when Lacey had to attend her meetings or run some personal errands.

Burton had also learned every aspect of his mother's care and actually looked forward to spending time with Janet and caring for her. He had always loved spending time with his mother. This was the woman who brought him into the world and raised him. The lady who had given birth to him, provided for him and taken care of him in every type of way. She had never really needed much from him besides a hello and a hug. Now Janet was in absolute need of care in numerous ways. In many ways he felt like this was his way of repaying her for everything she had done for him over the course of his life.

Janet needed a tremendous amount of care and supervision. Lacey had become his lifeline and she knew it. She conned him on the regular within the confines of their monthly agreement, which was two-hundred-twenty-five dollars a week and room and board. Burton would buy her cigarettes every day and he would keep food in the house so she could fix meals for herself. Burton was fine with that agreement as long as she took good care of Janet. Burton had a lot going on at the time. Every Sunday he was going to speak at various churches around the district including churches in other counties.

Burton was doing television interviews and running his campaign headquarters and his real estate business. With everything he had going on, the one most important thing he had to deal with was Janet's care. He sometimes felt like he was skating on thin ice because the minute he had no care for his mother, he was shut down and confined to the house. Lacey accommodated him and she did not hesitate to request her accommodations. Frequently Burton was basically confronted with situations where Lacey was telling him that if her demands were not met then she would have to go.

Burton wanted to make sure Lacey was accommodated as long as she took care of Janet's needs at the house. Lacey also had a host of friends, mostly male friends who visited her. Some of these guys Burton really did not want in his house, but he tried to be polite because she spent a lot of time there at the house, and it was somewhat unfair to now allow her to have any visitors. Burton was not concerned with her having a visitor as long as she remained there with Janet and made sure she was okay.

She had a number of men who would come and visit her as well as a host of female friends. Burton did not agree with some of her friends, but he was cordial and welcoming. Burton had always been a very private person who did not like having a lot of various and sundry people at his home. Primarily for security reasons, but also because he is a private person who remains protected and guarded about his home and where he lays his head as well as who might have access to his safe zone. He had a woman working in his home who he wanted to make sure she was comfortable and able to do her job.

It was a give and take. It was a deal between the two of them. They were like two parents who had never had sex taking care of their baby. Although, Lacey appreciated the job, and did a good job taking care of Janet occasionally she exploited her job and Burton's need to have her there at the house with his mom. However, Lacey often got on Burton's nerves. Sometimes she would call him while he was at work and ask him to get her some fried chicken or a whopper, which he did not want to do, but he did it anyway. Lacey would stay there in the house taking care of Janet for hours and days at a time. If a two-piece chicken meal with a side of pepper or a whopper which cheese was enough to keep her happy and there at the house working with Janet, certainly he was going to do it to keep her happy. Her work was not hard, but she was regularly confined to the house.

"Hey Burt," Lacey said. "You need to pick up some Cranberry Azo for Momma. I ran out and she also needs some Mucinex, she's a little congested."

"Sure, I'll try and get by the store a little later," said Burton.

"Also, I know it's not Friday yet but do you think I could get Forty Dollars," Lacey said. "I got a few personal items I need to get for myself. Just do like you do and deduct it from my money."

"Lacey it's already Wednesday and you've already got two draws this week," Burton said. "You can't just wait until Friday."

"Burton, I need some pads," Lacey said. "And I got to get my blood pressure meds."

"Pads don't cost Forty Dollars," said Burton.

"That's not all I need," Lacey said. "I told you I got to get my blood pressure meds and some other stuff. If you can't do it that's fine. I'll just have to get to walking and see if I can get it somewhere else. It's that time of month and I need some pads immediately."

"Whatever Lacey," Burton said. "Here, here's Thirty Dollars. That's all I have on me right now."

"Okay that'll work," Lacey said. "Can you give me that and just get me the other ten tomorrow."

"Sure," said Burton.

"I'm going to call a ride to take me to the store," Lacey said. "Will you stay here and watch Momma for a few minutes until I get back."

"Sure," Burton said. "Promise you won't take too long because I need to go back to work for a little while."

"It should only take a minute," Lacey said. "Thanks Burt, I'll be right back."

"Okay no problem," said Burton.

"There's one other thing I want to talk with you about," said Lacey.

"What's that?" asked Burton.

"I'm going to need some help," Lacey said. "I love Mamma and she has grown on me. I enjoy being able to work with her providing her care."

"And you've been doing a tremendous job by the way," said Burton.

"Thank you," Lacey said. "Every once and a while I need a little break and I know you need a break sometimes too. You might want to think about hiring somebody part time to help me. I mean I can handle this but we need a backup sometimes."

"What happened to Jayla?" asked Burton. "I haven't seen her lately."

"Jayla got another job and she's got her life," Lacey said. "Plus, me and miss thang got into it the other day. She wants to come around here getting an attitude with me and talking disrespectful to me."

"Jayla," replied Burton in a surprised tone.

"Yes Jayla," Lacey said. "Jayla can be as sweet as she wants to be sometimes but she's got her ways too, and I'm not going to have her talking to me any kind of way. I had to remind her that I was her mother and eventually I just told her to leave."

"Wow, I'm sorry to hear that," said Burton.

"She calls herself not talking to me now," said Lacey.

"I'm sure you guys will work it out," Burton said. "In the meantime, you let me know when you want me to call in someone to help you out. I have a few people."

"I haven't been to any of my meetings lately and I told you how important that was for me," Lacey said. "Every once in a while, you're going to have to start giving me some time off."

"Well sometimes on the weekend if you need to take off," Burton replied. "I'll be here with her, but I know you can't do it all by yourself and yes, I agree. I need to find someone who can fill in part time for you. Point well taken and I'll get to work on it."

"OK," Lacey said. "My ride's here. I'll be right back. See you when I get back. I just turned her and I should be back before it's time to turn her again."

Burton went into the room with Janet. She was sleeping peacefully. Burton stood there for a moment admiring his mother. She was still a very attractive woman for her age and even in her condition. He took his hand and gently stroked her head. She did not awaken at first. Lacey had been doing a tremendous job with Janet and Burton had no issues with regard to Lacey and her handling her job caring for Janet. Clearly Lacey had been going above and beyond the call of duty. So far, she had been such an enormous blessing. Burton was very thankful to her and for her. He was also thankful to still have Janet with him at home. Even though clearly and obviously her quality of life had been severely diminished and she was now confined to the bed among other things, he was still thankful that she was alive.

Burton finally got word that his divorce from Candace was final. Burton had originally filed for divorce in Mississippi about three years prior. However, after all that time in divorce court in Mississippi, he decided to dismiss his case in Mississippi and file in Alabama. They got some strange divorce laws in Mississippi called separate maintenance. He had one court date in Mobile before the judge granted his divorce from Candace. Burton could hardly believe it. Finally, after over three years. Apparently, the judge must have taken notice of the fact they had already been in divorce court in Mississippi and just decided to end it. All total they had two court dates which both occurred while he was involved in this campaign for Congress.

The first court date Candace showed up with her mother and proceeded to try and lie on him and slander him. She knew full well he was running for the Congressional seat, but she still proceeded to slander him in open court. Burton could not believe it and yet unfortunately he could. Surely, she must have known that if Burton won the election, she and the kids would be better off, but it appeared she simply did not care. She stated that Burton had a tendency to frustrate and anger judges. She suggested that he contact the judge in Mississippi and that is probably what he did. Otherwise, he could see no other reason that he granted the divorce so quickly and without another court date. Burton was finally divorced from Candace after eight years of separation. The next court date she asked the judge to set aside his Order granting the divorce. It was fully over.

Meanwhile Sandy called Burton and told him that her mother had to be hospitalized. Burton went over to the hospital with Sandy to visit her on two occasions. Each time she was in good condition and Burton was not sure what was going on with her as far as her health or why she was in the hospital. Burton thought her hospitalization was more or less routine but Sandy's mother was very ill. Burton was caught up with Janet and her issues. Mattie Lou was released from the hospital and subsequently passed away about three weeks later.

Ironically Burton had not talked with Sandy for a week or two before she passed away and did not realize her mother was still not doing well. Burton assumed that when she went home from the hospital, she was better. He saw Sandy about one day or two before her mother died. Sandy explained to him that Mattie Lou had not been doing well since she returned from the hospital. Sandy indicated that her mother's doctors stated he did not think she would live much longer. Burton felt sorry for Sandy, because he knew how close she and her mother had been. He was busy at the time, but told her he wanted to come by the house and visit her.

Burton did go by their house to visit Sandy's mother, Mattie Lou the next day and found her ill and yet still in good spirits. She was happy to see him, and Burton sat by her bedside and they talked for a moment. Mattie Lou died the next day. Sand and her family had a beautiful home going ceremony for Mattie Lou at a local church which was attended by all of her family.

Over the years, Burton had gotten to know Mattie Lou pretty well and she had become like a second mother to him. She was a country girl from rural Alabama. She was a very attractive old lady. Burton had seen pictures of her when she was a young woman and she was absolutely beautiful. She had her first child as a teenager. As a young woman she moved to Mobile to look for work. She worked as a seamstress and retired from the school system. She met Sandy's father after she move to Mobile. She had seven children after she married her husband. Several of her children had predeceased her.

Sandy was the baby of her family. Miss. Matie Lou was a sweet yet feisty old lady. She was actually pretty funny and liked to tell jokes sometimes. For the most part she and Burton got along well, except for that one time she called him and cursed him out and accused him of having taken her house. Otherwise, she was always cordial and for the most part enjoyed sitting on her sofa watching her television programs.

Burton's dealings with Mattie Lou helped him to understand how Alzheimer's affected many people in the same way. Based on differences in people's personalities and lifestyles Alzheimer's manifests itself in different ways with different people. Even though Mattie Lou and Janet both suffered from Alzheimer's they exhibited their signs in different ways and behaved differently. Mattie never became bedridden like Janet but she did have mobility issues and loss of balance.

For instance, whereas Janet was extremely active and always wanted to be out in the yard and constantly sweeping and mopping. Mattie Lou was more sedentary and liked to mostly sit at home and watch television. Burton wished sometimes he could convince Janet to sit down and watch television for a little while and stop getting into everything like a precocious and curious child.

However, they both experienced serious mood swings. Mattie Lou was constantly saying she lost something, particularly money. She would get confused and frustrated and go tear up the house looking for whatever it was she said she could not find. Frequently, she would accuse people, primarily Sandy, of having taken things from her.

Janet on the other hand, rarely said she had lost anything. Many years ago, Burton had simply stopped allowing Janet to handle any money. Janet would ask about her money. Janet would ask about her money and ask how they were managing to live and pay bills, but she never accused Burton of having taken anything from her.

Janet asked frequent questions about her parents and about where she was and about her home and her surroundings. However, Mattie Lou confusion and lack of memory was different. Sometimes Sandy's mother would just sit in her chair and cry for hours, but could not explain why she was crying. Janet willingly relinquished control to Burton as afar as the house and her life for the most part. Janet was not concerned with being in control of her house, car or money so much. She was more preoccupied with trying to figure out where she was. Her main contention of concern as far as control were that she was simply not going to be fucked with. If Janet felt like anyone stepped to her the wrong way, she was going to deal with you. Although in some instances someone having stepped to her the wrong way might be up for interpretation.

On the other hand, Mattie Lou was constantly seeking to maintain control of her belongings primarily her house, car and money. She too intended to deal with whoever she might have felt was the wrongdoer. She sought to establish that she was still in control of all those things no matter what. Her inability to recall and keep up with the things she wanted to be in control of frustrated her deeply and was displayed in different ways. They were both strong willed however, strong willed and determined women. The fact that they suffered from Alzheimer's did not seem to hamper their determination. Burton started to understand just how complex the disease was and how personality, sex, education level, surroundings and circumstances can often play a part in how it is displayed through a person's behavior, language, activity, temperament and affectations.

Herein Burton sought to understand how control is a major factor in a person's life as far as every aging person whether they have Alzheimer's, dementia or not. Obviously, a person who lives to be elderly had to live a long time. Therefore, at some point they had to be responsible for themselves and had to maintain authority over their own life and well-being. The word control is not used in a negative sense here in that every human being must manage their own lives.

It is frustrating for anyone to have a diminished ability to regulate what goes on in their life, and what they might feel is their right to exercise dominion over things they may have always exercised authority over, it is not easy to give up the authority and autonomy. Whereby most caretakers are confronted with autonomy, authority, self-reliance, ability, inability. Often, need versus not in need issues and they are usually struggling to comprehend and administer the proper level of care, understanding and patience.

Often this is not an easy task, because dealing with a person suffering from Alzheimer's is not easy. Burton thought to himself it appeared when working with someone suffering from Alzheimer's and dementia, you should always expect the unexpected. Unfortunately, you can be reasonably certain it will get worse before it gets better, no matter how many liars or motherfuckers you get called you have got to remain calm and not take it personal; expect unwanted intermeddlers who will seek to explain a situation; if you are caring for someone with diminished capacity people will try to make insulting spot second judgments about you and what you're doing; you could be prosecuted for abuse, neglect and wrongful death just to name a few. When it comes to Alzheimer's and dementia the devil is lurking.

CHAPTER SEVEN

The election finally arrived. The election for the seat that Burton had been running for finally arrived. Despite everything that was going on, Burton had managed to run a pretty tight campaign. He was running against a candidate who had considerably more political experience and much more money in his campaign. Burton's competitor had run for Governor and lost about two years prior to his campaign for Congress. In addition, the district that Burton was running in boasted that no Democrat had won that district in Fifty-Years. Burton was clearly the underdog and had always faced an uphill climb from day one. AL.com the Mobile newspaper, in one article wrote that anywhere else in America Burton LeFlore would be on his way to Congress, but not in Alabama District 01. On election day, despite Burton's best efforts he lost the election. He was crushed.

Anyway, how could Burton have realistically taken a job in Washington, D.C., with his mother Janet in the condition that she was in. Perhaps he could have managed somehow, but it would not have been easy. Similarly, it had not been easy running a campaign and managing a business and caring for Janet. He wanted Janet to be proud of him. He hoped that she would have lived to see him win a big election like this, but frankly speaking she probably did not even know what he was doing. It was still a tough pill for him to swallow. At the end of the day, he had to pick himself up by the bootstraps and keep it moving for himself, his children and Janet. When he got back to the house Lacey was there, and she had seen the election results.

"Hey, Burt," Lacey said. "Don't worry. Mamma is fine. I got her turned, gave her vitamins and meds, she's had a bed bath and she was asleep last time I checked."

"How are you?" asked Burton.

"I saw the election results on television," Lacey said. "All I can say is, it may not have come out in your favor, but I think you ran a hell of a campaign. Guess I'm not going to get that raise you said you'd give me if you won, but that's alright. You gave a lot of people hope in this community including me. I have to admit, I was very impressed, and I'm not really into politics like that."

"Thanks, Lacey," Burton said. "I appreciate that."

"You're a really good person Burton," Lacey said. "You're good to your mom. You've been good to me, and I hear you talking to your boys sometimes on the phone," she continued. "I can't wait to meet your children."

"I appreciate that," Burton replied. "I would like for you to meet my kids."

"I know you wanted to win that election and there's probably not much me or anyone can say right now, but you tried your best and that's all you can do."

"That's for sure," Burton said. "Even though I didn't win, I wish my mom could have been there tonight."

"I'm sure," Lacey said. "You know my mom has been dead for almost six years now, and not a day goes by that I don't miss her. I think that's one of the reason's I've become so attached to Mrs. LeFlore. You know I even call her Mamma now."

"I know and that's sweet of you," Burton said. "You know she needs all the love she can get right about now. I told you that Sandy's mom passed away last month," said Burton.

"You told me," Lacey said. "I called her and gave her my condolences."

"I want to tell you, I really appreciate what you've been doing for her," Burton said. "I think you're taking better care of her here for the most part by yourself, than they were doing when she was in the nursing home."

"She's a very special lady," said Lacey.

"You're saying that," Burton replied. "But I don't think you really realize just how special she really is. She is and was an awesome woman and an incredible mother. I wish you could have met her when she was younger. Before she got like she is now."

"I've seen a lot of pictures," Lacey said. "She was beautiful. She still is. As a matter of fact, one of the home health nurses who came by here the other day said Mrs. LeFlore used to be one of her favorite teachers."

"You know hardly a day goes by that I don't run into somebody who says she taught them chemistry," said Burton.

"Earlier today, I got her to talk to me," Lacey said. "We actually had a nice little conversation."

"She was talking today?" said Burton.

"Yep," said Lacey.

"This what I'm doing now," Burton said. "It's the least I can do to repay her for everything she has done for me. A few days ago, somebody said to me, Burton you have done some really awesome things in your life. I have to admit that practically everything I have done in my life she helped to make it possible. I love her so much."

"I know you do," Lacey said. "And it shows."

"I thank you so much for the words of encouragement," Burton said. "I'm drained. I just want to go and lay down for a minute."

"I got Mamma tonight," Lacey said. "I'm wide awake."

"You say she was talking today," Burton said. "That's good to hear."

"Yea she was talking to me," said Lacey.

"Let me go and check on her," Burton said.

He went into Janet's room and saw her there in her bed. She appeared to be happy and content. Now Burton was pretty much able to tell how Janet was doing by observing her. Since she was not talking as much now, he had to rely more on his intuition and his observations of her.

'Hey, Mom," said Burton.

"Hi, Baby," she replied. He reached over the railing of her bed, took her in his arms and gave her a big bear hug.

"You're talking to me today," Burton said. "I love you."

"I love you," replied Janet. "You know I almost became our next congressman today," Burton said. "I wish you could have been there today, even though I didn't quite pull it off. I gave it a good try though, and I know you would say to me that's all you can do. But one of the most important things I'm doing is right here with you."

Janet smiled at Burton for a moment and went back to rubbing the side of her blanket. She did not appear to be in any pain or discomfort tonight. Spending a few minutes there with Janet also helped to ease the pain he felt inside from losing the election. He had worked so hard, even though he knew it was a long shot from the jump. At least now he would have more time to focus on running his business, his children and taking care of Janet. He tried to remain optimistic, but being there in Janet's presence was comforting. He needed some comfort right now. Burton just took a moment to soak up that good old mother son bond. Simply being in her presence was comforting to him, and seeing that she was in good spirits made him feel much better. He still had a lot to be thankful for.

A few days later, Breton and Varina came to visit. Breton is a political junkie who follows politics very closely. He had given Burton a great deal of good information and statistics regarding the state and much of his advice Burton was able to use as talking points during the election. It had been over a year since Breton and Verina had seen Janet. Lately a lot of his conversations with Breton surrounded the election and what they felt was going on politically. Burton had not really taken time to fully explain to Breton everything that was going on with Janet. He knew that she had been in the hospital on several occasions, but Burton had not divulged the full range of Janet's current condition.

"Hey, Dad," Breton said. "How are you doing?"

"I'm hanging in there," Burton said. "It's good to see you."

"Hi, Mr. LeFlore," said Verina.

"Hi, Verina," said Burton.

"How's grandmother doing?" asked Breton.

"She's fine," Burton said. "It's been a while since you've seen her. I'm sure she'll be happy to see you guys."

"Where is she?" asked Breton.

"She's in her room," replied Burton.

"Is she asleep?" asked Breton.

"No probably not," Burton said as Lacey emerged from Janet's room. "Hey. I want you guys to meet Lacey. She helps me with your grandmother now. Lacey this is my oldest son Breton and his girlfriend Verina. They live in New Orleans. Of course, I've told you about Breton before."

"Yes," Lacey said. "It's nice to meet you both. I'm Lacey."

"Nice to meet you," they both replied.

"You didn't tell me you were coming," Burton said. "What brings you to town?"

"We just came in to see my boy Pat, he's having a baby," said Breton.

"He's having a baby," Burton said. "Oh really. When did guys start having babies?"

"You know what I mean, Dad," Breton replied. "Him and his girl. You know."

"Are they married?" asked Burton.

"Na, na. They're not married," Breton replied. "But he's really excited about the baby."

"When are you guys going to get married?" Burton said. "The two of you have been together forever."

"It may be pretty soon actually," said Verina.

"Well, Verina," Burton said. "I consider you my daughter in law now, and I will consider you my daughter in law then."

"Yea we've been talking about it," Breton said. "So how have you been doing since the election?"

"I'm good," Burton replied. "Life goes on."

"I think you would have made a great congressman for the people of this district, even though I think there were a few suggestions I made that I wish you had implemented. It is what it is."

"I certainly had a great political adviser," Burton said. "Come on and say hi to your grandmother."

"Where's Mae," said Breton.

"She doesn't work here anymore," Burton said. "Your grandmother is going to be so happy to see you."

They went into Janet's room. Janet was there in her usual space. "Mom, look who came to see you," Burton said. "It's Breton and Verina." Burton's back was turned to them as they followed him into her room. They were both very surprised. Breton tried to retain his composure as he walked over to the side of her bed.

"Hello, Grandmother," said Breton. Janet did not reply but she did look up at Breton and Verina. "Hi Mrs. LeFlore," said Verina. Janet still did not reply. Breton reached over and took Janet's hand. Verina just sort of stepped back from the bed and took a good look at Janet laying there. She noticed the feeding tube which was attached to the machine next to the bed with the bag of nutrition hanging atop of a pole. Verina was so overwhelmed that she started to cry. She was not expecting or prepared to see Janet like this, and it was such a drastic change from the lady she had met many years ago when she was a young girl in high school and first started dating Breton. Verina had actually majored in chemistry in college and was now working as a chemistry teacher herself.

Breton stood there holding Janet's hand. "Verina there's no reason to cry," Burton said. "She's had a long journey in life and she's just transitioning. It's going to be alright." Verina continued to cry for a little longer and then she also tried to regain her equanimity. It was obvious to Burton that neither one of them expected to find Janet like that. Burton thought perhaps he should have warned them. At any rate he was glad that Janet had gotten a chance to see them. Janet loved Breton so dearly.

"Hey, Dad. Will you take a picture of us with my phone?" asked Breton. Burton said he would. He took a few picture of Breton standing by the bed with his grandmother, and a few with Verina by the bed with Janet. The two of them stayed a while longer there in the room with her. They had both now gotten over the initial shock, and were a little more at ease.

"Mom, you see Breton and Verina?" asked Burton. Janet looked at Burton and nodded in the affirmative. She was pleased to see them. They stayed for a while longer before heading out to see their friends.

The irony of it all, is that they had just visited an old woman in her last days, as they were about to go to the hospital and visit a baby in the very first minutes and hours of its life. The wheel of life is constantly turning. People are leaving this life every day and people are coming into existence every day. The rest of us are just living, stuck somewhere in between birth and death. The amazing and wonderful thing about it all is that no matter what happens in the world, the wheel of life will continue to turn and forge ahead.

The world and the wheel of existence is infinitesimal and constantly emerging and ever changing. The entire process extends from one person to one tree or one flower to one animal to all that is you and me and every ancestor whose DNA is a part of our physical and biological makeup. The idea and reality of life relates to so many things we living beings still struggle to comprehend. Frankly speaking humans will never comprehend or fully understand. All we can do is just live. Another day the sun will rise and all we can do is try again.

    The amazing and awesome thing about the whole process is that reality extends from person to person and individual to individual and is omnipresent. It will always prevail. No matter what happens in a given life the only thing certain is there was life. Whether a life is beginning or ending or whether a life is still somewhere within this thing we call life. The world keeps on turning. The world always keeps it moving. The sun keeps on rising and setting and the stars still twinkle in the nighttime sky. Every being and organism is born from the earth, and its matter. Every living thing survives on the world's bounty and sustenance. The contour of a pregnant woman's stomach is round. Similarly, all life eventually returns to the earth. The world is shaped like a wheel and so is life, cyclic and ongoing.

CHAPTER EIGHT

Everyone always talks about the devastating effects of Alzheimer's on the people suffering from it; however, very often people fail to realize that Alzheimer's and dementia have a tremendous effect on a person's loved ones. Burton had been there for Janet from day one. From the point where his marriage with Candace disintegrated and he moved out of the house with his family, and moved into his mother's house. At that point, Janet was in the very early stages, but soon after he started staying with her, he started to recognize some of the telltale signs.

He also became aware of things going on that he did not necessarily know about before. Having resolved that his marriage was over and that he was going to do whatever he had to do to be there for Janet, and care for her. He started the process of caring for his mother while he watched this devastating disease start to slowly diminish her capacity, her ability to manage her affairs and now her ability to perform simple daily functions on her own. None of this was easy for Burton to handle or accept.

As the days, weeks and months of Janet being confined to the bed and completely immobilized continued to pass, he and his live-in caretaker Lacey went through the daily motions of helping Janet to survive. For so many years Janet had been one of the most vibrant, beautiful, intelligent, energetic and healthy women you would ever want to meet. Things had changed drastically. For the most part now, her existence on this earth was nearing an end, but she was still tenaciously hanging on to what little life she had left. Her quality of life had dwindled to little more than a bed, a room and a television.

However, her will to live was still unyielding. Her son Burton showed her a lot of love and perhaps that was one reason she continued to hold on because she wanted to continue to be there for him. Perhaps if it were not for all the love Burton had shown her, she would have been gone a long time ago. At this point, she was weak and vulnerable; however, she was well guarded, protected and cared for. Lacey was very protective of Janet. Burton watched over his mother Janet and cared for her like a loyal dog watched over their human.

Almost a year had passed now. Janet still had the gaping wounds on both sides of her buttocks. Lacey and Burton would always try to keep the covers pulled up under her arms and would often put a pillow under her arm. This was to keep her from getting to her bandages and wounds. One evening she managed to get her arm under the thick cover and she immediately went straight to her wounds. She took the bandages off and dug her fingernails into her raw flesh.

She scratched and scratched digging her fingers into her exposed flesh and it started to bleed. Janet continued to scratch and dig into her flesh and neither Burton or Lacey came into her room for a period of time. She scratched and scratched. The pain of her sharp fingernail digging in her flesh hurt but she could not resist the urge to continue to dig into her flesh. Usually although the wounds were open, as long as they were packed and covered in gauze and bandages there would be a minimal amount of blood and drainage from the wound.

Burton entered her room and immediately noticed the cover was not between Janet's arm and her body. Based on the position of her arm, he could see that she had managed to reach her wound. He went over to the bed and pulled the covers back. He saw that Janet had in fact been scratching her open flesh. There was blood all over her hands, the sheets, her diaper and bed pad. There was blood everywhere. It looked like some sort of crime scene. Even though it was painful, she continued to scratch. Burton grabbed her hand and pulled it away. She fought him and tried to snatch her arm away and continue to scratch, but he would not allow her to pull her hand away from him. He could see the tracks of her fingernail in her flesh as the blood continued to ooze out of her soar. Burton did not know what to do. He needed to change her sheets, redress her wounds, clean her hands and get her situated.

    Burton had learned how to turn Janet onto her side and roll the covers under her, and then turn her back onto her other side and ease the covers off the bed. He had learned a lot over the time he had been caring for Janet. He had to figure out how to get the covers in the washing machine and keep her from going back into her wounds. He also had to figure out how he was going to get to the antiseptic, tape and gauze which he needed to dress and clean her wounds. He was in quite a dilemma and had never faced anything like this situation.

    Janet was agitated and in excruciating pain. He tried hard to calm her down so that he could work with her and get her taken care of. He also needed to change her because she was soiled. Burton had to work fast. Burton was able to put her hand on the railing of her bed and ran into the laundry room with the bloody sheets and put them in the washing machine. He ran back into the room and started to wipe up the blood off of her skin. He cleaned her, wiped her and placed her diaper back on. She had pulled off the gauze and tape. Her wound on her left side was exposed.

    At that point, he started to do her wound care. Burton cleaned Janet's wound. He packed it with gauze and bandaged it. Now, he had to find some more cover to put on her bed. Burton had to go back into the laundry room and try to find a new sheet and blanket for Janet's bed. He had to hurry before she managed to get back in her wound again. Burton found a clean sheet and blanked. He tied the corners around the end of the bed and rolled it to her back. He then turned her over on her other side and pulled the cover back over the entire bed. Now Burton was able to put the cover back over Janet.

He was finally able to get her situated. He decided to go ahead and give Janet her vitamins and medicine. Burton went into the kitchen and crushed everything up and mixed it with water, so that he could give it to Janet. Burton then had to mix it all together and find a syringe. Now Burton had to disconnect her feeding tube. The tube consisted of one part that was attached to her stomach which extended out from her stomach about six inches. There was a receptacle at the end of the tube which could then be attached to the tube which allowed the nutrition to be pumped into her stomach. It could also be disconnected and the syringe could be inserted to give Janet her meds.

Burton was able to get the tube disconnected and insert the syringe where he slowly injected her medicine and vitamins into her system. After reconnecting the tube, he decided to go ahead and fill the bag which held her formula back to the top. Burton opened two cans of the formula and poured it into the bag. He had finally gotten Janet situated. That was a close call, and he had managed to do everything without Lacey's help or assistance. Burton was getting pretty good at all of this stuff which had frightened and intimidated him at the beginning. However, he was becoming more seasoned and professional about it.

Despite their best efforts, Janet would occasionally manage to get her hand underneath the cover and scratch her wounds. It did not happen often, but there were a few occasions when it happened and it was not a pretty sight. The wounds were constantly itching Janet and caused her pain; however, her level of cognitive recognition prompted her to want to scratch them even though scratching was much more painful than the incessant itchy felling.

"Hey, Burt," Lacey said. "I'm back."

"I'm back here with my mom," replied Burton.

"How is Mamma doing?" asked Lacey.

"She's fine now, but she managed to get her hand under the cover. She scratched her wounds pretty bad," replied Burton.

"Oh no," Lacey said as she pulled to covers back to take a look. "Mamma, how many times do I have to tell you to stay away from there. She's clean, you bandaged her back. You did a pretty good job Burt."

"Yea," said Burton.

"Mamma, I leave you for a few minutes and you just start getting into everything," Lacey said. "I'm back now. I'm here. I love you. Looks like Burton's been taking good care of you while I was gone."

"She wore me out," Burton said. "I'm hungry. I'm going to fix something to eat."

"I got some ribs while I was out," Lacey replied. "You're welcome to have some if you want."

"I'm good," Burton replied. "I've got something in the fridge. I feel like a salad."

"Burt," Lacey said. "I get so lonely up in this house with just me and your mom. I rarely get any visitors or company. Sometimes I feel like I'm about to lose my mind."

"I'm going to hire somebody to come in part time so that you can have more time off," Burton said. "I've been talking to someone about coming in and doing that. Trying to work that out with her now."

"Thank you that would be greatly appreciated," Lacey replied. "But I was wondering if you wouldn't mind if I got a little dog."

"Yes, he's the cutest little dog and he's house trained," Lacey said. "Please Burton, he's just a little dog and he's not going to get much bigger than he is now. My friend's dog had some puppies. I get so lonely up in this big house by myself."

"Sure," Burton said as he prepared his salad. "You can get a dog just as long as he's house trained, you're going to take care of it, keep him clean and make sure it doesn't get any fleas. I'm not going to have any fleas getting on my mom. Truthfully at this point, I don't have time for a dog. I don't have time to be taking care of any dog. I already got my hands full. But if you want a dog then sure we can consider it."

"Thank you," Lacey said. "He's such a cute little dog and I already know what I want to name him."

"I can understand how you would feel a little lonely at times," Burton said. "That's cool with me if you want a dog."

A few days later Burton got home from work and Lacey had a little dog. She named the dog Buddy Rho. Buddy Rho was seated on the sofa with Lacey watching television. He started to bark when Burton entered the house. Burton thought to himself this dog was barking at him in his own damn house and sitting on the sofa. He did not like the dog being up on the sofa. Buddy Rho was a little black mutt, not sure what type of mixed breed he was, but he looked like a mix between a miniature pincher and a wiener dog like Misty.

Misty who thought she was a greyhound and liked to run with the wind, had long since run out into the street and gotten hit by a car. Now Buddy Rho was the new dog on the scene. Lacey called herself introducing Burton to the dog, and the dog to Burton. Burton took a look, went into Janet's bedroom to check on her and went upstairs to his room.

"Burton, you know it's been several months since Madea passed," said Sandy.

"I know," Burton replied. "I know you must miss her. She was quite a lady. I miss her."

"I've been thinking," Sandy said. "Now that Madea is gone, I can devote all my time to caring for your mom. You could fire Lacey and hire me. After all I need a job."

"Sandy we've discussed this, and as far as that goes," Burton said. "I'm not firing Lacey. She does a good job and that's pretty much a done deal."

"You love Lacey," Sandy said. "Lacey, Lacey, Lacey."

"No, I don't love Lacey," Burton said. "I love my mom. Lacey works for me, helping me to take care of her. This has nothing to do with love. It just has to do with me doing what I've got to do to care for her."

"You said the only reason you hired her instead of me is because I was still taking care of my mom and you were right," Sandy said. "There's no way I could have taken care of Mrs. LeFlore and Madea at the same time, but now Madea is gone and all I have is time."

"I can hire you to come in part time and help," Burton said. "And there might be some other work I can give you, but taking care of Janet isn't the only job in town. If you want to work, find a job."

"Yea, but Lacey's got a job though," said Sandy.

"Let me tell you something," said Burton.

"You don't have to tell me anything Burton," Sandy said. "You got your girl Lacey there with you. Y'all are good. You couldn't possibly need me anymore. She's fucking you, and taking care of your mom. Y'all are one big happy family and there's no place for me."

"Lacey gets on my nerves most of the time, and I'm not fucking her," Burton said. "But I do appreciate what she does to help me with my mom."

"But I never did anything to help you with her," said Sandy.

"Did I ever say that?" Burton replied. "I never said that. I appreciate everything you've done to help me. But one thing you got to seriously understand is this isn't about you. This isn't a game I'm playing. This is for real, and I'm doing what I got to do. Even with Lacey here, there's still things I need help with, and if you're available then fine, but I'm not going to have you coming to my house causing confusion."

"Confusion," said Sandy.

"It's not about you Sandy," Burton said. "That's the first thing you need to understand."

"There never would have been any confusion if you had just been a man, and said 'Hey, Sandy. I hired this lady named Lacey to take care of my mom, and I don't need your services. Instead of not telling me or saying a word about it after you asked me to come over to your house and help you. You never came to get me and never called."

"Well, I'm sorry about that, but I don't have any apologies about my decisions, and what I'm doing in my house to make sure my mom is cared for," said Burton.

"But you love your Lacey though," Sandy said. "That must be some good ass pussy."

"Whatever man," said Burton.

"Can't even give me a chance," replied Sandy.

"You know what, you need to back the fuck up off me," said Burton.

"Burton, I already know you and Lacey had been together long before she ever started working at your house," said Sandy.

"I'm not going to keep on discussing the same thing with you," said Burton.

"I want you to know, I do care about your mom," Sandy said. "I care about you. I never asked for this. No matter what you think. I'm here for you if you need me. I know how much you love Lacey, her fat ass."

"I don't understand why you want to continue to make personal statements about Lacey," Burton said. "It's nothing personal here."

"If she's doing such a good job then why is your mom getting sores on her shoulders and ankles," said Sandy.

"She's been in the bed for a long time," said Burton.

"But you said she was doing such a good job," Sandy said. "The last time I was over there I saw sores on her shoulder and ankles," Sandy said. "You say she's supposed to be turned every two hours. Then why if she's getting turned every two hours, is she getting sores on her shoulders and ankles. I'm just saying. I took care of Madea for ten years or more with Alzheimer's. She never got down in the bed like that, until a few days before she died. She never got any bed sores."

"Well Sandy, I guess you're just better than me," said Burton.

"I'm just saying Burton," said Sandy.

"You know everybody is quick to criticize, but I'm doing the best I can with or without you. So, you need to wrap your mind around that. I'm not going to fire Lacey and hire you so if you got a problem with it, then we don't have anything else to talk about. If I need you and you're available then cool, if not then all good."

"Okay. I would never try and come between you and your precious Lacey," said Sandy.

"Why are you trying to make this about Lacey," Burton said. "My mom is on a feeding tube, she has to be changed, bathed, turned every two hours, and she has to have wound care on a daily basis. I appreciate you Sandy, but frankly speaking I think it's more than you can handle. I got someone who's been doing it now for almost a year. I'm going to keep rolling with what I got right now."

"I'm sorry Burton. I know it's a lot on you," Sandy replied. "I just wish you would let me help you and I think I can do a better job than her."

"I'll keep that in mind," Burton replied. "Like I said I have plenty of things I need to get done and I will certainly be needing help."

Sometimes Burton would go into Janet's room when he got home from work and just give her a big hug. Burton would tell Janet that he loved her. He liked to give her kisses on her forehead. Burton wanted his mom to always feel loved. He would often stay there at the side of her bed for long periods of time and just wonder to himself what was going on inside of her mind and her body. Janet rarely said anything anymore. She did not express her thoughts, if she had any. Janet never complained about being in pain. Although Burton had learned to interpret her movements and facial expressions.

Occasionally Burton would take her right hand and bend her contracted fingers outward and straight. Janet did not like when he did that, and she would always scream and tell him to stop. Even on days when she was not talking much, he could always get this response from her if he tried to straighten her fingers. Burton had also learned that when changing her or doing wound care, he could turn her on her side and put her right hand on the rail. Her fingers would easily fit around the bed rail and Janet would not let go of the rail. Even at this stage of the progression Janet would still let you know if something was hurting her or if you were agitating her or bothering her.

He also tried to get in tune with Janet. There she lay in front of Burton practically dead and yet very much alive. Janet would look him in the eyes and eye contact became very important between the two of them. Alzheimer's had slowly taken everything she had, but she continued to fight. Janet continued to display a will to live even in her current condition. Janet was such a proud and active person the majority of her life. Burton loved his mother more than ever. This was the one time in her life that she needed him, instead of the other way around. He realized her days with him on this earth where few and he wanted to make sure he showed her all the love he could while he still had her. There was no way he could imagine what her thought processes where like. Perhaps the Alzheimer's was on automatic pilot along with her basic human instinct to survive.

Burton did not really have the answers to all of the questions that went through his mind about Janet. All he knew was that he wanted her to feel loved. Burton wanted her to be cared for properly. Burton wanted for Janet to be comfortable and content. Burton was not ready to let go of her and sometimes felt selfish, like he was keeping her alive when she might be ready to die. One thing was for sure, he wanted to keep her alive and comfortable as long as he could. Even though caring for her was a pretty huge task. Sometimes he felt like he was skating on thin ice because a primary part of his care for his mother could walk out on him at any time and then what would he do.

Lacey had hung in there with him like a champ from day one, but the fact that he was so dependent on Lacey to provide Janet with the care and round the clock supervision she needed bothered Burton. He did not like that feeling one bit, or the various and sundry people she invited to the house. The fact that people would think he would be simple minded enough to try and put sex into the mix with this woman was absurd. She already figuratively had him by the balls, he certainly was not going to allow her the opportunity to have him literally by the balls.

Burton had one concern and only one concern. His primary preoccupation was caring for Janet, and making sure his mother Janet was supervised and cared for. He loved Janet as most every son loves his mother. All he wanted was what was best for her, just like she had wanted what was best for him all of his life.

"Burt, I need you to get me some KFC," Lacey said. "I'm hungry, and I don't have any cigarettes. I also need to get a Thirty Dollar advance on my money this week because I need to get my diabetes medication. I don't have any insurance. I got to pay it out of my pocket."

"Okay can I bring it to you about 9 o'clock when I get finished at the office," said Burton.

"Burt I'm a diabetic I have to eat my meals regularly, and you haven't brought any groceries in a few days," Lacey said. "There's nothing in the refrigerator to eat, you promised you would keep some groceries in the refrigerator so I can fix my meals. I'm starving, plus I'm out of my medication, and I need to take it. I have no cigarettes, none. I don't mean to bother you, but is there any way you can bring it now, I'm here with your mom. Please, if not, I'm going to have to go and borrow some money and find me a way to get something to eat, and get my medicine. You'll just need to come on here and take care of your mom."

"Yea, alright. I'll be there in a few minutes," said Burton begrudgingly as he hung up the phone.

Burton appreciated Lacey immensely and usually when she made her demands which were for the most part not unreasonable, he acquiesced. A three-piece box of chicken, cigarettes and money to get her medicine was not asking for much. After all, like she said, she was there with Janet. Even though leaving work right now would probably put another hour onto his day at the office, he would just go ahead and get her what she needed. That way she could go back to doing what he needed her to do. He could go back to doing what he needed to do. It was a give and take between the two of them.

Burton tried to keep her happy and provided for her needs within the confines of her weekly salary. Although she got on his nerves at times. The two of them occasionally clashed on a personal level, Burton was always respectful to her because she was dedicated, and did an incredible job with Janet.

Even though the work with Janet came in intervals. She had to be turned every two hours. Occasionally she had to be changed. Periodically her formula nutrition had to be replenished and was turned off for four hours a day. She had to have wound care once a day. But Lacey remained there at the house with Mrs. LeFlore around the clock. That's one of the reasons Burton agreed to let her get the dog. Lacey loved Buddy Rho and treated him like a spoiled little baby. Lacey was a very loving and nurturing person.

He detected this early on with Lacey when he saw how she worked with Janet. Lacey immediately tried to connect with Janet, and started to demonstrate signs that she felt protective of her from day one. Sometimes she would rub Burton the wrong way and there were a few occasions when Burton wanted to tell her to get her shit and go, but he dared not utter those words. For the most part, they got along though. Burton was determined he was going to get along with Lacey as long as she continued to maintain Janet's level of care. Lacey was a tremendous blessing in Burton's life and he was fully aware of it.

Burton had gotten into the regular habit of asking ladies dressed in CNA scrubs about their employment and possible availability for part time work. Lacey was there a lot, and he needed to find some regular relief for her, so that she could have some time off occasionally. Burton wanted to have some time off himself every once and a while. He did not want to spend the extra money but he had to do it. There was no choice. He had spent it many times in the past. The cost did not matter. Burton just hoped to find regular, consistent and trustworthy backup that he could call on when Lacey would go AWOL, or just so she could have a day or two off work. The lady put in a lot of hours for the meager pay that Burton gave her. She did not complain. Burton wanted to have some people he could contact to come in to work when he needed some additional help.

One day Burton was getting some gas and he noticed a young lady at the nearby pump. She was in uniform and wearing a name tag with the insignia and logo of a nearby nursing home. Burton decided to approach her and inquire if she was a CNA possibly available for part time work.

"Hi," Burton said. "Are you a CNA?"

"Yes," said Sophia.

"My name's Burton LeFlore," Burton said. "I'm looking for someone part time to work with my mother, she has Alzheimer's dementia. I have a full-time caretaker, but I'm looking for someone who might be available for part time work."

"My name is Sophia. I could be available for some part time work," replied Sophia.

"Nice to meet you Sophia," Burton said. "My mom is bedridden, she's on a feeding tube, she has to be turned occasionally. Are you familiar with that type of work?"

"Yes, that's what I do," Sophia replied. "I'm a CNA. I work at Garden Oaks, and I have three boys to support. I'm definitely looking for some part time work."

"Do you have a resume' and references," said Burton.

"Of course," Sophia replied. "You want me to email it to you. What's your email address?"

"Here," Burton said. "Here's my card. Just give me a call."

"Will do, and here's my number put it in your phone," said Sophia.

"Great so we'll talk next week," Burton said. "And you've got my office address and email address. Just email me that resume or drop it by my office. My fax number's also on there in case you would prefer to fax it."

"Okay nice to meet you Mr. LeFlore," Sophia said. "Didn't you run for office or something. Your name sounds familiar."

"Yes, I did run for office a while ago," said Burton.

"I thought your face looked familiar," Sophia said. "I voted for you."

"Thank you," Burton said. "Thank you. Thank you so much for your support."

"You're welcome," Sophia said. "I think you were a much better choice than that other guy."

"I certainly appreciate that," Burton said. "Why don't you get me your resume. When could you be available?"

"I work the night shift," Sophia said. "I can be available in the early morning or in the afternoon before I go to work or on my off days. I'll get my resume' to you."

"Great well I look forward to talking with you," said Burton as he got in his car and left.

Burton followed up with Sophia and got her resume' which was very impressive. She was working, had plans on going back to school and taking care of her three children. Sophia was quite an ambitious young lady. After they interviewed, he decided to hire her on a part time basis. Lacey had been saying that she needed some help and now Burton felt like he had found someone he wanted to hire. She said she could be available when not working their other job. Janet needed care and supervision around the clock. Either he was going to do it or he was going to pay somebody to do it.

He had no help or support from any other family members. It was all on him. He asked Sophia if she could come to the house for a few hours on the weekend when she got off work. Sophia agreed to come on the following Saturday for orientation, and the first day of her new part time job caring for Janet. Burton discussed with Lacey that she could have the day off and that he had someone to come in to take care of Janet for a while. The following Saturday Sophia showed up for work. She drove into the back yard, got out of her car and knocked on the back door. Lacey answered.

"Hi," Sophia said. "I'm here to see Mr. LeFlore. I'm here to help out with his mom."

"Yea I'm Lacey," said Lacey. "And you are?"

"I'm Sophia," Sophia said. "Is he here?"

"He's up in his room," Lacey said. "I'll tell him you're here."

"Thank you," said Sophia.

"Matter or fact can you loan me ten dollars," Lacey said. "I got something I need to do."

"Um sure I think I have ten dollars," replied Sophia.

"You know what," Lacey said. "I don't have a ride. Can you let me get your car keys for a minute, I won't be gone long."

"Um here's ten dollars," Sophia said. "Can you be sure to pay me back."

"Yea. I'm gonna pay you back," Lacey said. "And I'm going to get Burton for you. Come on in."

"Thank you," Sophia replied. "This is a nice house. Where is Mrs. LeFlore?"

"She's back here," Lacey said. "Come with me, I'll show you. I want to let you know if you try any funny business with Mamma, you got me to deal with."

"I'm just trying to help," Sophia said. "I'm a licensed CNA, and I care for patients day in and day out. I'm not up to any funny business."

"Just making sure," Lacey said. "By the way can I get your car keys I need to make a quick run."

"My keys," said Sophia.

"Yea, I'll get Burt for you in a minute. Let me show you what's going on with Mrs. LeFlore if you're supposed to be working."

"Yes, I'm supposed to be working this afternoon," Sophia said.

"I just turned her about fifteen minutes ago," Lacey said. "I also changed her a little earlier, so she should be fine. Every time you turn her you need to write it down in this notebook along with whatever else you did. All of her supplies are over here if you need to change her. Mamma's formula is over here if her feeding bag gets low. You say you're a CNA so you should know what to do."

"Is Mr. LeFlore here?"

"I said I'd get him for you," Lacey said. "So how much is he paying you?"

"He asked me not to discuss that with you," said Sophia.

"Oh yea, he told you not to discuss that with me," Lacey said. "I'm going to go and get him so you can talk to him. You think I can get them keys. I got something in need to do real quick. I won't be gone long."

"You don't have a car," Sophia said as she handed Lacey ten dollars.

"That's irrelevant," Lacey said. "Can I borrow your car? I'll be right back."

"Sure," Sophia said as she reached in her purse and handed Lacey her keys. "I don't have much gas in there."

"I told you I won't be gone long," said Lacey. "I'll put some gas in there."

"Can you get Mr. LeFlore," Sophia asked.

"I'm going to get him for you," said Lacey. "Hey, Mamma. This is, what did you say your name was again?"

"Sophia," replied Sophia.

"This is Sophia," Lacey said. "She's going to be here with you while I'm gone. If she doesn't take good care of you, you let me know. When you turn her be sure to tuck the cover under her arm."

"Trust me, she's going to be alright," Sophia replied.

"Hi Mrs. LeFlore," Sophia said. "I'm Sophia your son hired me to come here and help out with you. You sure are a pretty lady. It's so nice to meet you."

"I'm going to go upstairs and let him know you're here," Lacey said. "I'll be back soon."

"Thank you," said Sophia as she started to familiarized herself with everything.

Lacey knocked on Burton's door. She said she was leaving and that somebody was downstairs waiting to see him. "She said she was here to watch Mamma for me while I'm gone."

Burton awoke from his sleep when Lacey knocked. He put on his clothes and went downstairs to meet Sophia. Lacey was gone when Burton got downstairs. He found Sophia seated in the large lazy boy chair near Janet's bed. She was dressed in her uniform and reading a book.

"Hi Sophia," said Burton.

"Hey, Mr. LeFlore," said Sophia.

"You've met my mom?" Burton asked. "Mom, did you meet Sophia? She's going to be coming in part time to work here with you."

"Yes," Sophia replied. "She's very pretty. You didn't tell me your mom was so pretty."

"Did you hear that, Mom," Burton said as he stood by Janet's bed. "Sophia said you're very pretty."

"She's adorable," said Sophia.

"Thank you," Burton said. "Did she say anything to you?"

"Not really," replied Sophia.

"Mom, you're not talking today," Burton said. "Why don't you say hi to Sophia?"

"Hi," said Janet.

"Did you hear that," Burton said. "She said hi to you. I wish you could have met her before she got down like this. She was also very active until about a year or so ago."

"Miss Lacey pretty much showed me where everything was," Sophia said. "She said to write everything down in the notebook over there."

"So, you met Lacey," said Burton.

"Yes, I don't think she likes me though," said Sophia.

"Why do you say that?" asked Burton.

"I don't know," Sophia said. "She wasn't very nice. She did ask me how much you were paying me, and I told her you said not to discuss that with her."

"She already asked you how much I was paying you," Lacey said. "She didn't beat around the bush huh."

"Then she borrowed ten dollars from me," said Sophia.

"She asked you for ten dollars," Burton replied. "She just got paid yesterday. She shouldn't need to borrow any money."

"That's okay," Sophia said. "She said she would pay me back."

"Is she still here?" asked Burton.

"No, I think she left," Sophia said. "She borrowed my car too."

"She...she borrowed your car," Burton said. "Sophia. Hold up, you let her borrow your car?"

"She said she would be right back," said Sophia.

"First of all, Sophia," Burton said. "Don't let Lacey punk you. You're here to help with my mom. You're not here to loan her money and please don't let her borrow your car again. I don't even think she has a valid driver's license. If she wrecks your car, you'll be around here with no way to get your kids around or go to work. I'm so sorry Sophia. Lacey complains about not having any help, but when I try to bring in help. she gets an attitude about it. I appreciate everything she does to help me with my mom, but I need the extra help and so does she. Please don't allow her to intimidate you. You're working for me, not her. Just remember that."

"It's alright. I'm good," said Sophia.

"Okay well I'm going to go upstairs and lay down for a little while," Burton said. "It was a long week, and I was up late with my mom last night. If you need anything just let me know."

"We'll be fine," said Sophia.

"Don't mind Lacey," Burton said. "She's harmless. But if I were you though, I wouldn't let her borrow your car again."

"She promised me she would be right back," said Sophia.

"If you want anything to drink there's some juice and sodas in the refrigerator," Burton said. "You're welcome to it."

"Thanks, but I've got my water," said Sophia.

"It's nice to have you," Burton said. "I'll be upstairs if you need me."

Sophia worked with Janet for several hours. During that time, she had to change her once. She had to turn her a few times. She also emptied the urine from the bag that was attached to her catheter. Janet was calm and relatively relaxed today. She did not put up much of a fuss while Sophia was working with her. The television was on and for the most part Janet lay there watching television and quietly rubbing her hands along the covers on her bed. When Sophia was not working with Jane, she sat there in the chair near her bed reading her book and occasionally glancing up at the television.

Burton came downstairs a few times to check on Janet and to see how Sophia was doing, but for the most part he stayed upstairs in his room. It was a while before Lacey returned to the house. Actually, Lacey did not return until right about the time when Sophia was scheduled to leave. Overall, it appeared that Sophia had done a pretty good job caring for Janet during her shift, and Burton hoped she would not be dissuaded by Lacey behavior toward her into not returning to work at the house again. Lacey did return her car to her in one piece.

Later that evening Lacey approached Burton in the kitchen. She wanted to discuss Sophia and how much he was paying her. Lacey seemed sad as if she was about to cry. She stood there, eyes sobbing and her nose red. Burton knew right then what was coming. Although he did not want to have the conversation he was about to have, he knew it was coming. Lacey sat at the kitchen counter. Instead of walking away, Burton decided to stay and hear her out.

"I see you've hired little miss thang to help you with Mamma," said Lacey.

"Little miss thang?" Burton replied. "Are you talking about Sophia?"

"Yea Sophia," Lacey said. "Whatever."

"What about her?" asked Burton.

"I asked her how much you were paying her," Lacey said. "You told her not to discuss it with me."

"Yea and I really think it was inappropriate for you to ask her that," Burton replied. "And she said you borrowed ten dollars from her when you just got paid yesterday."

"Burt, I bust my ass for you taking care of Mamma," Lacey replied. "I'm here all the time making sure your mom is cared for, and I hardly ever even ask for a day off. Then you hire somebody and you pay them in a day practically what you pay me in a whole week."

"Lacey, you have voiced to me that occasionally you need some time off. I know you need some time off," Burton said. "I appreciate you immensely, but I need some time off sometimes too. As you know caring for my mom right now is a pretty big responsibility. I'm just trying to get some dependable consistent part time help so we both can have a little time off. You act like you got a problem with that."

"I don't have a problem with that," Lacey said. "It just hurts when I realize you're paying someone for a few hours of work practically what you're paying me in a week when you could just pay me that money."

"Despite what you may think," Burton said. "I don't have all the money in the world. I'm paying you. I'm paying other people. I got children to support. I got bills. I buy your cigarettes. I try and keep food in the house for you to eat, and I pay you a weekly or monthly salary. You do a tremendous job, but I'm not in a position to pay you anything more than what I'm paying you now and you deserve to have some time off sometimes. You complain about not having any help and then I get you some help and then you complain about that."

"I'm not complaining," Lacey said. "I'm just saying that really bothers me."

"If you ask me, you're concerning yourself with the wrong things," said Burton.

"You like her, don't you?" asked Lacey.

"I think she's very professional," Burton said. "And she did a pretty good job with my mom today."

"No that's not what I'm talking about," Lacey said. "You like her. You think she's all that, and like I'm just some garbage or something. 'She's very professional.'"

"Nobody said anything about you being garbage," Burton said. "Whoever, said that? I just told you, and I tell you all the time that you're doing a tremendous job. Please don't try to put words in my mouth. She came here and worked one day, and you've been here over a year now, here with me day in and day out. Don't be ridiculous."

"At least you recognize," Lacey said. "Alright. Hey, are you planning on going out tonight?"

"No," Burton said. "Why?"

"Burt, would you mind getting me a few beers?" asked Lacey.

"Lacey," Burton said. "You said you were in recovery."

"I am," Lacey said. "I haven't had anything to drink in over a month. I just would like to sit here and have a few beers tonight, come on. I'll give you the money if you'll go and get them for me. Please."

"Lacey the first thing you told me when you started working here was that you where an alcoholic and you were trying to keep alcohol out of your life."

"I am Burt," Lacey said. "I just want a couple beers. I'll be alright I promise you. I can handle a few beers. It's liquor I can't handle."

"Jayla said there are some people who should not be drinking and you're one of them," said Burton.

"Burt, are you going to get me the beers or not?" Lacey said. "I just want a few beers. It's not a big deal. If you're going to be here and help me with Mamma tonight. I'll have a few beers, take a nap and be up early to take over when you go to bed."

"Alright I'll get you a few beers," said Burton.

"Thanks," replied Lacey.

"What do you want?" asked Burton.

"Just get me a few Bud twenty-four ounce in the can," said Lacey.

"Okay," Burton said. "I'll get em."

"Here's the money," Lacey said. "I'm going to go and turn Mamma. It's time to turn her again and I'm going to do her wound care for this evening. I'll be waiting here when you get back. Yea and I'm out of cigarettes too. Be sure and get me a pack of cigarettes."

Burton took the money and left for the store to get Lacey's beer and cigarettes. Lacey proceeded to go into Janet's room. Janet's bedroom was painted a bright vibrant yellow. Around the walls there was crown molding. Her floor was made of bamboo. When Burton renovated her room for her several years back, and took out her old carpet. Janet said she wanted hardwood floors in her room instead of carpet. They decided on light colored bamboo for the floor. She had several paintings hanging on the wall. For the most part her curtains remained closed except during the day when Lacey would open one of them partially to let a little sunlight in.

Janet's room was filled with supplies for her care. There were supplies for her wound care; a suction machine to suction her mouth; large plastic syringes to administer her medications and vitamins; boxes with cans of formula for her tube feedings; a machine which provided her with nutrition; diapers along with her bed pads. Inside her bathroom was a bathtub with a chair in it for elevation and a wheelchair both of which she no longer used. Janet's room was fully equipped for her care and maintenance.

"Hey, Mamma," Lacey said. "I'm back. So, I see Burt's hired little miss thang around here, but Mamma you know who's been here with you from day one right," Lacey said. "I know you need somebody to be there for you. Just between me and you, as long as he keeps his end of the bargain with me, I'm not going anywhere. I'm here with you Mamma," Lacey said. "You need me I'm here. I'm going to have to do your wound care now," said Lacey as she held Janet by the hand.

She peeled off the bandages. Janet's tried to reach back there and scratch it, but Lacey instinctively caught her hand and redirected her while she continued to remove the bandages and gauze. She poured the antiseptic into her open wound. Janet flinched as every time this was done it was absolutely agonizing and painful. She repacked the wound with gauze which was no less painful to Janet since her ass cheeks where there exposed. This entire wound care experience was an absolute necessity, but it was total and complete torture to Janet even with the occasional pain meds. No matter how old her nerves became from age, pain medication or psychological detachment wound care was always an excruciating ordeal for Janet. Lacey bandaged her left side and then flipped her over to her right side where she did the same thing again and once again it was extremely hurtful and distressing to Janet. Janet had to undergo this painful and excruciating experience on a daily basis.

"Mamma, don't be mad," Lacey said as Janet continued to fight her. "We're almost finished. I'm going to get your arm and then we'll be done. I just want him to appreciate me. Is that so much to ask for. I mean I'm there for you Mamma no matter what and, he just hires that little thang and thinks it's all good. I told her she better not be up to any funny business because you're my responsibility. I do what I have to do, and I'm accountable for me." Lacey continued as she poured some additional nutrition into her bag that supplied her food through a machine in a tube in her stomach. She changed her diaper even though it was not soiled. "Mamma, I love you like you were my own mother. I can't answer for what somebody else does," she said as she finished bandaging Janet's right side.

"Don't you worry, I'm here for whatever you need." She crushed up her meds, vitamins and cranberry azo added water to it and gave it to Janet through her tube. She gripped her fingers around the edge of the tube to stop any overflow. "Buddy Rho, get out of here. I'll be with you in a minute. What did I tell you, Buddy Rho?" said Lacey as she finished giving Janet a cocktail of medication and vitamins. "Buddy

Rho, what did I tell you! Mamma, let me go and see what Buddy Rho wants. I'll be right back," she said to Janet as she just listened and continued to lay there watching television and rubbing her hands along the side of the comforter on her bed. Janet liked to be talked to even if she did not reply.

Burton returned with the beer and cigarettes she wanted. Lacey took her Budweiser and had herself a drink. Burton went into the den and found a movie on television. They were up most of the night. Burton stayed up watching movies and Lacey drank her beer. Lacey had regressed somewhat on her pledge to remain sober. She was not back to her old ways by any stretch, but she was indulging occasionally. Burton made a good enabler because he was going to give her what she wanted as long as she made sure Janet was good. Burton totally understood that he had to set up an environment where Lacey was happy and content. As long as he could continue to do this, he was reasonably certain she would remain and continue taking care of Janet.

However, Burton did tell Lacey that if she started drinking again, he would not allow her to continue working there at the house. He understood that she needed a break sometimes, but for the most part he needed someone with sober judgment to care for Janet. On the few occasions that she had consumed alcohol at the house, he noticed that she could drink like a fish. She would drink and drink and drink. Once after having had a considerable amount of beer, he heard loud noises of her vomiting in the back yard.

During Thanksgiving Burton brought a twelve pack. He drank two beers and a friend came over and he drank two beers. Lacey found out he had the beer in his truck. She asked if she could have one and Burton agreed. The next morning when he awoke the entire twelve pack was gone. Lacey was one of those people who as they drink, and the alcohol started to take effect, they start to think they were charming when in actuality, the people around them see them as obnoxious and a bit of an ass hole. However, this particular night was uneventful. She drank her beer and he took care of Janet.

As Janet continued to remain in a persistent vegetative state her legs continued to get more and more contracted. She was now basically in a fetal position. The bones in her legs had become brittle as her legs were practically fused together. She could no longer extend her legs because her knees were fixed in a bent position. It was also difficult to get her legs apart. Lacey and Burton usually kept a pillow between her legs to make her more comfortable and to keep her legs from rubbing together. When turning Janet, they would usually take one arm and put it behind her neck and the other arm would go between her legs and beneath her knees. Janet had to be turned approximately twelve times per day during a twenty-four-hour period. She would not do this on her own anymore. If let alone she, would remain in the same position indefinitely without moving or repositioning her own body.

One morning Burton woke up and realized that he had fallen asleep before turning Janet for the last time. He went downstairs to check on her. Lacey was still asleep. He checked Janet's notebook and saw that she had not been turned since the last time he turned her earlier that night. He went into Janet's room and found her also asleep. As much as he hated to disturb her rest, he pulled the covers off her and took her into his arms. He lifted Janet into the air and turned her onto her right side.

Janet did not want to be bothered and looked at him in an angry manner. He assured her that he was almost finished and he was going back to bed. When Burton tried to separate her legs a little so he could put the pillow between her legs, he heard something go pop. He stood there for a minute half asleep trying to figure out what was wrong. It did not take long for him to figure out that he had broken her femur. Lacey came into the room yawning and still half sleep followed by her dog Buddy Rho.

"I think her leg is broken," said Burton.

"Her leg's not broken," said Lacey.

"Oh yes it is," replied Burton.

"What makes you think her leg is broken?" asked Lacey.

"Trust me it is," said Burton.

"Well don't look at me," Lacey said. "I didn't break her leg."

"I didn't say you broker her leg," replied Burton.

"Oh okay," Lacey said. "What makes you think her leg is broken?"

"I turned her just a minute ago," Burton said. "I was trying to separate her legs a little so I could get the pillow in and I heard a pop. It was her bone. I know it was."

"Are you sure," said Lacey. "Oh, Mamma. I know you must be in pain. Burt give me some of her pain meds so I can give her some in case she's in pain."

"Yea, you know how stiff her leg was before," Burton said. "Now look how easily its moving."

"Oh, my goodness," Lacey said. "Her bone is protruding out of her wound. You can see it."

"I got to try and get her to the hospital," Burton said with a yawn. "I'm so tired."

"I'm up now. Do you want me to go to the hospital with her?" asked Lacey.

"It would probably be better if I go with her," Burton said. "I haven't slept hardly any at all last night," Burton replied. "Let me just get about two or three hours of sleep and then I'll call an ambulance so we can get her to the hospital."

"There's no more Narco down here," Lacey said. "Give me a few before you go back to sleep. I'll give them to her and I'll keep a close eye on her until you get back up."

Burton went upstairs and got a few hydrocodone pills out of his room. He gave them to Lacey so he could administer them to Janet. Burton kept the Narco in his room and did not keep it with Janet's other medicine and vitamins. He did not want Lacey to give her too much pain medication. He would only give her a certain amount per day to give to Janet, and keep the rest locked away in his bedroom. Lacey crushed one and mixed it with water and gave it to Janet as quickly as she could.

A few hours afterward, Burton awoke and called an ambulance to come and get Janet. They went to the Emergency Room. Janet was evaluated and it was determined that her femur was in fact broken. A jagged edge of her bone continued to protrude out of the side of her hip. You could literally see it sticking out as Lacey had indicated earlier. Janet was admitted to the hospital where she was seen by an orthopedic surgeon. They indicated there was not much they could do, and did not really expect it to heal. Burton got a little upset with the hospital staff the first day because they made her go over twenty-four-hour hours without receiving her nutrition through her tube. Burton asked them why they had not provided her with any nutrition. He told them he did not bring his mother to the hospital for them to starve her.

Janet was later taken to surgery where they basically shaved down the two jagged edges of her femur. The doctors told Burton there was no expectation that her bone would actually heal or fuse back together given her current condition. Since she no longer walked or ambulated anymore it was not necessary that they do anything to try and get the bone to heal.

Janet was not in the hospital for very long and was back home shortly after her surgery. Although it was unfortunate that Burton had broken her leg, in a way it was like a small blessing in disguise. Her legs had become so stiff and literally fused. The fact that her femur was detached on one leg made it easier for them to separate her legs when necessary. Whereas before it was practically impossible to separate her legs. Lacey stayed there in the hospital with Janet for those few days, but she still had a little break too since the majority of her care was up to the hospital staff while she had been there. Luckily, Janet did not appear to be in much more pain than usual after her surgery and return home.

CHAPTER NINE

Meanwhile, Janet had been home from the hospital after her surgery for a few weeks. One Saturday night Burton fried some fish, shrimp, and french-fries for dinner. Sandy was there at the house helping him with Janet. Sandy would come over to the house occasionally, but not too often because she claimed Lacey was not cordial to her. Over the time that Lacey had been there working, the relationship between Sandy and Lacey was amicable, and yet somewhat strained. Sandy did not really like Lacey and perhaps still wanted to be the person doing her job. Lacey did not necessarily like Sandy and had been very dry toward her because; according to Lacey, she still did not appreciate the way Sandy had acted toward her when she first started working for Burton.

Sandy had been there helping him with Janet most of the evening, and he had asked her to clean his room while she was there. Lacey was there at the house, but she was technically supposed to be off duty at the time. She had been in her room resting and had also got her hands on a few beers. Sandy had finished cleaning Burton's bedroom and he was about to take her home. Burton offered her some of the fried fish, shrimp, oysters that he had cooked. He and Sandy sat there at the kitchen table eating when Lacey came into the kitchen.

"Burt, I'm hungry can I have some?" asked Lacey.

"Sure, help yourself," said Burton.

"Thanks," Lacey said as she got a plate and started to get some food.

"Did you wash your hands?" asked Sandy.

"What do you mean did I wash my hands?" asked Lacey.

"Did you wash your hands," Sandy said. "Looks like you got little dog hairs on your fingers."

"My hands are clean. I always keep my hands washed," Lacey replied. "Did you wash your hands?"

"But you carry Buddy Rho around all the time in your hands," Sandy said. "It's not fair to everybody else if you put your hands in the food when you probably just had them on that dog."

"I just got through washing my hands a few minutes ago," Lacey said as she piled some shrimp, fish and oysters onto her plate. "Thank you." Lacey sat down at the end of the table and started to eat.

"Burton is that going to be enough for you," Sandy said. "She didn't leave very much."

"I'm good," said Burton as he noticed Lacey starting to glare angrily at Sandy.

"You act like you don't want me to have any?" asked Lacey in an angry tone.

"No, I'm sorry I never said that," Sandy replied. "You're a pretty big girl. You don't look like you're missing any meals around here."

"You trying to be funny," Lacey said. "Dada dee dada."

"Dada dee dada dumb," replied Sandy.

"Would you please pass the hot sauce," said Burton trying to defuse the situation.

"Yea I'm a big girl who will beat your ass," replied Lacey.

"Burton I'm finished eating," Sandy said as she put her plate in the sink and started toward the den. "Your mother's caretaker seems like she got a problem with me so can you take me home now. Can you hurry up. I'll be down in the den waiting for you."

"Let me tell you something," Lacey said as she got up and started to follow Sandy into the den. "You need to watch who you're talking to."

"All I asked was if you had washed your hands," Sandy replied. "I don't believe I was talking to you any kind of way. I always try to be nice and respectful to everyone. Even you."

"Just like that shit you said about my stankin' daughter laying on his sofa,'" Lacey said. "You got the wrong one baby. I've been putting up with your shit ever since I started working here and I'm not putting up with it anymore."

"Burton please come and take me home now," Sandy said. "You need to get me away from this crazy ass woman right now before I'mma have to hurt her."

"Bitch what you gonna do," Lacey said as she charged in Sandy's direction. "I'm not scared of you. I'm a big girl and I will beat the shit out of you."

"Lacey what are you doing?" Burton said. "Leave her alone. There isn't going to be any fighting in my house."

"It's obvious that you've been drinking," Burton said. "You need to chill out now."

"I'm tired of her fucking shit," Lacey said. "Ever since I've been working here. I'm not putting up with it. You want her to come and take care of Mrs. LeFlore then let her come and take care of her. She's not going to disrespect me, especially not on my damn job."

"Bitch you better put a little more distance between me and you or you might get slapped," said Sandy.

"I'll be the last bitch you slap," said Lacey.

"You're the one who came running up on me like you want to fight," Sandy said. "I'm not trying to fight you. But if you put your hands on me. Lawd have mercy."

"Lacey, you need to back off her," Burton said as he tried to step between the two of them. "Come on let me take you home. There isn't going to be any slapping or fighting."

"All this anger" Sandy said. "I just asked you if you'd washed your hands."

"Muthafucker, I wash my damn hands," Lacey said. "You don't have to ask me shit about have I washed my hands."

"Come on let me take you home," said Burton.

"Bye Lacey," Sandy said. "I hope you feel better."

"Respect is due to a dog," said Lacey.

"You got a lot of respect for that dog," said Sandy.

"Don't worry about my damn dog," replied Lacey. "He never did anything to you. Come here Buddy Rho."

"Sandy stop," Burton said. "Come on let's go."

"Buddy Rho did you hear what I said," said Lacey.

"I'll turn my mom when I get back," said Burton as he went out the door with Sandy.

On the way to her house, Burton apologized to Sandy for the way Lacey had behaved toward her. Very often during the time since Lacey had started working there, Burton had asked Sandy to apologize. Lacey's behavior that evening was totally uncalled for and inappropriate. Caregiver or not, Burton was not going to tolerate her lashing out at anyone in his house like that, especially when he knew that she had been drinking. In all truthfulness, she did have her hands on her dog quite frequently. Burton worried about whether or not she washed her hands and wore gloves when she was working with Janet.

Asking her if she had washed her hands when she practically took her fingers and dug into the food was not totally illogical or unwarranted. The manner in which she responded was unacceptable. He dropped Sandy off at her house and returned home. He watched movies on his computer in his bedroom and went into Janet's room about once every hour to check on her. Burton stayed up most of the night with Janet. Lacey stayed in her room for the most part and the two of them did not talk again that night.

Janet appeared to be recovering from having had her leg broken. Basically, now her femur was not attached anymore. She did not appear to be in any pain as a result of it. Burton was not sure anymore. He thought he could read her signs pretty well. This new formality actually made it a little easier to clean her and care for her. Although now when turning Janet, they had to be exceptionally careful not to just let her leg flop in any direction.

Both of her knees where brittle and locked more less in a bent position. Her right leg she did not move, and was becoming more contracted as the days and weeks and months went by. Burton was clearly aware that Janet would likely not be there with him much longer. He tried to mentally prepare himself, and yet it really was not about him. Janet was laying there before him having practically completely succumbed to the devastation of Alzheimer's.

That night Burton kissed his mom on her forehead every time he went into her room to check on her. He stood there just looking at her in the darkness as he could see her eyes as the light of the television behind him. Her television stayed on all the time. She did not like when the television was not on. Janet was also very much aware of Burton's presence. She appreciated and felt all the love he showed her.

She wanted to continue to live for him. Janet had practically forgotten everything she knew or had known in her life. But she always remembered Burton. Burton was all she had. She also remembered the round face and black hair of the lady who always came in there calling her Mamma. After turning her, he would just stroke his hand on her head and kiss her again and again on her forehead and cheek and tell her that he loved her.

He sensed and could clearly ascertain from her condition that it was possible that Janet was not going to live much longer. Sometimes he felt selfish for wanting to hold on to her even though her quality of life was so diminished at this point. Burton struggled to understand what Janet might be feeling at this point in her life, since she rarely said a word anymore. One thing is for sure, Janet had always made him feel loved. Now he just wanted to make sure that she felt loved.

Burton had watched his dad die some fourteen years prior and now after all this time he was watching his mother die. Janet was dying a slow and painless death. Alzheimer's had attacked her brain and nervous system. Over the years he had watched Janet forget and forget and forget. She struggled to maintain simple memories and recollection. Janet marveled at the times when she could remember everything, and now she had forgotten how to use the bathroom on her own, and how to walk. Janet had forgotten how to perform core human functions like what is practically an innate response for a person to turn themselves occasionally in bed even while sleeping.

Her nervous system was also making it more difficult for her to perform in a normal manner. But there she was still fighting and still holding onto life. Janet had been on a feeding tube for over a year. Burton was witnessing his mother's transition and frankly it was not easy for him. He longed for the days when he lived together in their old house on Davis Avenue. The days when he lived with his dad, mom and brother. His brother Champ and his father Walker were gone, and it was becoming increasingly evident that Janet was soon to join them.

The summer arrived and Burton's son Bryceton finished his first year at Ole Miss. Burton picked Bryceton up in New Orleans and he came to visit for the summer in Mobile. Burton was very happy to finally have his son, at least one of them there to with him. Ironically Bryceton was Burton's son, that was born not long after his brother Champ had passed away. Bryceton was now Nineteen years of age and had asked Burton if he would consider buying him a car.

Although at this point Bryceton did not have his driver's license, and did not know how to drive. He had done well in school that year and had stayed out of trouble. Burton was proud of Bryce and glad to have him at the house with him. It was a chance for the two of them to bond after a rather lengthy separation. Over the last few years since Candace moved away from Mobile, Burton had not seen his children as often as he would have liked. The stress between the two of them coupled with her unwillingness to allow Burton to spend time with them unless she tagged along coupled with Burton's increased amount of responsibility placed on him by

Janet's needs had resulted in long bouts of separation with his kids.

Burton brought Bryce to the house. As soon as he got him settled into his room, he took him downstairs to Janet's room so he could see his grandmother Janet. She was now a far cry from the lady he once knew. The lady who used to raise hell with them when they were little and being bad. The lady who busted his Candace's windshield with her broom handle. The beautiful lady whos pictures hung throughout the house. Bryce was surprised and did not know exactly how to respond or react. Burton urged him to speak to her. They saw Lacey in the kitchen on their way downstairs to see Janet.

"Lacey, I want you to meet my son Bryceton," Burton said. "Bryceton this is Lacey. Lacey helps me with you grandmother."

"It's nice to meet you, Bryceton," Lacey said. "My you're so tall and handsome."

"Nice to meet you Lacey," said Bryceton as the two of them shook hands.

"Mom, guess who's here?" Burton asked. "It's Bryceton. Do you see Bryce. Tell her hello. Don't be scared."

"Hi, Grandma Janet," Bryceton said. "It's me Bryceton."

"Mom, say hi to Bryceton," said Burton. Janet focused her eyes on her grandson but she did not say anything right away. "You remember Bryceton don't you?" Janet nodded her head in the affirmative.

"Hi, Grandma," said Bryceton.

"Say something, Mom," said Burton.

"Hi," replied Janet.

"Did you hear that," Burton replied. "Did you hear that Bryce. She said hi to you. She doesn't really talk much anymore."

"It's good to see you, Grandma," said Bryce. Janet perked up and looked at him.

"It's been a long time since you've seen her," said Burton.

"Yea it has," Bryceton replied as he pointed to the nutrition pump. "What is that?"

"She's on a feeding tube now," said Burton.

"A feeding tube," said Bryceton.

"She doesn't take much food orally anymore," Burton said. "Most of her nutrition is pumped directly into her stomach."

"Wow food, food is good man," Bryceton said. "I'm hungry right now. I don't know what I would do if I couldn't eat food."

"We also give her medicine through this tube," said Burton.

"Wow," Bryecton said. "A lot has changed since back in the day."

"Yes, a lot has changed and yet much stays the same," Burton said. "It's just life going through the motions. She doesn't get out of bed anymore. I know she's happy to see you though."

"I'm happy to see her," Bryceton said. "I am kind of hungry though."

"We'll get something to eat," Burton replied. "I just wanted you to see your grandmother."

"It's time for Mamma's wound care," Lacey said as she walked into the room. "Why don't you guys come back and visit with her in a little while after I'm finished."

"Wound care?" asked Bryceton.

"Come on let's go and get something to eat," said Burton.

"You know I don't eat meat anymore," Bryceton said. "I've cut meat completely out of my diet."

"That doesn't surprise me," Burton said. "I knew this day was coming when you would tell me that. Your grandmother doesn't eat meat anymore either."

"Y'all go ahead and get something to eat," Lacey said. "I'll be here doing Mamma's wound care."

Early that morning Bryceton awoke. Janet was on his mind. He went down into her room and just stood there for a moment looking at her trying to comprehend what life was really all about. His grandmother was there before him alive and yet almost dead. Even though nothing on her body seemed to move except her arms and head. She lay there looking at him as though she had something to say to him. He wondered to himself, what she would want to say to him, but his dad said she did not talk much anymore.

Bryceton wondered if he should try and talk to her and if she would respond to him. He said hello to Janet but she did not reply. She did however continue to gaze at him. She did appear to have something to say to him, but she did not utter a word. Bryceton remained there in the room with Janet for a while. It was not long before Lacey came in to turn her again.

"Good morning, Bryce," Lacey said. "How are you?"

"I'm fine," Bryceton replied. "How are you?"

"I'm good," Lacey said. "How's Mamma doing?"

"She's just laying there looking at me," said Bryceton.

"That's good" Lacey said. "I guess that means she's doing just fine."

"Mamma, let me check you out and make sure you haven't made a mess," said Lacey.

"It's been a long time since I've seen my grandmother, but I never imagined this," said Bryceton.

"This is all I have ever known of your grandmother," Lacey said. "I never knew her when she was a younger woman."

"Man, my grandma didn't take no shit," Bryceton said. "She was a kind person, but she didn't take any shit off me and my brothers and we knew it. Now she can hardly move."

"All you can do is love her and be there for her Bryce," Lacey said. "Your dad talks about you and your brothers all the time. He loves you guys so much. It's nice to finally meet another one of his children. I met your oldest brother and his girlfriend. They came to visit a few months ago."

"Yea you mean Breton and Verina," Bryceton said. "You met them."

"Yes, I met them and it's nice to meet you," said Lacey.

"Yea it's been a while," said Bryceton.

"So, you were in college right?" asked Lacey.

"Yea I was in college this year at Ole Miss," replied Bryce.

"That's great," Lacey said. "I know your grandmother must be proud of you. Your dad tells me she taught chemistry at community college. What are you majoring in?"

"I don't know," Bryceton said. "I was going to major in pre-med but my dad said I should get my general requirements out of the way and then declare my major. Truthfully, I'm just sick of school right now."

"Well school is better than a lot of the other alternatives," said Lacey.

"Yea it's alright I just feel like I need a break," said Bryceton.

"Your grandmother is glad to see you this morning," Lacey said. "They say being around young people, especially your children and grandchildren is good for elderly people. Part of Gods plan."

"Why does suffering and death have to be part of God's plan?" asked Bryeton.

"If I had the answer to that question, I would be a multimillionaire," Lacey replied. "If you figure it out let me know. Can you help me turn her?"

"Sure," said Bryceton.

"All you have to do is lift her up behind her back and legs and turn her over to her other side," Lacey said. "Lift her long enough so I can replace this pad under her. Can you handle that without hurting her. Be careful not to lay her on this feeding tube."

"Sure," replied Bryceton.

"Now she's going to pull at you and tug at you," Lacey said. "Just pick her up and turn her over to her left side."

"Not a problem," Bryceton said as he lifted Janet and turned her onto her other side. "Why do you have to turn her like this?"

"Because she won't turn herself anymore," Lacey said. "She has bed sores. You see that, those are her sores. She has them on her rear end, her arm and her ankles. It's very important those sores don't get worse or become infected."

"How long has she been like this?" Bryceton asked. "This is not the Grandma Janet I remember at all."

"Ever since I've been here, and I've been here almost a year and a half now," said Lacey.

"A year and a half," said Bryceton.

"Over a year and a half," said Lacey.

"Wow," Bryceton said. "So, this is what old age is all about."

"It could be better and it could be worse," Lacey replied. "Seems to me like the wheel of life and death doesn't always depend on a person's age. It's just a matter of when it's your time or not."

"I got her turned," Bryceton said. "I'm going to go upstairs and take a shower and wait for my dad to get up and see what he's talking about. I'll talk to you later."

"For sure Bryce," Lacey said. "I'm going to finish with Mamma and lay it back down for a minute myself."

"Okay I'll talk with you later," said Bryceton.

"You didn't tell your grandma bye," said Lacey.

"Bye, Grandmother," Bryceton said. "I'll be back down a little later to see you."

The next day Burton set aside some time to start teaching his child to drive. Bryceton was nineteen years old and he had never driven a vehicle. He did not take driver's education in high school, and he did not even have his drivers permit. Burton had to take him to the DMV so that he could obtain a permit to drive. He planned to start allowing him to get behind the wheel of his truck and teaching this boy how to drive as soon as he could. Burton wanted to buy him a car. Bryceton had done well in school, and had overall been a tremendous kid. He was helpful with his younger brothers and overall an exemplary teenager.

Burton wanted to try and get him a car to drive back to school while he was there in Mobile. As the weeks went by, Bryceton was learning how to drive but he still had not got his driver's license yet. Burton had also not made much progress toward his goal of buying him a car. They had looked at a few cars, but Burton was having some credit issues. Burton had been inundated with the cost of paying Lacey and other caregivers to help him with Janet. Although, Janet had some income her money only went to so far. Everything else on top of that was on Burton. He also had child support to pay and had endured a lengthy and costly divorce. He had also spent some of his own money on his campaigns for elected office. Burton was maintaining financially but his credit score was not where it needed to be in order for him to purchase the vehicle that he wanted for Bryceton.

Bryceton spent a lot of time at home with Janet and Lacey while Burton was at work. Lacey and Bryceton got along pretty well. A few weeks into Bryceton's visit, Lacey got ill, and had to go to the hospital for several days. Lacey was not in the best health herself, she suffered from diabetes and high blood pressure. When Lacey went to the hospital, Burton was forced to stay home from work for almost a week to care for Janet.

Although Burton was upset because he needed to go to work, he greatly enjoyed spending a few days at home with his son and Janet. Burton prepared some meals for he and Bryceton to eat while they were at the house. He and Bryceton spent a lot of time talking and watching movies together. They also spent a lot of time with Janet in her room. Although Burton did not ask Bryceton to take on any of the responsibility of Janet's care. He just appreciated having his son there with him and was glad to have a few days away from work to focus all of his time on his son and his mom.

During this time, Burton was not able to round up any of his part time help during the early part of the week so he did it all himself for several days straight. Burton did Janet's wound care every day; adjusted and monitored her feeding pump; gave her meds and vitamins; combed her hair; did her oral care; emptied her catheter bag; changed her; met with the home health care people when they came in and made sure she was turned every two hours. Burton was exhausted after a few days but he was determined he was going to do the bulk of it while Lacey was gone. During this time Burton also developed a greater appreciation for Lacey. He greatly appreciated Lacey but disliked feeling like he was dependent on her to care for Janet. He was determined that he was going to make sure she was cared for as good if not better.

"How much longer is Lacey supposed to be in the hospital?" asked Bryceton.

"I'm not sure," Burton replied. "Possibly a few more days."

"You think we can go and look at some cars while your off work?" asked Bryceton.

"Bryce how am I going to go and look at cars," Burton said. "I can't leave your grandmother here by herself, and I don't have anybody to stay here with her right now."

"I don't know," Bryceton said. "I just kind of want to get out of the house for a while. We haven't really been anywhere in the last few days."

"I understand and you're perfectly welcome to get out for a while if you want," Burton said. "I've seen you studying your driver's license handbook. Are you ready to take your license test? If you had your license, you could use my truck, but I can't just go off and leaver your grandmother here at the house by herself."

"Is there anything I can do to help?" asked Bryceton.

"Possibly," Burton said. "But I got it under control right now. You just take it easy."

"If there's anything you need me to do just let me know," said Bryceton.

"Just go in there and hang out with her and talk to her," Burton replied. "She might not say anything back, but she hears what you're saying. She might not be here with us much longer."

"Okay," said Bryceton.

"I appreciate you keeping me company," Burton said. "It's been a long time. It's good to have you home with me for the summer."

"It's good to be here too Dad," said Bryceton.

"It's cold in here," Burton said. "It's way too cold in here for your grandmother. I told Lacey to stop turning the air up so high even though it is summertime. It's way too cold in here for her. Bryce, will you turn the air down a little bit."

"Yea, it is chilly in here," Bryce said. "I got it."

"Thanks," Burton replied. "Your grandmother never liked a lot of cold air and now she hardly moves. She can't have all this cold air blowing on her continuously like this."

"Those scallop potatoes from Sam's were pretty good weren't they," said Bryceton.

"Yea, they are pretty good," replied Burton.

"Did you want some more," Bryceton said. "Because there's not much left and I was going to finish it off."

"Yea, go ahead," said Burton.

"Dad, do you think grandmother knows and understands everything going on around her?" asked Bryce.

"I'm not sure what she knows and understands anymore," Burton said. "Right now, she's just still holding on to life, what life she has left to live."

"How old is grandmother now?" asked Bryce.

"She's 88," replied Burton.

"Wow 88 years old," Bryceton said. "She's lived a pretty long life. Otherwise, her health is good."

"If it was not for the Alzheimer's she'd probably live to be a lot older," said Burton.

"These scallop potatoes are the bomb," Bryceton said. "It's been almost a year now since I went completely vegan, and I feel incredible now that I don't have any meat in my system."

"Coming from a guy who refused to eat pork and red meat at the age of three," Burton said. "It doesn't surprise me that you have finally decided to become a complete vegetarian. I on the other hand my friend still like meat. You got to put a little meat in your life sometimes. For those who chose not to, I'm not mad at you, but as for me."

"You should try it just for a few days Dad," said Bryceton.

"I've tried it before," Burton said. "I just like meat. I like vegetables too. I like having a well- rounded diet of animal protein and vegetables."

"I hear you," Bryceton said. "Well, that's the last of the scalloped potatoes. I wish we had some more."

"We'll get some more. It was good," Burton said. "I'll be damned Buddy Rho used the bathroom in the house again. This has got to be the dumbest little dog I've ever seen in my life. Buddy Rho you're going to have to go outside for a little while."

"Lacey treats Buddy Rho like he's human," said Bryceton.

"Yea I believe he thinks he's a human," Burton said. "He seems to prefer using the bathroom in the house too, and I'm not going to be cleaning up shit after you Buddy Rho. You are going to have to go outside until you use the bathroom and that's that. I'm finished with your grandmother for now. Let's go and watch another movie."

The next day Burton was so exhausted, he decided to call Sophia and ask her if she could come in for a little while before she went to work. Sophia worked the night shift from Seven until Seven. He asked her if she could come in for a few hours before she went into work and do her wound care. She agreed to come in to work. As soon as she got there,

Burton went straight to bed. Sophia filled in and did Janet's wound care and turned her a few times.

Luckily, she had a bowel movement while Sophia was there so all of that happened on Sophia's watch. Burton was able to get some rest. Bryceton remained there at the house working on his computer. When it was time for her to leave, she knocked on Burton's door and said she was on her way into her job at the nursing care facility. Burton thanked her and asked her to be sure and come to work at her usual time on Saturday.

Finally, Lacey was released from the hospital that Friday. She returned to the house and was pleasantly surprised that Burton had done an impeccable job with Janet for those several days while she was gone. Lacey informed Burton that she was glad to be back home and could work with Janet, but was still not quite in a bit of pain. Her health was an issue and she was concerned. She had a list of medications prescribed for her which she asked Burton to have filled.

Burton agreed to pay her even though she had not worked at all that week. In all reality, Lacey put in a tremendous amount of time with Janet for the small amount of money he paid her. He went ahead and paid her so that she could get her medicine and some other things she needed when she got home. He assured her that she would be able to turn Janet at her usual intervals during the night while he rested. He had lined up Sophia to come into work on Saturday so that she could get some rest and focus on her own recovery now that she was back at work.

The next morning, Burton woke up at about 11 o'clock. He noticed some missed calls from Sophia on his phone. She was scheduled to be there at 10 o'clock. He went downstairs to see if she was in Janet's room. He found Janet there by herself. He looked at the notebook and noticed that Janet had not been turned since about 7 o'clock that morning. He looked in Lacey's room and she was fast asleep with Buddy Rho. He went upstairs and found Bryceton awake stirring around his room and on his computer.

"Bryceton, did you hear anyone ringing the doorbell this morning?" asked Burton.

"Yea I went downstairs and there was a lady at the door," said Bryceton.

"Why didn't you let her in?" asked Burton.

"I didn't have a key," replied Bryceton.

"Well why didn't you wake me up?" asked Burton.

"I knew you were asleep and I didn't want to disturb you," Bryceton said. "I thought Lacey would let her in."

"You just left her standing out there and you didn't say anything to me or Lacey," said Burton.

"I assumed Lacey was going to open the door for her," Bryceton said. "She usually opens the door when those people come by the house."

"Never assume anything or you might make an ass of you and me. Lacey's still not feeling too well," Burton said as he dialed Sophia. "Hey, Sophia, where are you?"

"Hi, Mr. LeFlore," Sophia said. "I came at 10 o'clock. Your son came to the door but he said he didn't have the key to open the door. I asked him to tell you I was there. I waited out there for a good twenty minutes and nobody came to let me in. I called your phone a few times but no answer."

"Hey. I'm sorry about that, I don't know why my son didn't tell me you were here," Burton said. "He said he thought Lacey was going to open the door."

"Is Lacey home from the hospital?" asked Sophia.

"She just got home yesterday," Burton said. "But I still really needed you to work today."

"I was headed home, told my boys I would take them the park," said Sophia.

"Oh man," said Burton.

"But I guess I could come on back," said Sophia.

"Thank you, thank you so much Sophia," Burton said. "I'm exhausted. I've been here all week with my mom and even though Lacey's back, she's still needing to get some rest. If you could work today, it would be a tremendous help. I'm sorry about what happened when you came out earlier. I'll be here, but I'll just leave the door open for you."

"Okay I'll be back over there in a minute," said Sophia.

"I can't believe you left her standing out there all that time," Burton said. "She's here to fill in with your grandmother. I'm tired as hell and Lacey's still not feeling her best. This is serious man."

"Sorry, Dad. I thought Lacey was going to let her in," said Bryceton.

"Think son," Burton said. "You got to think sometimes. It wouldn't have taken much to make sure that I knew she was here. That was so rude. This lady's coming here to do a job. I need some rest."

"Okay. Well next time I'll know," said Bryceton.

Sophia eventually got back to the house but was not able to stay as long as Burton had originally planned for her to stay. Burton took an opportunity to introduce Bryce to Sophia. He explained to Bryceton that Sophia was one of Janet's other caretakers. Bryceton apologized for having left her standing out there so long, and not having made sure somebody let her in the house. Sophia graciously accepted his apology, and went about doing her job with Janet for the remainder of the time she was there before having to go in to work at the nursing home.

The following Monday Burton returned to work. He had a lot to get caught up on. He worked late into the evening before returning home. When he got home Lacey approached him in the kitchen. She said that she had been feeling much better and thanked him for remaining there and continuing to care for Janet while she rested. She told Burton that she had something she wanted to discuss with him. Burton was not exactly sure what she wanted to discuss but he stopped and listened.

"Burt, I overheard your son arguing with his mom on the phone today," said Lacey.

"Arguing about what?" asked Burton.

"Well, it's not any of my business," Lacey said. "But this isn't the first time since he's been here."

"What are you talking about?" asked Burton.

"Well on several occasions I've overheard him arguing with his mom and every time it seems to be about him being here," Lacey said. "It seems that she keeps telling him to come back to Mississippi or wherever they live. He said he's not ready to go back yet."

"Why does she have a problem with him being here?" Lacey asked. "I think he's a very nice and polite young man."

"My ex-wife has tried to use my children to get back at me for divorcing her," Burton said. "She acts like she's so pissed that he came to visit me, but he's nineteen and doesn't have to ask her for permission to come and visit anymore. She told me the other day, the only reason he came here was to get a car."

"He's a nice young man," Lacey said. "I've been enjoying having him here. It was just a little disturbing to hear him arguing with her like that especially about something as simple as him coming to spend a few days with you."

"I know," Burton said. "It doesn't make any sense whatsoever. She's such a selfish person. I'm sorry to hear that she's stressing him out about being here. Thanks for telling me. I'll have a talk with him. How has mom been doing today?"

"She's been good," said Lacey.

"How about you," Burton asked. "How are you doing?"

"I'm feeling much better now," said Lacey.

"I'm glad to hear that," Burton said as he went into Janet's room to check on her. "I'm going to talk with Bryceton."

"You missed me didn't you, Mamma," said Lacey.

"How are you doing, Mom?" Burton said. "Has she been talking at all today."

"No, she hasn't said much today," Lacey replied. "But she was smiling and I could tell she was happy to see me. Looks like you did a pretty good job while I was gone though."

"Of course," Burton said. "That's my mom and I love her. I love you, Mom. Do you know how much I love you?"

"Lacey loves you too, Mamma," said Lacey.

"Hey, Dad. How are you?" asked Bryceton as he came into Janet's room.

"Hey, Bryce," said Burton.

"Do you think we can get something to eat," said Bryceton.

"Sure," Burton said. "Let me finish saying hello to your grandmother, and we'll go get something."

Burton and Bryceton went out to grab a bite to eat. Burton allowed him to drive as they were still working on improving his driving skills and getting his driver's license. Bryceton wanted to go to a nearby Indian Restaurant. Bryceton loved that restaurant. Every time his dad asked him if he wanted to go out and eat and where he wanted to go, he always said he wanted to go to the Indian restaurant.

Burton wanted to talk with him about what Lacey had brought to his attention. They went to the Indian restaurant and they discussed a few things pertaining to the conversation that Lacey said she overheard between Bryce and his mother. Bryceton said he had several arguments with his mom and that she was putting tremendous pressure on him to come home, but he was enjoying himself and wanted to stay longer.

Burton told him that he was enjoying having him there tremendously. Burton said he did want to buy him a car and that he felt he deserved help purchasing a vehicle, but he was unsure if he would be able to make it happen this time around. He wanted him to get his license and they would continue to look around, but his credit score was not really where it needs to be. Bryceton said he understood. He said he really wanted a car but if he was not able to do it at the time then he would just have to make do.

Burton assured him that he would try and buy him a car but he did not want him to be too disappointed if he was not able to buy him the car this summer. Burton really wanted to buy him a car. Unfortunately, he had already been turned down several times. He also knew that Janet could pass away any day now and despite a small amount of insurance she had, it would not be enough to bury her and he would have to come up with the rest.

About a week later, Lacey was in Janet's room working with her. It was about midnight. Bryceton was upstairs asleep. Burton had gone back over to his office for a little while. Lacey was trying to turn Janet and she was fighting against her. Lacey was tired and struggling to get her turned onto her other side so she could lay down. As Lacey turned Janet her tube got caught between Janet and the bed. Janet's feeding tube dislodged from her stomach. It came out completely.

Lacey panicked and tried to see if she could get it back in. It was not long before she realized the tube would have to be put back in by a doctor who knew what he was doing. She contacted Burton and told him Janet's tube had come out, and asked him what he thought they should do. Burton said he thought she might need to go to the hospital so they could put it back in. Burton rushed home and called an ambulance to take Janet to the emergency room.

The ambulance arrived. They asked Burton where they wanted to take her and he said to take her to Mobile Infirmary. The ambulance drivers said the emergency room at Mobile Infirmary was full, and it might be better to take her to Springhill Memorial Hospital. After briefly considering how long that wait might be at the Infirmary, he told them to take her to Springhill Memorial and that he would follow them in his truck. The ambulance left immediately to carry Janet to the hospital. Burton left the house headed to Springhill Memorial to meet his mother at the emergency room. On his way to the hospital, he ran out of gas on the service road.

By now it was about 3 or 4 o'clock in the morning. There was hardly any traffic on the road and there was no one he could call at that time of night to help him out. He called the emergency room at Springhill Memorial and explained to them that his mother Janet LeFlore was there in the emergency room because her feeding tube had come out. He said he was trying to get to the hospital but had run out of gas on the service road. After about an hour or so he was still out there trying to figure out how he was going to get some gas in his truck to get to the hospital.

Finally, a police officer came driving down the service road. Burton stopped the officer and explained the situation. He asked him if he would take him to the gas station to get some gas. The officer agreed. Burton got his gas and finally made it to the hospital. It was practically morning by then. He arrived at the hospital and the doctor said her tube was back in and she could go home now.

As Burton followed the ambulance back to the house, he was somewhat relieved that Janet was alright, and they had been able to get it done so quickly. They returned to the house with Janet brought back inside and the comfort of her bedroom. Lacey reconnected her tube to the pump and resumed her feeding since she had not received her nutrition now in over five or six hours. Burton was tired after this experience that had turned into a night of him sitting in the middle of the service road trying to figure out how he was going to get some gas to get to the hospital to be with Janet. Thank goodness for the police officer who finally gave him a ride to the gas station. Thank goodness Janet was back home and everything was back to normal.

The rest of the summer flew by with a quickness and it was not long before it was time for Bryceton to return to college. Burton had not been able to get him the car. However, Burton had a chance to spend some good quality time with his son who was now a young man in college. Burton really needed that time with his son. He had become so consumed with Janet and her care. It's almost like he had forgotten he even had children. He was so caught up in the sorrow of watching his mother on the verge of death that he had forgotten the sweet joy of watching his children as they embarked upon their lives and their future.

He had allowed himself to become distanced and alienated from his boys, and it had deeply troubled him. Bryceton himself had said to Burton that his boys were tremendous human beings, and in his opinion, they were the best and greatest thing he had ever done. Bryceton had spoken some real truth that time. It was the middle of August when Burton had to put Bryceton on a bus headed to New Orleans. His mother would pick him up in New Orleans and take him back to Ole Miss.

"Burt, you need to get Mamma some Mucinex when you go to the pharmacy," Lacey said. "She has a little congestion in her chest."

"You know we could just turn down the air conditioner a little," Burton said. "I'm sure she does have some congestion because it's freezing in here."

"It's not that cold in here to me," Lacey said. "But you know I get hot flashes all the time."

"Lacey, I know you said you get hot flashes and stuff but it's too cold in here," Burton said when he returned to the house. "My mom can't handle all that cold air. Plus, the fact you can't just run the air all the time. I'm not trying to have a six or seven-hundred-dollar power bill."

"Burt what makes you think I run the air all the time," said Lacey.

"Because the air is running all the time. I turn it down, and you turn it right back up," Burton said. "She can't handle all that air. Look at her she's got goose bumps."

"Burt, it gets hot down here," said Lacey.

"I know it's hot it's August, but it's too much air on her," said Burton.

"Okay but I have hot flashes so bad," Lacey said. "And I haven't had my hormones lately. It doesn't seem that cold in here to me."

"I understand you have hot flashes, but we can keep the house cool without having it freezing in here like an ice box or something."

"Okay I'll keep the air down," Lacey said. "Be sure and get her that Mucinex and will you get me a Whopper with Cheese. I'm hungry."

"I'm serious it's way too cold in here," said Burton.

"I understand, I understand," said Lacey.

"Is there anything else you want me to get while I'm out?" asked Burton.

"Yea we need some garbage bags and some Cranberry Azo and the Mucinex and please don't forget my Whopper with Cheese and some fries and a large coke please."

"Yes, she does seem to be having a little wheezing when she breathes," Burton said. Alright well I'll go and get the stuff from Rite Aid and then get your Whopper," Burton said. "I'm serious about that air though. It's too much for her."

CHAPTER TEN

One night, Burton was up taking care of Janet. He was tired so he lay in his bed watching movies on his computer until it was time for him to go back down and turn her or check on her. The time came to turn her again so he went back into her room. She had soiled herself and Burton did not feel like changing her. She had diarrhea and it was pretty bad—having dripped out of her diaper and onto her pad. Burton decided to wake Lacey up so she could change Janet.

"Lacey, Lacey," said Burton.

"What, what is it?" said Lacey.

"Can you get up, I need you to come in here for a minute," said Burton.

"What's wrong," Lacey said. "Is Mamma alright?"

"She's fine," Burton replied. "She just needs to be changed."

"Changed!" Lacey said. "I've already changed her three times today. You woke me up out of my sleep for that."

"Well, it's pretty bad," said Burton.

"It was pretty bad the other three times," Lacey said. "Damn Burt you know how to change her."

"Could you please help me with this," Burton said. "And you can go right back to bed. I'll even be up at least long enough to turn her one more time before I go to sleep. Just handle this for me right here."

"You act like all I'm good for is to clean up shit," said Lacey.

"As much as your dog shits around this fucking house I wonder," said Burton.

"Why are you always talking about Buddy Rho?" asked Lacey.

"Look I'm not talking about Buddy Rho," Burton replied. "I'm talking about trying to get my mom cleaned up here."

"Buddy Rho, go back in the bedroom," Lacey said. "Go on now."

"If you can just help me with this you can go right back to bed," Burton said. "I'm tired too, but I will stay up and turn her at least one more time before I go to sleep. It's almost morning just please."

"Yea okay Burt," Lacey said. "I got this. Buddy Rho what did I tell you."

"Thank you so much," said Burton.

Lacey took over the cleanup job and Burton remained there to help her. The two of them were able to get it done relatively quickly. Lacey put a clean pad and diaper on Janet after cleaning her. They pulled the cover back over her and both went back to their rooms. Burton remained awake as he said he would. By now he had grown tired of watching movies and had started to listen to some music. He was a jazz lover and was in a tired and mellow mood as he tried to stay awake. Lately he had been listening to a lot of Robert Glasper. Burton enjoyed Robert Glasper's tunes since discovering him on the internet a brief period ago.

As the early morning neared, he decided to go and just sit there in the chair next to his mother's bed and listen to his music for a while. Burton thought Janet might like to hear some music too. He kissed Janet on her forehead as he did a thousand times and gave her a big hug. Burton sat in the chair next to her bed and listened to his jazz. He turned it up loud enough so Janet could hear it. A Robert Glasper remake of Music Soulchild's song "So Beautiful," started to play.

Burton liked this song. He placed his phone on the pillow next to her head so she could hear it. Burton wanted to share a moment in time with Janet as he stroked her head. He realized then, that this song would always remind him of her. He told Janet that he wanted to dedicate this song to her because she was so truly beautiful inside and out.

There are some things that will always remind you of someone special in your life. It may be something they used to say; it may be a food they liked to eat; it might be a joke they like to tell; it may be a smell or fragrance; something they used to wear; it might be a song; it might be something they liked to do and the list goes on and on. There were many things that reminded Burton of his mother Janet. At that moment, he had found something else to remind him of her. He would always think of this moment in time with Janet when he heard that song. Burton was tired but he just wanted to relish this moment.

As it became more and more evident that Janet was dying slowly and there was no telling how much longer Janet would be there with him. Burton started cherishing every moment more than ever before that he spent with Janet. No matter what, she was his mother and he loved her unconditionally. He was ready willing and able to do whatever he needed to do to make sure she was cared for and comfortable. As he played the song several times over and over, Lacey came into the room. She peeped inside at Burton there at Janet's bedside. She turned and went back into her room. It was morning and the rays of the morning sun could be seen through the closed curtains in Janet's room. Burton remained there for while with Janet holding her hand and listening to music with her.

The following day, someone from the hospice care came to visit the house. Burton had switched Janet to hospice care several months ago because she could receive more services and supplies though hospice. Lacey told them that Janet had been having a little difficulty breathing, so they arranged to have an oxygen tank and mask delivered to the house for her use. At this point Janet's room was about as equipped as any hospital room.

Rebecca from hospice care was in the room meeting with Lacey and showing her how to use the tank when Burton arrived. They had connected Janet to the mask for a breathing exercise. Burton walked in and Lacey introduced him to Rebecca. Burton wanted to speak with Rebecca so he walked outside with her as she was leaving.

"Lacey said Mrs. LeFlore was having a little difficulty breathing so we decided to get an oxygen machine," said Rebecca.

"That's fine," Burton said. "Thanks for coming over to check on her on a weekend."

"Not a problem," Rebecca said. "I lost my father about ten years ago and my mother about two years ago. So, I know what you might be experiencing right now."

"Right now I'm just taking life one day at a time," Burton said. "I just want to love her as much as I can while I still have her here."

"I can tell you love your mom a lot," Rebecca said. "But your mom has lived a great productive life and you need to think about what you might do in the event that she were to start to pass."

"What do you mean?" asked Burton.

"I'm saying if your mom were to start transitioning," Rebecca said. "If she were to start to die. I'm a hospice worker and I've been doing this for over twenty years now. I have seen a lot of people die over the course of my career."

"I don't really know how I'm going to handle that," said Burton.

"Sometimes there's a point when a person has reached the end and there is little more that medical science can do other than prolong their pain and suffering," Rebecca said. "You need to give that some thought. Mrs. LeFlore is dying and you need to be ready for that."

"I know," said Burton.

"We believe in death with dignity," Rebecca said. "There's the pre-active stage and there's the active stage of dying. And you may be at a point where you're going to have to make some end-of-life decisions for her. If you feel like your mother is nearing her final stages, you might not want to take her to the hospital. I don't think she wants to suffer any longer."

"I understand what you're saying," Burton said. "But you can rest assured that if I think mom is dying, I'm going to seek medical attention for her. I can't watch her suffer and not try to help her."

September had arrived ushering in cooler autumn air and bright sunny blue skies. Burton left work to meet the ambulance at the house to take Janet for her wound care appointment. Wound care management had been extremely important over the months since Janet had her surgery which resulted in her having permanent wounds. She also had developed other bed sores on her ankle, arms and back from the prolonged period of time she had been informed. It appeared that Janet may have been developing an infection. She was under the care of Dr. Damian Collins at the Infirmary Wound Care Center. Her wound care appointment was practically the only time Janet went outside the doors of her house and bedroom.

Burton always went with her to the wound care appointments. Today he needed to discuss antibiotics with Dr. Collins, because Janet occasionally needed the antibiotics to prevent infection. Burton and her doctor Damian had been friends since childhood having grown up in the same neighborhood and gone to school together. Janet arrived at the wound care center on a stretcher and was moved from the stretcher to the exam table. The nurses immediately began to check her and do her wound care. This was always painful for Janet as she lay there trying to scratch. Burton held her hands so the nurses could do her wound care.

Janet's wounds were examined by Dr. Collins. He said for the most part they looked good, but he was concerned about the one on her right hip which appeared to be a little infected. Damian indicated that he wanted to prescribe some antibiotics for her without Burton having to ask him. Burton was glad there had to be no further discussion about the antibiotics for Janet. After completing the exam, he and Burton talked briefly there in the exam room while the nurses finished bandaging and taping her. The appointment was relatively quick as they usually got Janet right in and right out.

They returned to the house where Janet was taken back to her room and placed back in bed and her feeding pump was reconnected. Janet was starting to look like all of this was starting to take a toll on her. Day by day she was struggling to survive but slowly succumbing to her circumstances. They say that often men usually die quickly when they are ill, but women on the other hand tend to linger on for a while. Janet was definitely lingering like the true lady she was. Often Burton would wonder if perhaps she was waiting. Maybe she was waiting to see her sisters and brothers before she died. Maybe she wanted to see her grandchildren. Perhaps there were a few friends she wanted to see. Maybe it was Mamma, Pappa and all those who had gone before her. Possibly both or perhaps none of the above.

She was a woman trapped between the doorway of life and death. Holding onto life was all she instinctively knew how to do. Despite the tremendous impact she had on the lives of so many people. She lay there for the most part alone and forgotten. Her brothers and sisters never called, not even to ask about her. She had seen some of her grandchildren, but not all of them. The only friend she had who came to visit her and check on her regularly was Earnestine. Other than that, all she had was her son Burton and his employee caregiver Lacey. Janet was very much alive and seemingly disregarded by practically everyone who should have held her in regard. Yet she continued to persevere. She continued to find solace in living and in being alive. Burton showed her all the love he could. Lacey was also a loving and compassionate caregiver as well.

Burton had been going through the day-to-day process of working with Janet until the past two years had been practically a blur to him. Despite everything Lacey hung in there with him, and continued providing competent care for Janet. It was only a matter of time though. As the seasons were changing so was Janet. As the world continued to move with its ebb and flow where people come and people go. There are only two things that remain constant: life, death, and rebirth. Life is the only real constant.

One night, Burton was in the kitchen fixing himself something to eat. He had just turned Janet and made notations in her notebook. It was about 4 o'clock in the morning. Lacey was in her room, and her light was on but he was not sure if she was asleep or awake. He did not bother to disturb her. All of a sudden Burton heard the back doorbell ring. He was startled by the doorbell ringing at such an inordinate hour of the morning. Burton walked to the door to see who it was. He looked out the window and saw the figure of a man standing there.

"Who is it?" asked Burton.

"Is Lacey here?" asked the man.

"Hey, man. It's 4 o'clock in the morning," Burton said. "Who is this?"

"This Melvin," said the man.

"What the fuck are you doing at my door this time of night?"

"I came to see Lacey," the man said. "Is she here?"

"I'm gonna tell you what," Burton said. "You're not gonna see Lacey or anybody else here this time of night."

"Can you ask Lacey to come here," said the man.

"Nah I'll tell you what, I'm finna go and get my gun. I'll be right back. When I get back. When I get back, I'm going to see if you're still standing out here at my door." He said, "Just wait right there. I'll be right back."

Burton went upstairs and got his gun. He quickly came back downstairs and returned to the door. The man at the door had disappeared. That was about the best thing for him to have done, because Burton was thirty-eight hot about him showing up at his house that time of morning unannounced.

"Lacey," said Burton.

"Yea," replied Lacey.

"Don't have people coming over to this house this time of night," said Burton.

"I didn't invite anybody over here," said Lacey.

"Then why would he come over here," said Burton.

"I don't know," Lacey said. "I'm trying to get some rest so I can get up with Mamma. Who was it?"

"He said his name was Melvin," said Burton.

"Melvin, I don't know why he would be coming over here," Lacey said. "I didn't invite him over here. You remember Melvin, he was over here one night and you took him home."

"I don't give a damn if I remember him," Burton said. "I just saw some fucker on the back porch at this time of morning. I don't mind you having company, and you know that, but please have some respect for my house. "

"I do respect your house," said Lacey.

"No fool is going to show up at somebody's house at 4 in the morning unless somebody knows they're coming," argued Burton.

"Burt I'm not trying to have any company this time of morning," Lacey said. "And I didn't invite him here, and I didn't know he was coming. I don't know why he came over here."

"I mean that shit Lacey don't have people coming up to this house this time of night," Burton said. "I almost shot his ass."

"Burt he won't come over here again," said Lacey.

"He better not bring his ass over here this time of night again," Burton replied. "This is ridiculous."

"I agree so can you leave it alone," Lacey said. "My head hurts,"

"I'm serious!" said Burton.

"Good night," Lacey said. "Good morning or whatever. My head is throbbing. Please."

"Good morning, Mamma," Lacey said. "My head still hurts so bad. How are you doing? You probably hurt to don't you. Let me give you some pain meds. I guess you heard Burt fussing at me. It's so hot in here. I must be having another hot flash. Mamma did you ever have hot flashes when you were going through menopause? He's going to get mad, but I'm going to have to turn up the air" Lacey continued as she pulled back the covers and started to turn Janet onto her right side. "I don't know why that fool came over here. I didn't tell him to come here, and I get cussed out as bad as my head is hurting. Stop Buddy Rho, sit down Buddy Rho," Lacey said as she checked Janet to make sure she had not soiled herself. "You looking good right now Mamma. I'm going to give you some pain medicine so you won't be hurting this morning. Buddy Rho I'm not going to tell you again."

Lacey crushed the Narco tablet and mixed it with water. She sucked the water in the syringe and pumped it into Janet's stomach. She placed the line from her feeding pump back onto the end of the tube attached to her stomach and turned the pump on. "Mamma I'm going to go back to bed and lay down for a few more minutes. Hopefully my headache will go away soon. I'll see you in a little while. Buddy Rho come on."

Janet lay there watching Lacey as she walked out of the room. Lacey turned up the air conditioner again and went back to her bedroom. Janet lay there silently rubbing her hand against the comforter on her bed. The television could be heard as some newscaster was talking about local news. Janet was still breathing but with a slight degree of difficulty. She got goosebumps on her frail little arms as she felt the cold from the air hitting her skin. She was cold. She took her finger and poked it in her hair. Burton walked into her room again and saw that she had been turned. He kissed her once again before he went back into the hallway and cut the air off again.

The following Saturday Burton's friend Meat was outside cutting the yard. As he mowed the grass and made his way around the yard, he saw a used condom laying on the carport. Meat thought that he might mention this to Burton because he knew it probably did not belong to him, since arguably no self-respecting man would throw a used condom on his own carport and leave it there. Meat was finishing up cutting the grass, which would hopefully be the last cut of the year before winter. He was just about finished with his work when he noticed a woman pull into the driveway. It was Sophia arriving for work. Burton met Sophia at the door and let her inside. A few minutes after Sophia came inside, Meat rang the doorbell to let Burton know he was finished.

"Burt I'm finished," said Meat.

"How much I owe you?" asked Burton.

"The usual," Meat said. "Eighty-five dollars."

"No, Meat. It's usually seventy-five," said Burton.

"Yea, that's right seventy-five," Meat said. "That's a fine little lady you got there."

"Who you talking about?" Burton said. "Na, man. She helps me with my mom. You want to meet her."

"Man, you know I already got my hands full with this one I got," said Meat.

"If you want to meet her just let me know," said Burton.

"You know you got a used condom laying out on your carport," said Meat.

"A condom," Burton said. "Where?"

"Out there on the carport near the edge," said Meat. "Shit, when I saw her drive up, I thought she was the reason you had the condom on your driveway."

"Nah," Burton said. "Why the hell would I want to throw a nasty ass condom on my driveway. That's a bit uncouth don't you think," he said as he walked out into the yard with Meat who showed him the condom on the ground. "I'll be damned," he said as he got a stick.

"How does your yard look?" asked Meat.

"Looks pretty good," Burton said. "I need you to come back and do the hedges, but I can wait until after it gets cold. Hopefully, this will be the last time I'm going to have to cut grass until Spring."

"That's going to be a little more money," said Meat.

"Yea, I know Meat," Burton said. "Everything is going to be a little more money. Here and don't forget to get the lot over on Congress. Get that done by the end of the week, and I'll pay you for that."

"Appreciate you, I'll see you next week," said Meat.

"Hey, Lacey," Burton said as he returned to the house. "Can you tell me why there's a used condom in the back yard?"

"What, what a condom in the yard?" Lacey said. "Why are you asking me?"

"Because I didn't put a condom out there," Burton said. "I want to know what the fuck a condom is doing on the carport."

"I don't wear condoms. I'm not a man," Lacey said. "And I have a room. If I wanted to be with somebody, I would have them in my room and not out on the carport. Maybe you should ask little miss thang Sophia how the condom got there."

"I surely will ask her," Burton said. "But somehow I believe I would be asking the wrong person."

"I don't know anything about any condom in the driveway," Lacey said. "Hey. It looks like my ride is here. I'm gone. I'll see you."

"Before you say anything," Sophia said. "I heard what Lacey said about, I was probably the one who left a condom in your yard. I didn't leave any condom in your yard. I haven't been here in over a week. I just drove in the yard, got out of my car and came in the house. I've been sitting here with Mrs. LeFlore ever since I got here."

"Sophia, I know you didn't leave a condom in my yard," Burton said. "She is so full of shit. I don't care what she does. If she had sex with somebody, whatever. She's a grown woman and she can do what she wants. But don't be so tacky as to let some guy just throw the damn thing on the driveway. That's nasty and disrespectful as hell. Who does that?"

"Why would she try to pull me into it?" said Sophia.

"Whenever she's put in a compromising situation and doesn't have a plausible answer for why she did what she did" Burton said. "It's blame somebody else. I already know that."

"Goodness," said Sophia.

"Just like some guy showed up here ringing the doorbell at 4 o'clock in the morning a few days ago," Burton said. "Who comes over someone's house at 4 o'clock in the morning."

"Yea, especially when they should know it's that person's job," said Sophia.

"I don't mind if she has friends come over here," Burton said. "Since she is here all the time. Sometimes they might be over here kind of late. I don't mind that as long as she's here with my mom and doing what I need her to do. But anybody with sense knows you don't just come up to somebody's door at that time of night and ring the doorbell like it's all good."

"Do you know who it was?" asked Sophia.

"It doesn't matter," Burton said. "He almost got himself shot."

"I heard that," said Sophia.

"All I'm trying to do right now is make sure this lady here is taken care of," Burton said. "Lacey has been there with me since day one, and I appreciate everything she does to help make sure she's cared for properly. Is it asking so much to ask her that she make sure that people she knows respect the fact that this is her job and respect the fact that this is not her house. "I don't think that's asking much at all," said Sophia.

"I'm a very private person," Burton said. "I don't have anybody and everybody at my home. There's been times she had people over here that I probably wouldn't have invited to my house. Those are her friends. I try to understand because I know she feels isolated, but have some respect, damn."

Sophia stayed there with Janet until it was time for her to report to her job at the nursing home. For the most part Burton was there at the house relaxing. Lacey had not returned yet so he called Sandy and asked her to come and help with Janet. At first Sandy was reluctant because she said that Lacey had been so rude to her and acted as if she wanted to fight her. Burton assured Sandy that Lacey was not there and he did not expect her to be back until late Sunday sometime. Finally, she agreed to come over and help him for a little while.

"You know. I don't know how much longer mom is going to live," Burton said. "I don't know how much longer I'm going to last."

"Burton, it's not easy, take it from me," Sandy said. "It's not easy taking care of them and it's not easy losing them, because you love them. It was hard sometimes taking care Madea, but I loved her. She was my mom, and there wasn't nothing I wouldn't do for her. When she died it was one of the saddest days of my life."

"No matter what, she's my mother," Burton said. "I don't know what I would do if she died."

"You know Burton you are such a strong man," Sandy said. "Even though I talk about Lacey because righteously

I'm jealous of her being here with you all the time taking care of your mom instead of me. But I admire you so much and what you've tried to do for your mom."

"I appreciate that," Burton said. "Lacey gets on my nerves though."

"Well, that's your Lacey," Sandy said. "You chose her and you're not going to get rid of her so why are you telling me?"

"This morning Meat was over here cutting the grass and he found a condom on the carport," said Burton.

"Oh yea," said Sandy.

"Yea and the other night some dude came over here at 4 o'clock in the morning," Burton said. "Seriously that time of morning. There's other little shit she does."

"Burton you've been knowing this for a long time," Sandy said. "Isn't it time to go and turn her again."

"Yea," Burton said. "Thanks for coming over and helping me."

"No problem," Sandy said. "I'm getting paid right, because I don't have any money. You show me what you need me to do and I'll do it. Just give me a few dollars when I leave so I'll have a little money in my pocket."

"Sure," said Burton.

"Looks like she needs to be changed," said Sandy.

"Yes, it does looks like she needs to be changed," said Burton.

"Will you hand me those gloves right there and hold her hands for me," Sandy said. "I got this."

"Thanks," said Burton.

"Mrs. LeFlore let me get these off you so we can change you and get you cleaned up," Sandy said as she loosened the taped edges of her diaper. "Those sores on her butt aren't going to heal are they?"

"They haven't healed yet and it's been over a year," said Burton.

"She's so precious, she just lays there like a baby in the womb," Sandy said. "I remember when Mrs. LeFlore used to raise pure D hell all the time."

"Yea," said Burton.

"You got any wipes over there," said Sandy.

"They're right behind you," Burton said pointing at the wipes on the table. "See them."

"Okay, Mrs. LeFlore," Sandy said. "We got you all cleaned up."

"Grab that pad underneath her," Burton said. "When I lift her slide it out and put a new one there."

"You lift her and I'll slide the pad under there," said Sandy as Burton lifted and she changed pads.

"Okay, Mom," Burton said. "You haven't seen Sandy in a while. Did you say hi to Sandy?"

Janet laid there in her usual fetal position. She was very alert and her eyes were wide open, but she did not say anything to either one of them. Her right leg had become so contracted that when she opened her eyes, she was literally staring at her knee. The femur on her left leg was still detached. Her left leg was just as contracted, but it could be positioned in a way that it would not be directly in her face.

Her ankles were taped as well as her shoulders. Burton decided he would go ahead and do Janet's wound care while he had Sandy there to help him. Sandy had no experience doing wound care. He told her that he was going to teach her how to do wound care.

Burton took off the bandages, cleaned and dressed everything on her right side. He then turned her over, and did the same thing to the bed sores on her left side. As usual it caused Janet a considerable amount of pain. Burton asked Sandy to hold her hands since she fought more than usual when people where messing with her wounds. She tried hard to pull her hands away from Sandy as Burton worked to change and clean her soars. Sandy continued to hold her hands as Janet frowned with pain. Burton worked as quickly as he could. Burton finished and put the covers back on top of Janet.

They went into the den and watched television for a while. Later that night he took Sandy home and dropped her off. He returned home and stayed up for the remainder of the night with Janet. Lacey was off work and did not return that night. She was gone for the majority of the day on Sunday just as he knew she would. Burton remained there at the house with Janet the entire weekend. It was late Sunday night before she returned. When Lacey returned Burton was there at the house having a beer with his friend Alexis and William.

"Burt you're sleeping with that girl, aren't you?" asked Alex.

"Yea, I think he is," William said. "He just doesn't want anybody to know."

"How many times do I have to tell you?" said Burton.

"You got this woman living in your house and you're not getting any," Alex said. "Seriously, are you serious right now."

"The fact that he's not getting any doesn't surprise me because we all know LeFlore's not getting any," William said. "That's a well-established fact."

"Now you got jokes," said Burton.

"You got that pretty muther fucker living up in here with you, and you're not hitting it," said Alex.

"No, I'm not hitting it. She works for me that's it," Burton said. "If you think she's so pretty then you holler at her, because I'm about ready to tell her to get her shit and get the fuck out."

"Why you say that?" asked William.

"Nothing man. I don't really feel like getting into it," Burton said. "She does a good job with my mom, but me and her clash sometimes on a personal lever. She's good people, but she got some real ghetto ass ways sometimes."

"You need to put the hammer on her," said Alex.

"Why do you keep saying that?" Burton replied. "You're a manager and have been a manager for many years. I don't see you trying to sleep with not one of your employees. So why do you insinuate that I need to sleep with mine? If you think somebody needs to sleep with her so bad, then maybe you need to go and sleep with her. Maybe that's what you want to do."

"Tell you what, can I have another beer?" William said. "How about that, I would like to have one more beer before I go home. Can you do that for me?"

"Mine is getting pretty low right about now too," said Alex.

"Two beers you got it," Burton said. "Just understand that her being here is not about me. It's about my mom. So it really bothers me even though I know you're just joking or half serious, that y'all keep saying that. I have the most important thing in my life besides my children here, and I'm living life by faith from day by day. Today I don't know what tomorrow will bring and my mom might not be here much longer."

Janet was having increased difficulty breathing. Lacey and Burton would give her oxygen via the oxygen mask; however, she still had increased difficulty with her intake. Lacey continued to blast the air condition every waking moment. Burton would turn it down, but as soon as he would go to work, she had the air back on. The month of September was coming to an end. The Autumn months in sunny Mobile were extraordinarily pleasant as always. Perfect temperatures and beautifully sunny skies. The two best times of year in the south were always early Autumn and early Spring.

During the winter southerners stayed confused by the constantly changing weather from warm to cold. During the summer in the south, it was hot all the time and the mosquito's and flies can make it difficult at times. On the other hand, Autumn and early Spring in the south was always a time when people felt new and refreshed. Janet was waning and growing weaker by the day. Alzheimer's, old age, and debilitation was taking its effect.

That night Burton came home from work and he was tired. He wondered how he was going to manage to stay up tonight to turn Janet. He went to his room took off his clothes. He selected a movie and popped it in his computer.

Burton went back downstairs and checked on Janet. She was laying there in her bed resting. Lacey had put the oxygen mask on Janet's face. He checked her notebook to see when was the last time Lacey had turned her.

He went ahead and turned her before going back upstairs to his room. He watched movies many nights while he stayed awake to turn Janet a few times while his caretaker, Lacey slept. Sometimes she would watch a movie five or ten times just trying to stay awake. The last turn of the night, Burton took off the oxygen mask and turned off the tank. He did not want Janet to continue to rest with that mask on her face. He listened for her breathing and he heard her breathing. He went up to his room and fell asleep.

CHAPTER ELEVEN

The next morning Lacey was knocking at his door telling him to come downstairs. The hospice people where in Janet's room when Burton walked in. He greeted them and went to Janet's bedside and saw her. The hospice staff did not say much afterward. Janet looked unusually pale and jaundiced. Her oxygen mask remained on the nightstand where he had left it the night before. She was still breathing but appeared to be in a considerable amount of distress. Burton took a look at Janet and then he looked around the room at the hospice staff and Lacey. He took another look at his mother. He got out his cell phone and called for assistance to take her to the hospital.

Once at the hospital she was immediately rushed to an examining room in the hospital emergency medicine facility. They put her on oxygen practically as soon as she arrived. It was clearly obvious that she was having trouble breathing. Janet was struggling and fighting to breath. She could have given up right then, but she did not appear to have any thought of giving up. Janet was trying with all she had to breath and to live.

After running some tests on her, it was determined that she had pneumonia. Janet's X-rays and tests further revealed that Janet had a considerable amount of fluid in her lungs. Actually, it was ascertained that the majority of the fluid was in one lobe and the other lobe was not constricted.

Throughout the years when Burton would talk to his mother Janet about being cold and exposing herself to the frigid elements, she would tell him that she had never had a cold. Janet would say have you ever known me to have had a cold. Burton's response would always be, mom the first cold you get might be your last. His grandmother Teah always talked about pneumonia. Pneumonia is the absolute worst cold which can and has been fatal over the course of the human population and civilization. When Burton would tell Janet the first cold she got could be her last, he was talking specifically about Pneumonia. Now he was here in the emergency room with her and doctors had just informed him that Janet had Pneumonia. It was almost like déjà vu, all these years he had been telling her to be careful when it came to the weather, and now as a result of no fault of her own, she had Pneumonia.

Dr. Rousso attended to her again. That morning Burton was made aware of their diagnosis, he indicated that she would be admitted. Rousso said she would be treated in the intensive care unit. Janet was obviously and noticeably in distress but she still continued to express and display a will to live. Burton was there with Janet when his phone rang. He noticed the 215 area code. Someone from Philadelphia was calling his phone. He recognized the phone number as being that of her sister Anna.

He wondered how and why she had the wherewithal to call at this particular moment. Burton told Janet that he was going outside and the he would return soon. He answered the call from Philadelphia and it was indeed his mother's sister. Ann started off the conversation by saying she was so sorry to hear about Janet. Burton wondered how she even had any information to talk about how she was sorry about Janet.

He explained to Anna what was going on and stated he had stepped outside to talk with her. Burton said he needed to return to Janet's bedside, and wanted to know what it was she had to say. Simply Anna said she was sorry to hear her sister was not doing so well. Burton concluded the conversation and told her that he was about to go back into the emergency room where Janet was undergoing treatment.

He was cordial and said he would talk with her at some point in the near future. Burton ended the conversation and went inside to be with his mother. A few minutes later Burton's phone rang again. It was Janet's sister Anna. She called again like she did not remember having already called a few minutes prior. She actually phoned once more like Burton had not just politely told her it was nice to speak with her, but he had way more pressing matter to deal with.

Anna called him again after they had just finished talking. Burton wondered to himself why she called him and why after all these years she had not called or inquired. All of a sudden, she wanted to call. Burton explained the situation and said he would speak with her later, but he had neither the time or the luxury of trying to evaluate her or her motives. Dr. Rousso and the other staff members told Burton that Janet would be given a bed within the foreseeable future. Burton watched his mother Janet putting everything she had into trying to breath and her survival. No matter her condition.

No matter what, Janet was his mother and she deserved the finest healthcare available. Although he was in denial, and had no clue as to what might be down the road for Janet and for him. He was there and he had no idea what was going on with her sister who all of a sudden out of the blue decided to call and call again five minutes later, talking about she was sorry. He had heard that Ann was showing signs of having Alzheimer's. It seemed ironic to him that the sister who waged war on Janet when she first started showing signs of Alzheimer's and dementia might now be showing signs of it herself.

Janet was admitted to intensive care at Mobile Infirmary. The same hospital her husband Beck had served and worked at for so many years. She was on oxygen, a catheter for her urine, in need of daily wound care, incontinent, dependent on a feeding tube for sustenance, her legs totally and absolutely contracted, still able to display a range of motion relegated to her arms and hand. Janet was totally alert and engaging. She was a woman fighting for her life and her son was there willing to make sure she was provided with all the necessary sustenance and care. The only problem was this was beyond his ability. Janet was completely debilitated. She was absolutely and completely incapacitated and dependent. One thing Janet had taught him over the course of his life was that you should not allow yourself to be dependent on anyone. There may be many instances when someone might be dependent on you, but the ultimate goal in life was to remain autonomous.

The ultimate goal in life was to be totally independent of anyone or anything. Janet taught Burton that in life there was nothing more supreme than to love and serve God. Janet would always tell him that life was a journey and not a destination. She would say to him that life was for the living and that death was for the living. He felt like he did not know anything anymore. He loved Janet and did not want to see her suffering.

It was not long before they transferred her to the ICU. Burton went up to the ICU with her and gave the attending nurse all the information he needed about her medical history. Janet remained on the oxygen while the hospital staff in the intensive care unit started hooking Janet up to machines and IV's. Janet was still very much awake and alert. She was looking around and blinking her eyes. For a moment there it appeared that her breathing had become less labored, but she was still having difficulty. The nurse named Ed, explained that the intensive care unit had very strict visiting hours and that Burton would be expected to adhere to the times posted on the front door of the ICU.

Burton agreed and he asked Ed if he needed anything else from him in terms of her information. He stated that he was finished. Burton told him that he was aware that visiting hours were over, but he wanted to remain there with his mom for a moment before leaving. Burton held Janet's hand and told her to be strong and she would get through this. He assured her that he would be with her every step of the way and asked her to hurry up and get better so she could come home. Burton was starting to feel confident that Janet was stabilized, and she would be on her way to recovery.

About twenty minutes later, at around midnight, Burton finally left the hospital and got in his truck to head back around to his office for a minute. In the ICU Janet's nurse remained in her unit. Janet was still very much alert as she continued to wheeze. There was a gurgling noise in her lungs. You could hear the fluid in her lungs as she continued to fight to breath. Not long after Burton left the ICU, Ed noticed a change in Janet's breathing patterns.

Based on the changes in her breathing patterns, the ICU staff was able to determine relatively quickly that the aid of the oxygen mask was not enough. It would not be long before she would stop breathing. Burton had not been gone very long, not more than ten or fifteen minutes. The nurse contacted Burton on his cell phone. Burton had just reached his office which was not far from the hospital. He was pulling into the parking lot when his phone rang. He recognized the number and knew the call was from Mobile Infirmary.

"Hello," said Burton.

"Mr. LeFlore this is Ed, your mother's nurse for the night," said Ed.

"Yes, how are you," said Burton.

"I'm calling about your mom Mrs. LeFlore," said Ed.

"Is everything alright?" Burton asked as he started to become a little worried about the reason for his call.

"It appears Mrs. LeFlore is not breathing well at all," the nurse said. "It will probably be a matter of minutes before she stops breathing. She's not going to make it through the night."

"What!" said Burton as his heart dropped at what the nurse had just said.

"Do you want us to just let her pass away, or do you want us to intubate her?" asked the nurse.

Burton was silent for a moment as he thought to himself. Here he had left her side only a few minutes ago, and she appeared to be stable. Now within a matter of minutes her nurse was saying she had taken a sudden turn for the worse. Burton thought to himself how he could possibly utter those words let her die. He thought about how she had appeared to him during the hours he had been there with her at the hospital. Janet was fighting for her life and struggling with everything she had to breath. Janet did not seem to Burton as though she was ready to give up, or perhaps Burton mistook his unwillingness to let go of her for Janet's thought and wishes.

There was no way Burton could tell the nurse to just do nothing and let her pass away. He could not bring himself to say it. He opened his mouth to speak and no words came out. He took a deep breath and told her nurse to intubate her. Burton asked the nurse if it would be alright for him to come back to the intensive care unit in about an hour or so to check on her again. Ed indicated he would let the other staff know that Janet should be intubated, and they would get to work immediately before she stopped breathing. He also told Burton it would be alright for him to come back to the ICU in about an hour or so if he wanted to check on her.

The ICU staff immediately started preparing to intubate Janet. It was a stat emergency in the ICU as they rushed into her unit and started the process of running a tube into her mouth and down her throat. Janet did not like it and she resisted but she was so weak and helpless. They held her arms. As all this was going on, Janet looked around to see Burton, but she did not see him. All she saw was these strange faces around her pulling at her and holding her arms down as they continued to run that tube into her throat. All of a sudden, she felt oxygen being pumped into her lungs. She was breathing and it was not such a struggle anymore. It was not long before she drifted off to sleep.

As Burton sat at his office trying to finish up the little bit of work he had hoped to get done before he went home for the night, all he could think about was his mother Janet there alone without him in the ICU with her. He wondered if he had made the right decision to allow them to put her on a ventilator. Although in his heart, he knew Janet was nearing the end and her quality of life was severely diminished, he also figured that in a few days the fluid on her lungs would go down and she would be able to breath on her own again. He resolved at the moment that he had made the right decision. It was the only decision he would have felt comfortable with. The other alternative decision was still not an option for him.

He sat there at his desk thinking. Burton reflected back to the time he and Janet had traveled to Wilmington, North Carolina during the Spring of 1982. They arrived in Wilmington and found his grandmother Mable with both of her legs as swollen as they could be. Mable's legs were swollen like inner tubes, all the way from her ankle to just below her knees. Burton recalled the conversation between Mable and her daughter Janet when she told her they were going to the hospital. Mable told Janet that she did not want to go to the hospital. Mable said she feared that if she went to the hospital, she would never return home and she just wanted to die peacefully at home.

Janet told Mable they were going to seek medical care for her she did not want to hear any more talk about dying. According to Janet, they were only going to go to the hospital so they could get the fluid off her legs, and she would be right back home within a few days. Mable pleaded with Janet not to take her, but Janet insisted. Despite Mable's objections about going to the hospital, Janet managed to convince her to go. Burton remembered how he had helped his grandmother down the back steps of her house and into the car.

Mable continued to say she did not want to go; however, it was not long before Janet pulled up to New Hanover Memorial Hospital where Mable was admitted. Within a day of being in the hospital, Mable had a heart attack. When asked whether or not to resuscitate Mable after the first heart attack, Janet told them to resuscitate her. Her brothers and sisters started calling and arriving in Wilmington not long afterward. A few days later, Mable had another heart attack and they all told the hospital to resuscitate her again. Burton had seen a lot of death in his life but this was the first time he had actually seen dying before his eyes and the drama that went along with eight children trying to figure out how to save their mother.

Burton and Janet remained in Wilmington for almost three weeks afterward. After being revived and resuscitated and remaining on life support for an extended period of time Mable finally passed away. Now in 2015 Burton was sitting there thinking about that experience which affected him and changed his outlook and perception on life very much as a young man. Watching Janet and her eight siblings holding on to what was left of their dying mother had really blown his mind. Watching his grandmother undergo that long and labored ordeal of dying in that hospital when she had begged to just stay at home and die in peace was vivid in his mind.

However, he fully understood how Janet could not in good conscience go along with such a plan when there was still hope that it would not be so serious and everything would be alright. Perhaps Mable already knew or felt reasonably certain she was going to die. But how was Janet supposed to know. It looked manageable and treatable at the time.

When they encountered her at her house in Wilmington, she was sitting up talking and holding her swollen legs out in front of her. Why would anyone in their right mind have said, "Yea, Mom. Forget about seeking medical care for yourself. Let's just let you stay at home and die?" On the other hand, now Burton was facing the same or similar circumstance as he had experienced with Janet and her mother Mable. All he knew how to do was to try and keep her alive, because he loved her. Some people would say, if he loved her, he would have told the ICU nurse to do nothing when he called and said she was going to stop breathing. Actually, he could have just remained at home with her and the hospice staff earlier in the morning and not called an ambulance to take her to the hospital.

Despite Janet's physical and cognitive condition at this point in her life, Burton felt pneumonia was curable and there was a strong possibility that Janet could continue to live. So why not seek medical attention for her and why not place her on a ventilator for a day or two to give the antibiotics a chance to get in her system and hopefully decrease the level of fluid in her lungs. He was not ready to let go of her yet, after all, there was still hope, he thought to himself. Before going home that night, Burton went to the hospital again. He contacted Janet's nurse who said they had successfully intubated her. She was breathing with the aid of the ventilator and appeared to be resting.

Burton was allowed to enter the ICU again where he spent a few more minutes with Janet. She was in fact breathing and resting as Nurse Ed had stated. After a while, he was able to go home knowing that his mom was still alive and he would be in a position to evaluate her progress over the next few days before making any further decisions about her course of treatment. He arrived home that night and found Lacey there anxious to know what was going on.

"Burt, how's Mamma doing?" asked Lacey.

"She almost died tonight," Burton said. "She's still in the ICU. They had to put her on a ventilator. They say she has pneumonia."

"I got my bag packed if you want me to go over there and be with her," said Lacey.

"She can't have anybody staying overnight with her in the ICU," Burton said. "They have restricted visiting hours. I would like for you to go over there and spend some time with her during visiting hours though if you would."

"I don't mind," Lacey said. "Burt, I feel like I might have to go to the hospital myself. My head is hurting so bad, and I feel like my blood sugar is high. I didn't want to bother you while you were with Mamma, but would you mind taking me to Burger King so I can get something to eat."

"No problem," said Burton.

"She's got pneumonia," Lacey said. "That's why she's been having trouble breathing."

"Yea Lacey," Burton replied. "That's why I repeatedly asked you to not keep that cold air running all the time in her room."

"I have hot flashes all the time," Lacey said. "Ever since you said it, I have been keeping the air down and you come and turn it off practically every time it comes on, so please don't say that to me. I've been here taking care of Mamma round the clock for almost two years now. I love your Mamma just like she was my own. My mother passed away in 2006 and I love Miss. Janet."

"Look you do a tremendous job," Burton said. "I'm just saying."

"So, if your Mamma passes away, you're just going to kick me to the curb huh," Lacey said. "You won't need me anymore then."

"If she passes, I'm going to kick you to the curb," Burton said. "What are you talking about."

"You heard me," Lacey said. "You won't need me anymore. You're going to just put me out and kick me to the curb, aren't you?"

"Nobody said anything about kicking anybody to the curb," Burton said. "You said that."

"I'm not feeling well at all," Lacey said. "I'm starving, will you please take me to get something."

The next morning Burton got up and went straight to the hospital to check on Janet. He entered the ICU and went to her unit. Burton found her there still on the ventilator. She was alert, wide awake and looked him right straight in the eyes. There had been no conversation between Burton and Janet prior to her going to the hospital like the one she had with Mable some thirty years prior. Even though there had been numerous conversations between Janet and Burton about Mable over the course of the years. At the moment he simply rejoiced in being able to look into her eyes once again and know that she was still alive and there for him to love and care for. Despite everything he was in tune to Janet and even though she no longer communicated, the two of them still had communication. She communicated with him in many ways and he fully understood her.

One day with Janet in the intensive care unit turned into one week. After one week there still had not been any significant changes in Janet's condition. She was still on the ventilator and there was evidence of fluid remaining in her lungs. Lacey had also managed to be admitted to the hospital. Now Lacey and Janet both were at Mobile Infirmary receiving medical care. Burton talked about Lacey sometimes and she was not always perfect, but she did the job. She did that. He got mad at her and sometimes they argued like siblings, but he thanked God for her every day. There was no doubt she was starting to regress into her old ways. She had remained dedicated and devoted to Mrs. LeFlore's care. It was somewhat paradoxical that Janet and her caretaker both ended up in the hospital at the same time.

The hospital staff took it upon themselves to explain to Burton that Janet did not have a living will with advanced directives. They wanted him to understand that if Janet started to have a heart attack it would not be favorable to her to do any type of chest compressions or to tamper with her rib cage in an effort to get to her heart. The intensive care unit wanted to know exactly how far he was planning on going with this thing. There was clear and convincing evidence that she might have died relatively peacefully a few days prior, but for his request and insistence they employ extraordinary measures to keep her alive, they did so. So far there was no marked improvement. Dr. Bell had a stroke not long after the last time Janet had been hospitalized and was not available to attend to her. Burton contacted Dr. Hunte and asked him to go and see about her. He promised he would but would not be able to serve as her primary physician. He was stuck with the hospital staff physicians.

On or about the 14th of October Janet experienced marked improvement. Four days is about the maximum a person should be on a vent, but Janet had been on a ventilator for almost two weeks now. Burton went in to spend some time with Janet. He kissed her and took her by the hand. The 14th of October was the day his father, her husband Walker B. LeFlore had passed away some fourteen years prior. Burton noticed her renewed energy and vitality. Burton was optimistic at this point they would say the fluid in her lungs had cleared up enough to take her off the ventilator and let her breath on her own.

CHAPTER TWELVE

"Mom, it's October 14th," Burton said. "This is the day we lost Daddy. I love you so much. Please forgive me if I did the right thing or the wrong thing. All I know how do is keep hope alive. You are my hope, my blessing, my mother. All I can do is keep on loving you and trying to do what's best for you. Maybe, in all reality, what's best for me isn't what's best for you. I don't know. I feel like I don't know anything anymore. All I know right now is that I want what's best for you. I don't want you to die, but I don't want you to suffer any more if you're tired of suffering. Oh, by the way, Lacey's here in the hospital too. On the same floor as you. Mom, I want you to get better and come home." Burton continued, "I remember when we went to Wilmington and found Grandma with her legs swollen. I admired the way you handled the situation despite the fact that Grandma said she didn't want to go."

Janet perked up and displayed her full range of motion. She was alive, alert and energetic. The ICU staff said she was breathing for the most part on her own. They had turned the ventilator down. She was looking Burton in the eyes and she was much more animated than usual. The expression on her face was clearly that she was ready to get off that machine. She had already been on the ventilator much longer than was recommended. Burton stayed in the unit with Janet as long as he could. When he left the hospital, Burton felt very optimistic that perhaps tomorrow they would say it was alright to take her off the vent. Actually, Janet appeared to be doing better today than she had in a long time.

The next day, Burton called the ICU to ask how Janet was doing. He spoke with the nurse who was attending Janet. He was expecting the nurse to tell him that Janet was doing well and the doctors were planning to take her off the artificial respiration as soon as possible. Unfortunately, the nurse did not give him a rosy report. She stated that Janet's heart had been beating at a high rate, and the doctor had to give her something to slow down her heart rate. The nurse also stated they had to turn the respiration rate up on the ventilator and she was taking few and less breaths on her own.

Burton could not understand what he was hearing. He felt certain when he had left her room the day before that she was going to continue down the road to recovery. He was hopeful yesterday when he visited her that she was recovering from the pneumonia. He went to the hospital and found Janet there in the unit. Nurse Darlene went out so that Burton could have some time with Janet. Janet was resting as Burton took her by the hand. It was his way of letting her know he was there. It was just as she had said. She opened her eyes and made eye contact, only this time her expression was much different.

The day before he honestly thought Janet was getting better and showing improvement. Now the picture and prognosis was looking a little bleaker and more grim. On a few occasions over the last few days when Nurse Darlene had been attending to Janet, she had made statements to Burton which in essence suggested in a very kind way, why are you doing this when you know your mother is not going to live and her quality of life is severely diminished. She did not say it in those exact words, but she alluded to it and it did not take Burton long to figure out what she meant by some of the comments she made.

The next day Janet was taking on fluid. Burton inquired about it but the ICU staff said they were not sure what was going on. They had been pulling fluid out of her lungs for days. The fluid looked like mucus. On this day, the fluids being pulled from her lungs was dark in color, almost like the color of dirt. Burton asked the nurse what was going on with her and they had no real answers. Janet was weary and disheveled but she made eye contact with Burton and maintained her focus on him for the majority of the time he was there with her. Burton held her hand the entire time he was there with her. Visiting hours where over and he had to leave. It was difficult for him to leave her there by herself.

Later that evening when vising hours resumed, Burton returned to Janet's bedside. She was being cared for by Nurse Fran. Burton liked Nurse Fran. She was very caring and attentive to Janet. She was also personable. She and Burton talked frequently on the nights she had been working with Janet. Burton inquired again to see if they had any idea why she was taking on fluid in her arms and legs. Fran informed Burton that Janet's kidneys had failed.

Fran pointed to the bag hanging from Janet's bed. The nurse pointed out to Burton there had been no urine in that bag for over twenty-four hours. She also said Janet had a considerable amount of fluid in her lungs. She had for the most part gotten rid of the fluid in her lungs from the pneumonia. Now she had more fluid in her lungs making it difficult for her to breathe again. They were continuously giving her intravenous fluids, and her body no longer had a way to excrete those fluids. When the news finally sunk in, Burton found it hard to fight back the tears. He stood there listening to Fran and tears started to stream down his face. He was so sad.

On Saturday Burton went to the hospital as soon as he got up. He found Janet pretty much in the same or worse condition that she had been the day before. Her extremities were more swollen. The tube which was draining fluid out of her lungs was full of this dark fluid. Burton came into the room and took Janet by the hand as he always did. Janet was laying there in bed awake and alert. He tightened his grip around her hand and she tightened her grip of his hand. He said hello to her and asked her how she was doing. Janet did not reply. She did not look in his direction. Burton tried to make eye contact with Janet but she would not look at him. Her eyes were wide open but she would not look at him. Her gaze was fixed at the corner of the ceiling in her unit. Burton walked around her bed and once again tried to make eye contact with his mother Janet, but she would not look at him or even glance in his direction. She continued to stare at the ceiling.

Percy and Gladys Johnson came into Janet's unit. Burton was happy to see them. Janet barely acknowledged them. She continued to stare of into space. Burton said a prayer for his mother with Percy and Gladys. They stayed for a while there with Janet and Burton. Visiting hours were over in the ICU. Burton had been asked to do a low country boil for his club. Burton was a pretty skilled chef especially when it came to seafood. The Low Country Boil was shrimp, sausage, corn and potatoes. He had agreed to do it several months ago and despite everything going on he went a cooked the food for the group. As he cooked the food, he observed how everyone was having a great time and enjoying themselves.

Although, he was not having one bit of fun. All he could think about was his mother there at the hospital dying and he not by her side. He did not feel like there was anyone there who he could talk to about it, nor if anyone really cared. As he finished the food, he walked past the party room and saw everyone dancing and having a good time.

He thought about some of the times he had brought Janet to parties at the club. He thought about how she danced, ate, and laughed. However, now Janet could not dance anymore. Her legs were contracted and one of them had a detached femur. When she opened her eyes, the first thing she saw was her knee which was practically in her face. She could not go to a party. She did not laugh and she could not eat any food.

Janet was not at a high point in her life. She was in constant pain. She had not gotten out of bed in almost two years. At home or in the hospital, she was confined to the bed and her room. She was totally dependent and had no autonomy or control over her own life. Day in and day out she lay there lifeless and yet very much alive. Burton knew he had to end this. He had to accept the fact that his mother was going to die. There was nothing he could do to stop it or prolong it.

There was much communication in Janet and her son Burton's eye contact. Janet had communicated loud and clear to him earlier today. She was swelling up like a balloon and must have been in a considerable amount of pain. She had a tube down her throat for over two weeks now. From the time Janet had arrived at the hospital, the staff at the ICU had basically been asking Burton on a daily basis to make a decision. He kept telling them, his decision was they needed to do everything to make sure his mother was alive and cared for. Deep down inside he knew what decision they were really asking him to make. He was finally ready to tell them. As much as it hurt his heart to think about it. It was time for him to accept the reality of the fact. Janet was dying. She had been dying and almost dead for a long time despite having lingered on for an indefinite period of time.

She was indeed suffering and he could no longer prolong her suffering. Burton could no longer in good conscience try to deny the inevitable. Actually, it did not matter much if he was willing to accept it or not. He went to the hospital and called the ICU and asked if it was alright for him to come and see Janet. Nurse Fran said that even though it was after hours she would request that he be allowed to come into the unit.

Before going back to the hospital, Burton dropped to his knees in tears. Burton prayed and asked God to please stop this. Burton pleaded with God to please end his mother's suffering. Burton cried and cried there alone at his bedside. He begged God to please take Janet if that would end her pain. Burton prayed and prayed. He said he trusted in him and that he was putting it in his hands.

He had done all he could. He had loved her and cared for her all he could and knew how to do. He had held on to her as long as he possibly could. He begged the dear lord to take her into his hands, into his heart. Burton asked God to welcome her into heaven and free her soul from this torment and a body which had become useless to her. He prayed and prayed and he cried and cried.

When Burton went up to the unit later that night her chest area now appeared to be swelling. He was glad Fran was the nurse on duty that night because he had found it easy to talk to her over the last few occasions she had been Janet's nurse. Nurse Fran explained that Janet was taking on more and more fluid due to her kidney's having failed. The nurse basically indicated to Burton in as kind and compassionately as she could that they could end it right now.

They could start to reduce the rate on the vent and begin administering her morphine. Burton asked Fran if there was any way he could just take her home so she could pass away at home. Of course, they both knew that Janet probably would not survive long enough to even make it home. Burton indicated to Nurse Fran that he was ready. He did not want to prolong this anymore. Then, instead of just giving her the go ahead, he said he would come first thing in the morning when the doctors where there and talk with them and give them permission to take her off the artificial respiration.

This was the day Burton always knew would come, unless of course his day had come before hers. The day had come that every son and daughter must face. There was no denying it. There was no miracle about to happen. Janet was not going to suddenly and miraculously improve. Janet was not going to be a candidate for dialysis. His mother was not going to be able return to the house and pass away quietly at home. She was being called to heaven to be with God, and the only home she was going to was a funeral home, which would likely be her last stop on the way. The only miracle that was about to take place during the impending hours was that God was going to end Janet's suffering and pain with or without his help. Burton could not handle seeing Janet continue to suffer. He had set it all on the table with his God. Burton had given it to him and put it completely in his hands.

Burton left the intensive care unit that night about 2 o'clock in the morning. The staff in the ICU began to slowly initiate comfort measures for Janet. The ICU started the process of discontinuing Janet's treatment and weaning her off the ventilator. Burton went to bed that night heartbroken, but he had prayed about it, and made peace with the fact that he could no longer request that the hospital continue any sort of extraordinary measures to keep her alive which would only prolong her suffering. Actually, it was obvious at this point there were no more extraordinary measures that could be initiated on her behalf. He was prepared to accept that Janet was going to pass away and that was all.

Janet was 88 years old. She had lived a wonderful life. She and her husband had been very successful and happy for the most part. She had grown up a small-town country girl from a semi well to do family with a lot of brothers and sisters to love and to love her. Janet had a loving mother and father who she loved and cared for.

She had two children which she loved and adored. For the most part she had good health all throughout her life. She was blessed in so many ways. Janet gave of herself and helped so many along the way as a teacher, mother, wife, daughter, sister, and friend. Asked if she had any regrets in life, her answer would have been she had no regrets. The ICU staff proficiently and deliberately went about doing their job. Her lungs were full of fluid and she could not breath anymore. Actually, the artificial respiration was making it worse, and the IV's where only complicating the situation further.

CHAPTER THIRTEEN

On Sunday morning, Burton awoke about 8:45 am. The first thing he did was contact the ICU and asked if any of her doctors had arrived on the unit. They indicated none of her doctors were there yet. He told them he would be there shortly, and he was ready to talk with the doctors about discontinuing the artificial respiration and any other treatment. Burton was mentally exhausted. He buried his head in his pillow and prayed again. This time he asked God why was he going to the hospital to ask a bunch of doctors questions that only he had the answers to. Burton laid there for a few more minutes praying. He concluded his prayer. He sat on the side of the bed and was about to get dressed.

As he sat there on the edge of the bed, his phone rang. It was the ICU, who indicated that Janet had coded. Janet was dead. He took a quick shower threw on his clothes and drove to the hospital. He went into Janet's unit in the ICU and saw Janet's lifeless body lying there. They had disconnected all the IV's and the ventilator. Her unit was bare, there was no more medical equipment around her bed or against the wall. There was nothing in her room but a hospital bed which contained her dead body. Burton was overcome with grief as he slowly approached her bedside.

He touched Janet's arm and her body was still warm. He suddenly felt completely alone as if he had nobody in this world anymore. Burton was hurt that he had not been there when she passed. One of the nurses drew the curtains to her unit so that Burton could spend a few moments with his mother before they removed her body to the morgue. Burton stood there looking at Janet as the tears ran down his face. His wonderful and precious mother had gone to be with God. God had heard his prayers and ended her suffering and pain. Surely, he would feel the anguish of her loss for some time to come, but her journey was ended and she was finally at peace.

After a while he was able to walk away from her bedside. He emerged from the hospital on that sunny and clear October morning. The sky was a beautiful blue and the autumn weather was pleasantly warm. On his way to his truck, he gazed into the picturesque sky and thought to himself that Janet was finally free. He wondered if her soul was dancing joyfully in the sky. He hoped she was finally smiling again and in the company of angels and all of the people she had loved and lost over the many years. He had not seen her smile in such a long time.

How ironic that both Janet and Beck had died on a Sunday in the month of October. Beck had passed on October 14th and Janet on October 18th. Burton hoped Janet had finally been reunited with her husband Beck who she adored with all her heart. As he approached his vehicle, he still could not take his eyes of the sky. Perhaps that is what she had been trying to tell him the day before. Perhaps she was trying to tell him to look up to the sky, and that is where you will find me.

While still in the parking lot, he felt so alone at the moment and he decided to call some of Janet's family to let them know she had passed away. For some reason, the first person he decided to called was his cousin Cheryl. Burton called her almost instinctively because he knew something certain, besides Ann's call on the first day she went into the hospital, he had not heard much of anything from Janet's siblings. He was sure they had not been talking much to him, but they had been talking. He did not know why he called her first, but something told him to call her.

"Hi Cheryl," Burton said. "This is Burton."

"Good morning Burton," Cheryl said. "How are you?"

"I just wanted to call and let you know my mom passed away this morning," said Burton.

"Aunt Janet passed away," Cheryl said. "I'm so sorry Burton. I'm so sorry to hear that. Aunt Bethany and those guys have been saying they're not going to worry about trying to come to Mobile. They're planning to possibly have a service for her up here. Maybe sometime during the summer when the whole family is here. I'm sorry Burton. I'm so sorry that Aunt Janet is gone."

"Hey. I just wanted to let you know," said Burton.

"Are you alright?" asked Cheryl.

"Yea, I'm as alright as I'm going to be right about now," replied Burton.

"Do you want me to let some of the family know Aunt Janet passed?" asked Cheryl.

"Sure," Burton said. "I'll get around to calling them but yea you can tell them."

"Are you sure you're alright?" she asked again.

"Yes, I'm fine," Burton said. "Hey. I'll talk with you later."

"Bye, Burton," Cheryl said. "You'll be in my prayers."

Burton hung up with Cheryl, he was still out in the parking lot of the hospital. He was thinking to himself, how could anyone be discussing his mom's funeral and she just died a few minutes ago. Frankly speaking, he was not surprised and right now he could not waste any time concerning himself with that conversation. He needed to call the funeral home and make arrangements for them to come and get his mother. He was exhausted mentally and physically. He had gone to bed late and had not slept well. Burton knew he had a long busy week ahead of him trying to get her funeral arrangements made. Burton was in mourning for his beloved mother Janet. He just wanted to take a moment and wrap his mind around all this. He wanted to lay down for a moment, and then get himself in gear for what he was going to have to do during the upcoming week.

Burton contacted Christian Benevolent Funeral Home and arranged to meet with them a few hours later at the hospital. He went home and relaxed for a few minutes. Burton must have cried the entire time he was there at home waiting to meet with the people from the funeral home. He contacted a few of his friends and told them his mom had passed. They assured him they would come by and see him later. Burton took a quick nap. He woke up and contacted Christian Benevolent again to see if they were ready to come and get Janet.

About an hour later he met with them at the back door of the hospital morgue. As he stood there looking at that door behind the hospital, he wondered how many dead bodies had been wheeled out that door. The fact that thousands of dead people had probably been taken from this facility through that door was no consolation to him. He thought back to the day they carried his dad's body out the back door of their house when he died, and how it felt to him knowing Beck would never return through that door. Now after all these years, he was waiting to claim and receive his mother's body. Both of his parents were gone. The funeral home arrived as they stood outside the morgue waiting for them to release Janet's body.

They wheeled her out on a gurney in a body bag. When they got her to the parking lot, Burton checked the body bag to make sure it was his mother. She was so swollen all over and now for some odd reason her head and face where swollen. Burton could barely recognize her. Although he knew it was Janet. He signed the paperwork for the hospital and released her body to the ambulance to be transported to Christian Benevolent. Burton followed the ambulance to the funeral home.

He always knew this day would come, but that did not make it any easier. Burton had tried so hard to prepare himself but he realized there were some things you could not be totally prepared for. This was a piece of reality that he simply had to face as it was nothing more than a part of life. Reality that had been spinning and unraveling before him for a long time.

There was nothing he could do to change it. Wisdom says God give me the serenity to accept the things you cannot change. Burton admitted Janet to the care of the funeral parlor. At that point it dawned on him that he had a busy week coming up and that Janet still needed him one last time. She needed him to plan and arrange her funeral and burial. Naturally, he was also going to have to come up with the money. Janet only had two small life insurance policies. The two policies together would probably not amount to enough money to cover all of her expenses. Burton had never planned a funeral and he had no one to help him.

The following Monday Burton busied himself preparing for Janet's funeral. He made an appointment to meet with the funeral director and later that day he went to Christian Benevolent to meet with her. As he entered the large front doors of the ornate historic house located in downtown Mobile's business district. He met with Beverly Cooper, the funeral director and owner of Christian Benevolent Funeral Home. Beverly knew Burton, Janet and his entire family.

Beverly's husband Gary and Janet had been very good friends over the years. The Cooper and LeFlore families had always been close throughout the years. Even though the family had traditionally used a different funeral home. Burton decided to use Christian Benevolent this time. He walked into Beverly's office and found her there at her desk.

"Hi Burton," said Beverly.

"Beverly how are you," replied Burton.

"I'm good," Beverly said. "How are you. I know this isn't easy for you Burton, but just know I'm here to help you through this as much as I can."

"Thanks Bev," Burton said. "I appreciate that."

"That's what I do," said Beverly.

"Do you think you could adopt me, cause my mom is gone," said Burton with a chuckle. "I miss her so much. Bev, can you help me make this funeral happen and how much are we talking about?"

"I believe we can do that," Beverly said. "Your mom was an incredible person, and not to mention my husband Gary thought she was the most beautiful woman in the world, so you know I wasn't thrilled about that. I admired Janet so much though. All of her students always spoke very highly of her. Everyone who knew her spoke highly of her."

"Thank you, Bev," said Burton.

"We have some fees that are pretty much our set expenses and fees and then anything beyond that is your decision as far as choosing a casket and other things regarding her arrangements," Beverly said. "Here's a form which pretty much outlines those basic charges," she said as she handed him the form.

"Okay," said Burton.

"Your mom wasn't from Mobile was she?" asked Beverly.

"No, actually she was from North Carolina," Burton said. "She was a transplant to this area. She moved down here when she married my dad."

"I thought so," Beverly said. "I'm a transplant to this area myself. I was born in Virginia and moved down here when I met Gary."

"I didn't know that," Burton said. "I thought you were from here. A lot of her family lives in Virginia around Hampton."

"Oh really," Beverly replied. "I'm from Richmond."

"She has family in North Carolina, Virginia, and Philadelphia," said Burton.

"Are you expecting any of her family to come in for the funeral?" said Beverly.

"Oh yes. My mom came from a huge family in North Carolina, I'm expecting them," Burton said. "You know how it is with family, sometimes when it's necessary they'll show up. They show up no matter what. They show up."

"I'd love to meet some of them," said Beverly.

"I'm sure you will," said Burton.

"Burton, whatever you need I'm here for you," said Beverly.

"We've got caskets upstairs or you can look at some of them on our website," Beverly said as she showed him the various items she had available. "If there's something you want, we can have it for you in a few days."

"I like that one," Burton said. "It's white and her favorite color was white. It also says, 'Let my work speak for me.'"

"We can have that one for her within two days," said Beverly.

Burton decided to make some phone calls to Janet's family members to let them know she had passed away and he would like to request their presence at her funeral. First, he decided he would call Peter, Bethany, Ann and Julia. Afterward he would contact some of his cousins. He figured some of them would not have the money to come, unless of course they decided to be resourceful in some sort of way which was not likely to happen.

Based on the conversation with his cousin, Cheryl, Burton was aware they had ample information, speculation, corroboration coupled with time to think, reflect, make arrangements, and make plans to pay their respects to their sister. They say death and funerals are not for the dead, they are for the living. In actuality they are for the dead and for the living. A funeral is a time when the living and the dead come together for one another. Burton prepared a news release which went out to local newspapers and television stations. He set about writing Janet's obituary. He also decided to contact her siblings. Burton decided he would contact Peter first.

"Hey, Peter. How are you?" Burton said. "This is Burton."

"Hey, Burton," said Peter.

"I was calling to let you know that my mom, your sister passed away yesterday," Burton said. "More than likely her funeral will be on this coming Saturday. I hope you will be there."

"Burton, I heard Janet had passed away," Peter said. "I'm sorry to hear Janet passed. I loved my sister very much. She was one of the kindest and sweetest people you would ever want to meet. She'll be greatly missed. In a lot of ways, she was like a second mother to me and the rest of them. You know I was the baby of the family."

"I'm working toward setting a definite date for her funeral," Burton said. "The tentative date right now is this Saturday coming up. Do you think you will be able to make it?"

"I don't know, Burton," Peter said. "I don't think I'm going to be able to make it."

"If it would help, I can push the date back a day or two," Burton said. "That's why I wanted to check with you guys and see if that date would work for you."

"I don't think I can come," Peter said. "I have bad back pain, my sciatic nerve. I can send you some money or something if you want, but I'm not coming."

"I didn't call to ask you for any money," said Burton.

"I'm sure that funeral is going to be expensive," Peter said. "I'll send you a little something to help out with the funeral, but I don't think I'll be able to make it."

"Okay. Well like I said," Burton replied. "I just wanted to let you know. Talk to you later."

"Hello," said Burton as he answered the phone.

"Burton, I'm so sorry to hear about my sister Janet," Julia said. "I loved your mother so much. I will always love her.

Janet was like a mother to us all, and I will miss her with all my heart."

"How are you?" asked Burton.

"I'm fine, just so heartbroken to hear this sad news about Janet. Heaven has gained a real angel," Julia said. "How are you doing?"

"As well as can be expected," Burton replied. "I've been busy preparing for a funeral."

"Have you made the arrangements yet?" asked Julia.

"Right now, it looks like her funeral will be this Saturday," Burton said. "I might be able to push it back a little if that would make it easier for you to get here."

"Burton, would you be very disappointed if I didn't come?" said Julia.

"Truthfully, yes I would," Burton replied. "She's your sister, what you do is up to you. I think it would be really sad if you didn't come and pay your last respects to her."

"I'm going to talk with your Aunt Ann and see what she says," said Julia.

"Like I said," Burton replied. "It's looking like her funeral is going to be this Saturday. Check back with me tomorrow, and I'll be able to let you know if Saturday is a definite, but that what it looks like."

"Burton, I just want to tell you that I love you so much," Ann said. "I know this is not an easy time for you. My sister Jeannie is gone. I can't believe it. Burton would you be offended if I wasn't able to make it?"

"Yes, I would be offended," Burton said. "But it's not about me. They say funerals are for the living. My mom did a lot for you and others over the years. Whether or not you attend her home going service is on you."

"Well, old age is a factor at this point," said Ann.

"People go where they want to go," replied Burton.

"If you really want us to come," Ann said. "Perhaps we can try and make it."

"It's not so much a matter of whether or not I want you to come," Burton said. "We're going to be fine one way or another. The question is do you want to come? She's your sister. I know if you died, she would come to your funeral if there was any way she could make it."

"Julia just called me," Ann said. "Let me discuss it with her and we'll see."

"Anyway, just let me know what you're going to do," Burton said. "At this point it looks like her funeral is going to be Saturday."

"Hi, Aunt Bethany," Burton said. "This is Burton. I was calling to let tell you my mom died."

"Oh yea, I know," Bethany said. "I'm deeply saddened to hear my sister Jeannie passed. Your mother was the salt of the earth. I know you're going to miss her. We will all miss her dearly."

"At any rate I was just calling to let you know," Burton said. "Her funeral is tentatively set for this Saturday coming up. I wish you would be there. If you think you would need a little more time to get here, I might be able to push it back just a little."

"I'm not going to be there, Burton," Bethany said. "My husband's got hemorrhoids. I'm can't leave him right now."

"I'm sorry to hear that," Burton said. "I certainly understand how you wouldn't be able to break away from him, even for a day to attend your sister's funeral."

"London might want to come," said Bethany.

"Maybe London could help you with Lester for a day or two so you could come," Burton said. "She's pretty much right around the corner, isn't she?"

"Yea but I can't put that on her," Bethany said. "I can pretty much tell you now, I don't think I'm going to be able to make it. We were thinking about having something for Jeannie in Virginia this summer. We're trying to get all of the family together this summer for a family reunion. You should come and we'll do something for your mother then."

"Her funeral is coming up this week, as I said it's set for this Saturday," Burton said. "That's when her funeral will be held and she will be available for family and friends to say their last goodbyes to her. I won't be attending anything in Virginia this summer. Her funeral will be held in a few days. If you don't think you can't make it, I understand."

Over the last few hours Burton had spoken with all of Janet's surviving brothers and sister about Janet's funeral and her upcoming arrangements. All of them had basically declined to come. Burton thought it ironic that these were the same people who, about nine years prior brought an action in court alleging they loved Janet so much and were so seriously concerned about her, as well as her well-being and her money. They all made multiple trips back and forth to Mobile then, even Peter with his sciatic nerve which he was always complaining about. Janet was gone, Burton had no reason to be concerned about them. There was nothing they could get from her, trick her into signing. Otherwise, there was no way they could take advantage of or capitalize on her to her detriment. All they could do was come in peace.

All they could do was come in peace to love and serve the Lord, and say their last goodbye, their final farewell to their sister who they had once claimed to be so concerned about. Burton had given some of them the cold shoulder over the last few years, but he was still a reasonable person who would not have made them feel unwelcome at a service where they might have wanted to pay their last respects to their late sister who basically raised all of them.

Certainly, the thought of being there for him had obviously not crossed their minds either. Burton was inundated with the plans for Janet's funeral and he was not going to continue to dwell on her siblings and their dispositions. He had to do what he had to do in order to provide Janet with an appropriate and suitable home going service. She still needed him and he had progressed into the stage of mourning which most people experience when they lose someone they love. It is the process in morning where you're loved one still needs you to come up with that money and put together a funeral for them.

"Hey, cuz. I wanted to tell you, in case you haven't heard," Burton said. "My mom passed away."

"Oh Burton, Janet passed away," Burton's cousin Amir said. "Man, cuz. I'm saddened to hear that devastating news. When did she pass?"

"Yesterday," Burton said. "She passed on Sunday."

"Have you talked to Bethany, Peter, Julia and Ann yet?" asked Amir.

"Yea I've talked to them," replied Burton.

"When are they going to be there in Mobile" asked Amir.

"I don't know," Burton said. "Peter and Bethany said they weren't coming. The other two say they're still thinking about it."

"What, man that's some bullshit," Amir said. "They're talking about not coming to Aunt Janet's funeral after all the shit she did for them. Burton believe me, I'm the oldest grandchild of Mable and Angle. My mother El was the oldest in the family. I grew up with all of them. Do you know them mutherfuckers wouldn't have had shit if it hadn't been for Aunt Janet."

"Cuz, if you want to come," Burton said. "You and your wife are more than welcome to stay here at the house."

"OK, Burton," Amir said. "I'll probably come. Let me discuss it with my wife and we'll see if we can plan to make it."

"Thanks Amir," Burton said. "I'll talk with you in a day or two."

"Burton this is your Aunt Ann and Aunt Julia," Anna said. "I got on a train and came down here to Richmond. I'm at Julia's house."

"Hi Burton," Julia said. "Ann is here and we're going to see if we can make it for our sister's funeral."

"That would be great," Burton said. "I've been busy with the arrangements. Like I said it looks like Saturday, but I could push it back a day or two if that would make it easier for you guys to get here."

"We should be able to get there by Friday," Ann said. "It's only Tuesday now."

"Burton, we just want you to know we are trying our best to get there for our sister Janet's funeral," said Julia.

"Thank you," said Burton.

"We'll get back with you as our plans progress," Anna said. "Just know we are making plans to be there for Jeannie."

"Okay well keep me posted," Burton said. "I'll keep you posted on the funeral arrangements."

The following morning Burton's friend Michael stopped by to drop off a few items he had purchased for him. Michael had some cokes, sprites, paper plates and forks that he brought over to the house. Burton greatly appreciated Michael, coming by the house to visit with him as well as the items he brought would definitely come in hand.

"Burt, I want to let you know you have my heartfelt condolences," said Michael.

"I appreciate that," said Burton.

"I brought you some things that you may need over the next few days," Michael said. "It's been almost two years since my mom passed so I know this is not an easy time for you. I appreciated you being there for me, and I want to be there for you."

"Thanks," replied Burton.

"You expecting a lot of family for the funeral?" asked Mike.

"A few," Burton replied. "My mom came from a big family. Some of them can't afford to come, but I do expect some of her family to come. You know that's how family is, sometimes they show up when you need them."

"You know I remember Uncle Buddy," Mike said. "I had an uncle named Buddy. He was from Ohio. I remember everybody loved Uncle Buddy. We would be so excited when Uncle Buddy came to town to visit. It was always Uncle Buddy this, Uncle Buddy that. But when Uncle Buddy died, nobody went to his funeral."

"That's fucked up," Burton said. "There are some family members who probably can't afford to come but you know sometimes there's a time when family will show up. I don't know about Uncle Buddy, but I'm expecting some of her family to come."

"Anyway, I got a few things I need to do today before I got to go home and get ready for work tonight," Mike said. "I just wanted to drop those things off with you and check on you and make sure you're alright."

"Right now, I'm at that stage of mourning where I have so much to do to get ready for my mom's funeral and I don't have any help," Burton said. I don't have a lot of time right now to think about me or to get into my feelings. I miss my mom with all my heart, but right now she needs me to take care of this business and arrange for her burial. She's gone on to be with God. My dad, God rest his soul, used to say sometimes, maybe death isn't so bad. You never see anyone kicking and screaming to get back here once they're gone."

"Your dad was a smart man," said Mike.

"Yes, he was, and I still miss him too," Burton said. "It's been fourteen years since he passed on October 14th, 2001. It's weird how both my parents passed away in October. Her on the 18th and him on the 14th. Mom held on to life as long as she could. I'm miss her but I'm glad she's at peace and she's not suffering anymore."

"If you need anything don't hesitate to call me," Mike said. "I'm going to run, but I'll try and touch base with you a little later. Hang in there my friend. I'll see you later."

"Thanks for coming by," Burton replied. "I appreciate you."

Burton had contacted his children and asked Candace if she would bring them to their grandmother's funeral. She would not make it possible for them to come and visit her when she was sick and in the hospital. The way his ex-wife had behaved toward Burton since she moved away from Mobile during their separation and subsequent divorce with regard to their children was disheartening to him.

She had even vigorously objected to him having any sort of custody or visitation with his children during their divorce proceedings. Despite an order from the court granting Burton custody and visitation every other weekend and on alternate holidays. She still flat-out refused to allow Burton time to spend with his children without her wanting to tag along.

Burton busied himself again going through the motions of getting with his church to plan a funeral. He had decided what pictures he wanted to put on the funeral program and he also had to order flowers. In addition, and most importantly he had to take some money to the funeral home. He was grieving and at this point, he had fixed his mind and spirit on the particular task in front of him.

There was still a lot to do in a short period of time. He had to pick out something for her to wear and finalize the program with Good Shepherd Church. He paid the funeral home some additional money in the form of signing over one of Janet's life insurance policies which was not enough to cover the expenses. He found some additional funds in Janet's savings which he paid over to the mortuary. He had not quite paid for the total cost in full but he had paid enough for Christian Benevolent to feel comfortable moving forward with the service.

CHAPTER FOURTEEN

Since losing his mother, Burton felt like he had no one in this world. Both of his parents were dead and his children lived in another state. He hardly ever saw his children, and now his mom was dead. Burton tried hard to fight back the feelings of loneliness, sorrow, and depression as he worked toward providing for Janet's final home going service. It would not be long before he would commit his mother to the earth alongside her husband Beck. Janet's life had not been a crystal stair since Beck had passed away some fourteen years previously.

Her battle with Alzheimer's had been a long and slow process of regression and death. Many years ago, Beck told Burton that he hoped he would predecease Janet. His dad said he did not know what he would do if he lost his wife, besides go back to drinking. There was one thing for sure, Janet and Beck loved one another and her spot next to him was soon to be dug open to receive her remains.

Despite the fact that Janet had been on deaths bed for many months, Burton still struggled to fully accept that Janet was actually gone. Upon hearing of Janet's having passed away there was a pouring out from the community of Mobile with condolences, cards, flowers, prayers and love for Janet and the LeFlore family. Former students of Janet and former colleagues as well as friends all expressed their sympathy. Many of Burton's friends rallied to his comfort and aid during his time of grief.

However, Burton received word from her sisters Julia and Anna, they would not be coming to the funeral. It did not appear that any of her nieces and nephews were planning to come either. Burton was very disappointed but not surprised. Janet came from a huge family of nine brothers and sisters, four of who were still living. She also had many nieces and nephews, none of who said they were coming to be with him when he buried his mom. All of Janet's life, her family had been one of the things she held most dear to her heart and to think none of them was even going to bother to show up and pay their last respects to her was saddening.

Saturday morning Burton arrived at Good Shepherd Church. Burton got a final glimpse of his mother Janet before they lowered the casket door over her lifeless body. Burton could not keep back the tears when he took that last glimpse of her face. He knew he would miss her, but he also knew her time had come and he would simply have to deal with it. She had lived a long, productive, prosperous, and happy life. Surely, she was now in heaven with God. The church was filled with friends of Janet and Burton. Shortly after the funeral began, all of Janet's grandchildren arrived with Candace. The only one of her grandchildren that was not there was Breton.

The funeral was a beautiful service. Janet and Beck's friend the Reverend Percy Johnson did the eulogy. Percy had also done the eulogy for Beck's funeral. Burton decided to ask Percy to do the Eulogy because he felt that he and his wife Gladys knew Janet personally long before Beck passed and she started suffering with Alzheimer's. The new pastor of Good Shepherd had never really met Janet. Percy did a tremendous job of eulogizing Janet. The service turned out to be a fitting and appropriate funeral for a woman who had given so much of herself to so many over the course of her life.

From the church they drove to Magnolia Cemetery where Janet was finally interred next to her husband of over fifty years to begin her eternal rest. As he did when his dad was laid to rest in that cemetery, he remained there at her grave site until they lowered the vault and completed the burial. Janet's poignant and somewhat poetic journey with Alzheimer's had finally culminated in what will be everyone's eventual destination. Her remains were reunited with the remains of the love of her life. The two of them would now lay side by side into eternity, which is where she wanted to be when she died.

Janet was laid in her final resting place. Burton left the cemetery with his children. In his sorrow, loneliness, grief and pain he also found tremendous peace. Janet was finally at peace. She was no longer alone, confused, lost, hurting, forgotten, or misunderstood. Alzheimer's was no longer stripping her of her memory, her ability to live as an independent person, her will to live, her knowledge of self and her fundamental motor skills.

When Burton found himself becoming extremely sorrowful, he had to remind himself of what a struggle life had become for Janet in her last years. As much as he hated to hear people say that someone is in a better place when they die, he hoped she was in a better place. It was time for him to go on with his life which is exactly what his mother Janet would want him to do. He had done all he could and now it was in God's hands. Hopefully, she was in God's hands.

Hopefully, she was somewhere in heaven dressed in a beautiful gown at a grand party with Beck, Champ, Mamma, Pappa, Warren, El, A.B., Carol, Evangeline, Teah, John and a host of her other relatives and friends, laughing and smiling and happy to be free of the burdens of this world we live in. Free of her flesh which had become old, tattered, mangled, wrinkled, contracted, and physically compromised. Free of her mind that could no longer recall that she had even existed, while only knowing that she did exist.

As more and more Americans are living longer, and an increasing number of people are suffering from what used to be called senility, before medical science coined the terms Alzheimer's and dementia. Around 1910, Dr. Alois Alzheimer noticed changes in the brain tissue of a woman who had died of an unusual mental illness. Many fail to realize the devastating effects this disease has on the loved ones of people suffering from Alzheimer's. Burton felt shell shocked like a soldier emerging from a long hard battle. His mother had fought Alzheimer's and he had been right there with her in the war.

Oftentimes, society overlooks the fact that Alzheimer's is not easy on caretakers and family. Trying to cope with a loved one's detachment from reality; often emotional bouts with confusion and disorientation; sudden mood swings; frustration; forgetfulness; sometime odd behavior; actual isolation and feelings of isolation; continual and sometimes necessary resistance and suspicion of others meddling in their lives; constantly repeating the same questions and statements; wandering off or potentially eloping and getting lost if not properly watched and supervised; vigorous struggles to maintain independence; inability to perform on their own basic human functions like using the bathroom and feeding oneself; other neurological impairment and the list may vary from person to person and go on and on.

Alzheimer's is a horrifying disease and it has its way of taking a toll on everyone involved in the process. Very often there are caretakers who are so overwhelmed with the stress and responsibility of caring for a loved one that they end up predeceasing the loved one or family member with dementia. Burton did not feel the sense of relief and guilt that professional psychologists claim loved ones and caretakers often experience. He found some relief in the fact that Janet was no longer suffering, but he felt no personal relief from the arduous responsibility of caring for his mother, especially during the later years of her life when she entered the final stages.

Almost instinctively, it was then that he loved her most when she needed him the most. As he struggled with the grief of the loss of Janet, his most sincere necessity was to cope with the pain of what they had endured for so many years. Burton was with his mother Janet from day to day as this condition progressed, and it was far from a beautiful day in the park. However, shortly after Janet's death Burton joined thousands of people in Langan Municipal Park for the March to End Alzheimer's.

It was liberating for him to celebrate Janet's life and join in with so many other people who had family members, loved ones and who were themselves afflicted as well as those committed to elder care and somehow finding an end to this atrocity called Alzheimer's and dementia. Thousands of people raising money and walking to support such a worthwhile cause. It brought healing to Burton's heart to walk with them. While walking the park with all the other people, Burton thought about his mom, her life and what he wanted to write on her tombstone.

After completing the trail around the park at the Walk to End Alzheimer's Burton took two of the colorful windmills and wrote 'In Memory of Janet," on the windmill. He would stick one of them in the ground at the park with the other windmills and he planned to take the other one home with him. Burton missed his mother greatly. As he stood there surrounded by all of the people at the Walk to End Alzheimer's, he felt totally alone and in his own world. A few people spoke to him, and he replied, but he did not talk to one person there, simply because he was filled with sorrow and did not have a word to say to anyone.

After a considerable amount of thought and deliberation, he decided to write the following epithet on Janet's stone. Burton wrote the following words which he felt in his heart were befitting of her and her life:

"A loving Mother,

Supportive and Dedicated Wife.

Dutiful and loving grandmother,

Tireless Teacher and Chemist,

Dutiful and Devoted Daughter,

Loyal and Understanding Sister,

Beloved and Trusted Friend.

Philanthropist and Humanitarian.

A Sultry and Hot Summers Day,

The Transformation of Autumn Leaves,

Welcomes the Cold Winds of Winter,

And the Rainy Days of Spring,

Which Beautiful Flowers Bring.

The Kindest and Most Generous, Woman I Have Ever Known.

May Your Soul Dwell In Peace,

Eternally in Heaven, At God's Throne."

After finishing writing those words, he drove out to the family plot at Magnolia Cemetery where his family is buried. He sat there on the small bench he and Janet had purchased for the plot when his dad had passed away. He sat there staring at the barren spot where Janet had been buried there next to his father. Burton cried and cried and cried and cried. He kept saying "Mom, I miss you so much. I miss you so much. I miss you." After a few minutes, he regained his composure. He went back to his truck and drove back to the house. Once at home he went up to his room and fell to his knees and prayed. He prayed. He could not help but to feel like he had no one in this world anymore. The only woman who had even loved him unconditionally was not dead and gone.

Janet lived a noble life, and as Burton stated in her tombstone. She had been a wonderful mother to him and his brother. She had always tried to be supportive of her husband and dedicated her life to loving him and being there for the man she always referred to by his middle name which was Beck. She remained steadfast in being there at his beck and call as the common phrase is commonly stated. Janet spent most of her life teaching. She had worked on the high school level during her early career and then spent the remainder of her time teaching Chemistry on the college level. She was always concerned about her parents and Beck's parents. She loved her brothers and sisters so dearly with all her heart and did whatever she could to help them. Which is why it hurt her so deeply when they turned their backs on her when she started experiencing signs of possibly having Alzheimer's.

Although Janet very often put her family first in her life; her husband, her children, her parents and in-laws; her sisters, brothers, nieces and nephews, she had a host of acquaintances and a handful of people she called her close friends. Janet was a good person who was selfless, unselfish and giving almost to her detriment at times. Janet had been very blessed in so many ways and she would not hesitate to help someone in need. His son Breton would later remind him that he forgot to include on her headstone that she was a good grandmother.

Janet was an extremely kind hearted person. Sometimes she and Burton argued on numerous occasions when he would try to caution her about being less trusting of people and being more cautious when conducting herself with strangers who might try and pray on her because she was elderly and often alone.

Janet was the type of person who always looked for the good in everyone and thought every human being had some inherent good in them. Janet also had a deep faith in God. She looked for the positive in the world and viewed the world in the way she thought it should be, perhaps more so than the world really was. She did not always take well to having someone attempting to take her out of her mindset bubble with regard to trusting and caring for total strangers. Perhaps God had his hand on her and she did not waste a lot of time worrying or being afraid. She led a blessed life and had touched and helped so many. She was such a kind and compassionate individual.

Janet was also extremely healthy. Had it not been for the severe effect of Alzheimer's on her life and mental capacity Janet probably would have lived to be a very old lady. Of course, Eighty-Eight is pretty old. Alzheimer's had slowly and consistently robbed her of her memory and ability to recall. She was a highly educated woman who prided herself on her intelligence, ability to learn and recall. A scientist who understood, embraced, and understood the complex world of chemistry. Alzheimer's and dementia had caused her to reach a point where she even forgot it was customary to get out of bed at some point. Alzheimer's quietly progressively resulted in her being decreasingly debilitated. She was a person who was loved and adored. She was a lady who gave her very best no matter what.

As a young woman she was vibrant, beautiful, intelligent, and ambitious. Janet was born in Wilmington, North Carolina during the 1920's. The daughter of a postman and farmer with what eventually ended up as a family of ten children. Janet adored and emulated her mother Mable—who, for the majority of Janet's life, was a housewife, mother, and homemaker. Janet had married Beck in her mid-twenties and her first son was born when she was in her mid-twenties. She was almost forty when Burton was born. She and her husband Beck where finally starting to live the dream life they had worked so hard to achieve. They had both struggled through school together. Janet obtained a master's degree in chemistry and her husband Beck an M.D.

Janet found a position that gave her the opportunity to teach chemistry which was what she enjoyed most. Beck established an extremely large, lucrative, and successful medical practice in Mobile, Alabama after having moved back to Beck's hometown from Philadelphia. She and her husband who were both depression babies. They were able to achieve the financial security which they had always longed for and worked so hard to achieve. The two of them where both hard working and yet still very frugal in the way they lived, and spent their money. Janet's life had not been a crystal stair by any means; however, all the same, her life had been a good one. She had two wonderful children, an adoring husband and a huge family of siblings.

According to the natural order of things, the sun rises in the morning and eventually will set in the evening. A person is born and pursuant to their gift of life, we all face the inevitable certainty of death. Janet fought the battle against Alzheimer's and old age like a grand lady. She was a true champion who embraced life and loved living. Janet had endured the heartache of losing her oldest son and then her husband. She had experienced the pain of having her siblings who she loved so dearly turn their backs on her and treat her with a total lack of compassion. She had lost siblings that she loved dearly. She had seen many people come and leave this world during her lifetime. However, all the same, even in the bleakest darkest hours of blissful, painless oblivion and inability to recall much of anything Janet persevered because that was who she was.

Made in the USA
Columbia, SC
23 April 2024